PHIL SPECTOR

Tempo
A Rowman & Littlefield Music Series on Rock, Pop, and Culture

Series Editor: Scott Calhoun

Tempo: A Rowman & Littlefield Music Series on Rock, Pop, and Culture offers titles that explore rock and popular music through the lens of social and cultural history, revealing the dynamic relationship between musicians, music, and their milieu. Like other major art forms, rock and pop music comment on their cultural, political, and even economic situation, reflecting the technological advances, psychological concerns, religious feelings, and artistic trends of their times. Contributions to the **Tempo** series are the ideal introduction to major pop and rock artists and genres.

The American Songbook: Music for the Masses, by Ann van der Merwe
Billy Joel: America's Piano Man, by Joshua S. Duchan
Bob Dylan: American Troubadour, by Donald Brown
Bon Jovi: America's Ultimate Band, by Margaret Olson
British Invasion: The Crosscurrents of Musical Influence, by Simon Philo
Bruce Springsteen: American Poet and Prophet, by Donald L. Deardorff II
The Clash: The Only Band That Mattered, by Sean Egan
The Kinks: A Thoroughly English Phenomenon, by Carey Fleiner
Kris Kristofferson: Country Highwayman, by Mary G. Hurd
Patti Smith: America's Punk Rock Rhapsodist, by Eric Wendell
Paul Simon: An American Tune, by Cornel Bonca
Phil Spector: Sound of the Sixties, by Sean MacLeod
Ska: The Rhythm of Liberation, by Heather Augustyn
Sting and The Police: Walking in Their Footsteps, by Aaron J. West
U2: Rock 'n' Roll to Change the World, by Timothy D. Neufeld
Warren Zevon: Desperado of Los Angeles, by George Plasketes

PHIL SPECTOR

Sound of the Sixties

Sean MacLeod

ROWMAN & LITTLEFIELD
Lanham • Boulder • New York • London

Published by Rowman & Littlefield
A wholly owned subsidiary of The Rowman & Littlefield Publishing Group,
Inc.
4501 Forbes Boulevard, Suite 200, Lanham, Maryland 20706
www.rowman.com

Unit A, Whitacre Mews, 26-34 Stannary Street, London SE11 4AB

British Library Cataloguing in Publication Information Available

Library of Congress Cataloging-in-Publication Data

Names: MacLeod, Sean, 1971– author.
Title: Phil Spector : sound of the Sixties / Sean MacLeod.
Description: Lanham : Rowman & Littlefield, 2018. | Series: Tempo, a Rowman & Littlefield
    music series on rock, pop, and culture | Includes bibliographical references and index.
Identifiers: LCCN 2017015245 (print) | LCCN 2017018711 (ebook) | ISBN 9781442267060 (elec-
    tronic) | ISBN 9781442267053 (cloth : alk. paper)
Subjects: LCSH: Spector, Phil, 1939– | Sound recording executives and producers—United
    States—Biography. | Popular music—United States—1961–1970—History and criticism.
Classification: LCC ML429.S64 (ebook) | LCC ML429.S64 M3 2017 (print) | DDC 781.66092—
    dc23 LC record available at https://lccn.loc.gov/2017015245

♾ ™ The paper used in this publication meets the minimum requirements of
American National Standard for Information Sciences Permanence of Paper
for Printed Library Materials, ANSI/NISO Z39.48-1992.

Printed in the United States of America

CONTENTS

SERIES EDITOR'S FOREWORD

Of the many contradictions threaded through the most culturally transformative decade of the twentieth century, over there in the popular music sector was Phil Spector. Chief among the 1960s story of looking for release from control was one who gripped the means of production so tightly that he seemed to rather effortlessly pop out hit songs and hip personalities one after another, such that sixties youth cultures had plenty of encouragement as they pushed for liberation and a future in which popular culture would (ironically) define what a free society looked, felt, and sounded like. This Tempo series of books examining rock, pop, and culture keeps an eye out for sites of tension and couldn't have found a much better one than in Phil Spector. Precisely because Tempo books are about marking the cultural times and analyzing the forces that change these times, they look into the contradictions in popular music and the people who lived the tensions artfully and disruptively. Phil Spector's knack and nuance for developing musical performers, recording their talents in a big way, and then seeding the bed for the empowerment of the teenager, one single record at a time, was his art and his cultural disruption; Spector's narcissism, need for control, and paranoia overshadowed his art and became more destructive than disruptive, not for him alone but for some who worked with him too.

Sean MacLeod helps us mark Spector's fervor and fury behind much of the sound of the sixties by bringing his appreciation and intelligence into a dialogue with what others have said about Spector, including those who worked directly with him. Presenting the arc of Spector's career in critique and relief against the fraught and complicated plotline of the sixties, and many of its major musical characters, will give readers a greater sense of the Spector-sixties entanglement.

Scott Calhoun

PREFACE

Ever since I was a boy the pop music and pop culture of the sixties has been a big part of my life. My introduction to one of the century's most colorful decades, however, was shrouded in sorrow, since it directly sprang from the killing of John Lennon in December 1980. The TV and radio were buzzing with tributes and commemorations of the former leader of pop music's most celebrated group, the Beatles, whose charm, humor, music, and style was still as alluring at the beginning of the eighties, at least to an eight-year-old such as me, as it must have been twenty or so years earlier at the height of Beatlemania. It wasn't long before I was eagerly exploring the treasure trove that was sixties pop culture, bringing me in touch with the great music of the Beatles, the Rolling Stones, the Beach Boys, and the Byrds.

Although I was aware of Phil Spector, it was only peripheral, and it wasn't until many years later when I came across *The Best of the Ronettes* CD that I first began to realize just how significant he was to the sixties. Every song was a virtual sonic masterpiece, and although I was familiar with his big hits, such as "Be My Baby" and "Then He Kissed Me," I couldn't quite believe how the magic of songs such as "Do I Love You," "Is This What I Get for Loving You," "The Best Part of Breaking Up," and "Walking in the Rain," had passed me by for so many years. No wonder he had been so highly thought of by people such as John Lennon and the Beach Boys' Brian Wilson. This music, as was much of the girl group music of the early sixties that Spector had done so much to create, with groups such as the Ronettes, the Crystals, and Darlene Love, was very unique and special, while the sonic textures were way beyond anything else the other more successful groups of the time were producing. I became nearly infatuated with the girl group genre, so much so that I wrote a book on it.

After writing *Leaders of the Pack: Girl Groups of the 1960s and Their Influence on Popular Culture in Britain and America*, and before beginning this book, I thought I was familiar with most of Spector's work, the girl groups specifically, as well as the work with the Righteous Brothers and John Lennon's and George Harrison's post-Beatles work, but there was more to Spector than that. So much more. His work in the 1970s with the 1950s singer Dion, although not a commercial success, is a real lost classic, not to mention his earlier work with the Teddy Bears, Connie Francis, and Gene Pitney, as well as his inspirational work with the Paris Sisters, whose songs alone are worthy of securing him a place in pop music history.

Although, for some, such as songwriters and producers Jerry Leiber and Mike Stoller and Terry Melcher, Spector was a hustler who just got lucky; to many of the pop aristocracy of the sixties, such as Brian Wilson, John Lennon, and Carole King, Spector was a musical genius. Without doubt, Phil Spector was a complex, mercurial figure full of contradictions and insecurities, and yet, to a greater or lesser degree, Spector and his music had a significant impact on the pop music of the 1960s.

Phil Spector revolutionized the recording process as well as shaped the business and marketing approach of the music industry, which was in its infancy at the time. He raised the bar and standards for other musicians and producers to follow and gave a voice to the newly emerging socioeconomic group of teenagers, as well as other groups struggling to achieve equality during the sixties, particularly women and African Americans. Spector, however, was a complex character whose need for control brought much damage and confusion into the lives of those around him, as well as into his own career and life.

This book primarily focuses on the following themes: his early life and formative years; his significance as a pop music impresario and music business entrepreneur; the impact his visionary approach to pop records had on the musical landscape of the time; his influence on the sociopolitical climate in regard to youth culture, the rise of feminism, and the civil rights movement; his influence on many of the new generation of pop and rock musicians; his egocentric need for control and power, both personally and professionally; the significance of his role in the post-Beatles' careers of both George Harrison and John Lennon; and his final decline and ignominious fall from his position as pop music's greatest producer to his imprisonment for murder.

INTRODUCTION

Between Elvis and the Beatles

BEFORE ELVIS THERE WAS NOTHING

The devastation of two world wars and the threat of fascism, along with the massive consumerism that had developed hand in hand with the industrial advances of postwar America, meant that life after World War II was being experienced in dramatically different terms than prior to it. Following the war, the United States had become the foremost nation on earth, acting now as the guardian of freedom and democracy while simultaneously promoting capitalist and consumer ideologies. For many young people outside the United States, who were still suffering from postwar depression and the restrictive hierarchical traditions of their own cultures, the American way of life, intrinsically associated with freedom and wealth, became an increasingly more attractive idea.

The postwar years had created a growing youth population, and with plenty of part-time work and few financial responsibilities, the new youth, which became known affectionately as *teenagers*, were considered one of the most lucrative, as well as one of the most impressionable, groups in society and were an easy target for manufacturers, who indulged their fads and trends (Judt, 347–50). It was for this very reason that Colin McInnes, in his 1959 novel *Absolute Beginners*, which depicts the burgeoning youth culture of the time, exclaimed that "the teenager is the new economic class." This new subgroup, with its own language, pastimes, fashion, and cultural representatives, encouraged the beginning of a whole new era, primarily interconnected with the fleeting trends of consumerism, otherwise known today as pop culture. In her book *Where the Girls Are*, writer Susan Douglas observed that

> for kids born after WW2, the media's influence was unprecedented. . . . Much of this media was geared to the fastest-growing market segment, baby boomers. Media executives knew if they were going to succeed with this group, already known for its rising rebellion against '50s conformity, they would have to produce songs, movies or TV shows that spoke to that rebellion. They would have to create products specifically for teens and definitely not for adults. (14)

The new sound of rock 'n' roll, which was enthusiastically embraced by the postwar youth, had its origins in the African American communities and as a result rejected the color prejudices that had existed in American society up until that point. Music publishing executive Arnold Shaw recounts that the stirrings of something new became obvious when a sweet white Jewish girl called Georgia Gibbs started to hit the charts with covers of the black "gritty" blues singers, such as LaVern Baker ("Tweedle Dee") and Etta James ("Dance with Me Henry"). "Old line publishers," Shaw suggested, "who had dominated the hit parade for years couldn't understand it. They both feared and hated it without really knowing what it was" (Shaw, 3), and when the young, slim, and attractive figure of Elvis Presley made his first appearance on *The Tommy Dorsey Show*, on January 28, 1956, "the music industry saw the writing on the wall, for all was about to change" (Shaw, 11).

While parents detested Presley, thinking he was obscene, the kids loved him and recognized that he was the voice of their generation, leading them, pied-piper-like, into an era that would bow to their every whim. It wouldn't take long before fifties advertisers and marketing men realized the commercial potential of this new youth market, and soon media outlets, TV, radio, and magazines began to heavily promote the new consumer culture.

In Britain, the older prewar values were outrightly rejected by the young in favor of the more consumer and egocentric values projected abroad from the United States. The Rolling Stones manager Andrew "Loog" Oldham describes the mesmerizing effect that the Technicolored lifestyles of the new American teenager had on their wide-eyed British counterparts:

> Those of us punters not yet part of the new intelligentsia nurtured the hope that someday soon our lives would resemble the American movies we loved, we'd trade places with a miserable young James Dean in a flash. We had no perspective on Britain's glorious and unrecoverable past, so we lived in a make believe present time inspired by Hollywood and rock 'n' roll. . . . Dreams were important because our elders had run out of them and therefore aspiration belonged to the young. Rock 'n' roll was ours because it was American and our parents didn't want it. (Oldham, *Stone Free*).

While the consumer-driven culture of the fifties and sixties created an economic boom that "engulfed the adult population," the blatant manipulation of the young generation by unscrupulous businessmen cast its own dark shadow that "left the idealistic young feeling hollow and unfulfilled" (Doggett, *There's a Riot Going On*, 15); or as Shaw chillingly expressed it, "Considering the animadversions about teen-age taste by the older generation, its readiness to trade on genuine adolescent feelings provided its own cynical commentary" (Shaw, 171). Many artists and intellectuals voiced their opposition to consumerism, seeing it as "an antithesis to America's notion of freedom and democracy, as it trapped people in a state of consumer-driven anxiety and distanced them from the true goal of personal self-development" (MacLeod, 6).

Along with the increasing attitude of cynicism toward the postwar consumerism, there loomed an even deeper sense of unease due to the imminent threat of a nuclear war between the world's two opposing superpowers—the United States and the Soviet Union—that had emerged in the aftermath of the war. This constant threat led to a new generation growing up in an atmosphere of permanent fear and dread.

Not only did the fear of impending nuclear war cause anxiety that had to be masked by a consumer culture, but also the banality of suburban life, which was inadvertently created by the consumer culture, distracted society from the glaringly obvious personal, domestic, and social issues that the Western world, particularly the United States, was undoubtedly experiencing and added to the anxiety already felt in modern life.

Rock 'n' roll was intrinsically linked to this feeling of alienation and held up those disaffected malcontents, such as Elvis, Marlon Brando, and James Dean, as its heroes; these were figures who strongly connected with and strengthened the inner emotional experiences of the new youth culture and those at odds with the all-consuming self of society's "happiness machine" (Curtis).

TOWARD SOCIAL REFORM

While black communities benefitted largely from the postwar prosperity, finding jobs in manufacturing plants, particularly the automobile industry, in areas of the north, such as Detroit, there was a heavy migration of blacks from the south who came to seek opportunities and escape the terrible racism they were subject to (Diana Ross's father Fred and Motown's founder Berry Gordy were examples). Under such circumstances many black families found comfortable housing, such as the Brewster Housing projects, and steady employment to help raise their children and provide them with at least a basic education (Marable, 29; M. Wilson, *Dreamgirl*, 10, 11; and T. Wilson, 18–20).

Despite the change in circumstances for the black communities, there was still a feeling of inequality. Many blacks in the towns of Boston, Detroit, and New York began to realize that, although they had more opportunities and rights than those blacks in the south, they were still discriminated against and were thus moved to bring about change by campaigning and protesting. Black soldiers, who were treated as equal among the European countries they liberated from German occupation, had a greater feeling of self-worth and refused to give up their right to equality when they returned home (U.S. Diplomatic Mission).

While the government had made attempts to outlaw segregation throughout America and to ensure equality for all citizens, civil rights were still being violated. Organizations such as the Black Muslims, the National Association for the Advancement of Colored People (NAACP), Martin Luther King Jr.'s Southern Christian Leadership Conference (SCLC), and the Revolutionary Action Movement evolved in order to put an end to racism once and for all.

Young whites began to absorb black culture through the fusion of black and white music; Elvis was liked by both black and white kids

(Shaw, 50); and his mix of country, blues, and gospel was a good example of this racial crossover, while live performances of black artists, particularly, attracted a mixed-race audience. The rock 'n' roll star Little Richard was another example of how such performers broke down racial taboos when demand for personal appearances from him, even in the southern states, was by a predominantly white audience (White, 69). Rock 'n' roll, as writer Mark Kurlansky observed, was "profoundly about racial integration" (2), while Susan Douglas described this changing attitude, particularly in regard to young black female artists, as

> the vibrating voices of black teenagers, often trained in the gospel traditions of their churches, [that] suggested a perfect fusion of naiveté and knowingness. . . . Black voices conveyed both a moral authority and a spirited hope for the future. These were the voices of exclusion, of hope for something better, of longing. They were not, like Annette or the Lennon Sisters, the voices of sexual repression, of social complacency, or of homogenized commercialism. (S. Douglas, *Where the Girls Are*, 95)

Encouraged by the civil rights movement, women too began to assert themselves and break free from the traditional but extremely restrictive role of "finding a husband and bearing children." Prior to the Second World War women had made a certain amount of headway in having their civil liberties respected, due mainly to the suffragette movement in the 1920s, and during the war women played a pivotal role, taking over traditionally male jobs, while the men were away fighting. Once the war ended, however, a vigorous campaign started, "fueled by the fear that there wouldn't be enough jobs for returning servicemen" (S. Douglas, *Where the Girls Are*, 47), to encourage women back into the home (Wolf, 64). One commentator, particularly, observed that

> social mores, indeed, were changing and so were the expectations for marriage. Sexual enjoyment and companionship in marriage altered women's private worlds and thoughts. But if women dared to chart a course for themselves outside the traditional family sphere, they were either chastised or ultimately forced to surrender to their "natural feminine instincts." (Gluck, 6)

Throughout the 1950s and 1960s many feminine groups formed to support and encourage women in their fight for equal rights and independence (Judt, 338, 339, 487), and soon many women were occupying positions in politics, business, and media that were once only filled by men.

The legalization of the contraceptive pill, in 1961, brought with it sexual freedom, which fit neatly into a youth culture influenced by feminism, rock 'n' roll, economic prosperity, and the birth of the teenager. Both men and women could now experience and express themselves sexually, without the fear and stigma of an unwanted pregnancy.

All of these new freedoms and attitudes fed into each other and produced a society of young people, who were freed from the drudgery and responsibility of becoming young adults as soon as they left school. The new youth had greater and more exciting opportunities than had their parents. They had money to buy things, fueling the consumer culture, and the means (particularly with the postwar boom in the motor industry) to go places, as well as greater sexual freedoms that previous generations couldn't even imagine. Most importantly, this new youth culture had its very own style of music—rock 'n' roll, a virtual euphemism for sex, (Shaw, 106), which provided the perfect soundtrack to the new generations' journey to freedom and personal happiness.

THE SCENE IS SET

The advent of rock 'n' roll had set a teenage Phil Spector on a course of personal adventure, while the new consumer culture created opportunities for individuals such as him to become very wealthy and successful. The new trends and fashions in teen consumerism meant that teenagers with any drive were seen as gold dust among clever marketing and businessmen, who wanted access to the teen markets, as well as a product that would attract the potential teen consumer. The young Spector with his musical ambition and talent fitted this profile perfectly and was virtually dollar signs in the eyes of marketing men of this type.

The waking impulses of the civil rights movement and the cultural acceptance of black music not only influenced and encouraged Spector to develop his sound but also allowed him to operate in an industry that could draw on the wonderful resources of black vocalists, as well as the teenage sensibilities that the young teen songwriters, who had begun to emerge, were able to tap into. All this provided Spector with the elements he needed to create a successful brand of pop music. Also, growing up in the postwar era as the first wave of teenagers meant he was already attuned to the outlook and emotional responses of his own audience. By the time he had developed his production and songwriting skills, he was already experiencing and feeling the things that his teen audience were also experiencing and feeling, ultimately making his music the perfect musical accompaniment to their lives.

TIMELINE

Phil Spector	*Cultural Events*
January 10, 1903: Benjamin Spector is born.	
July 15, 1911: Bertha Spector is born.	
November 27, 1911: Bertha Spector arrives, with her family, in America.	
June 1913: Ben Spector arrives, with his family, in America.	
1934: Spector's parents marry.	
1935: Spector's sister, Shirley, is born.	
December 26, 1939: Spector is born.	
	Dec 7, 1941: United States enters World War II after Japan attacks U.S. naval base at Pearl Harbor.
	May 8, 1945: Germany surrenders.

Phil Spector   *Cultural Events*

Aug 14, 1945: Japan surrenders.
Bombs dropped on Hiroshima
and Nagasaki. End of World War
II; peace declared.

June 1945: Following the Allied
victory in World War II, the first
of the U.S. soldiers begin
returning home from Europe, the
Pacific, and Asia.

Oct 1945: Setup of the UN in the
aftermath of the war.

April 1948: Marshall Plan
established to provide aid to
Europe in the aftermath of the
war. Britain in the grip of
recession and rationing. The
Marshall Plan aims to get Europe
back on its feet.

January 5, 1949: Truman
presents his proposal for a "Fair
Deal," which provides great social
and economic reform in the
United States following World
War II.

April 20, 1949: Spector's father
commits suicide.

June 25, 1950: North Korea
invades South Korea. United
States comes to the aid of South
Korea, bringing them into a three-
year-long war.

July 1950: Marlon Brando makes
his first movie appearance and
shakes the cinematic world with

Phil Spector

Cultural Events

his new acting style. His 1953 film *The Wild One* makes a big impact on the postwar generation.

April 1951: European Union begins with the France/Germany Coal and Steal Treaty, otherwise known as the Paris Treaty, reinforced six years later by the Treaty of Rome.

November 1952: The world's first music chart is compiled in the UK.

December 26, 1952: Spector gets his first guitar.

1953: Spector's family moves to LA.

June 1953: The coronation of Queen Elizabeth II.

July 1954: Elvis Presley records with Sam Philips at Sun Studios. Eighteen months later "Heartbreak Hotel" is released to completely transform popular music and culture.

Fall 1954: Spector enters Fairfax High School.

March 9, 1955: James Dean makes an impact with Steinbeck's *East of Eden*.

March 19, 1955: Bill Haley's song "Rock around the Clock" features in the film *Blackboard Jungle* about juvenile delinquency

Phil Spector

Cultural Events

and begins the craze for rock 'n' roll.

September 30, 1955: James Dean dies in a car accident. *Rebel without a Cause* is released in the wake of Dean's tragic death. The film makes an huge impact on the teen culture that begins to emerge.

July 30, 1955: The United States proposes to send "artificial" satellites into space, beginning a space race with the USSR, which was supposedly won by the United States when they eventually "landed" a man on the moon.

December 1, 1955: In Montgomery, Alabama, Rosa Parks sparks off the civil rights movement by refusing to give her seat on a bus to a white passenger.

December 26, 1955: As a birthday present Bertha and sister Shirley take Spector to his first major musical experience, Ella Fitzgerald. He is most impressed with her guitarist, Barney Kessel, who becomes a major inspiration for Spector.

Fall 1956: The Suez Canal Crisis has a disastrous effect on the UK and establishes the United States as the world's leading superpower. The British Empire begins to unravel its commonwealth as

Phil Spector

Early 1957: Spector forms his
first rock 'n' roll group with
friends from Fairfax High School.

Spring 1957: Spector makes his
first TV appearance on a late-night
show called *Rocket to Stardom*.
He also starts an apprenticeship,
of sorts, in Gold Star Recording
Studios.

June 1957: Spector graduates
from Fairfax High School. He
studies French at Los Angeles
City College. He also takes a
course in court reporting in a
business college. He works as a
court stenographer on the famous
Lana Turner/Cheryl Crane and
Johnny Stompanato murder trial.

May 20, 1958: Spector forms the
Teddy Bears with Annette

Cultural Events

Australia and Canada begin to
seek their independence. India
and the West Indies too seek their
independence; Britain allows its
subjects from these countries to
enter Britain.

September 1957: Jack Kerouac's
book *On the Road* creates a new
literary style and draws attention
to the beat poets and certain
unsavory elements of American
society.

October 4, 1957: USSR beats
United States in putting the fist
satellite, *Sputnik 1*, into orbit.

Phil Spector

Kleinbard and Marshall Leib and records a demo, "Don't Worry My Little Pet," in Gold Star.

July 3, 1958: Spector and the Teddy Bears sign to Era Records.

Summer 1958: Spector records "To Know Him Is to Love Him." The song is released at the end of September.

November 28, 1958: Spector and the Teddy Bears appear on *American Bandstand* to promote the single.

December 1958: Spector has his first number one with "To Know Him Is to Love Him."

Late December 1958: Spector leaves Era Records to sign with Ricky Nelson and Fats Domino's label Imperial.

Cultural Events

January 12, 1959: Berry Gordy establishes Motown record company. The Miracles release the label's first major hit, "Shop Around," the following year.

February 3, 1959: Buddy Holly, Richie Valens, and the Big Bopper are killed in a plane crash.

March 1959: Spector begins recording tracks for the *Teddy Bears Sing* album.

Fall 1959: Spector officially breaks up the Teddy Bears. Soon after, he manufactures a group

Phil Spector   *Cultural Events*

called the Spector Trio for which
he writes and produces the
material. It lasts only a brief time.

Summer 1960: Music industry
professional Lester Sill, Spector's
friend and future partner,
arranges for Spector to go to New
York as apprentice to the highly
successful production duo Leiber
and Stoller.

Fall 1960: Spector records
"Corrina Corrina" with Ray
Peterson, his first big hit since "To
Know Him."

October 20, 1960: Spector had
cowritten "Spanish Harlem" with
Jerry Leiber; he begins recording
the song with Leiber and Stoller.
The song features Ben E. King on
lead vocals.

November 8, 1960: John F.
Kennedy is elected president of
the United States.

Spring 1960: Spector has four
songs in the charts: "Corrina
Corrina," "Spanish Harlem,"
"Pretty Little Angel Eyes," and
"Some of Your Lovin'."

1961: Spector records Bert Bern's
"Twist and Shout" with a group
called the Topnotes for Atlantic
Records. Spector ruins the song,
which would become a hit by the
Isley Brothers a year later. The
Beatles would cover it on their

Phil Spector

first album and make it a rock 'n' roll classic.

1961: Spector records a number of records with Gene Pitney.

May 24, 1961: Spector's first recording with the Paris Sisters, a song called "Be My Boy," is released. The song makes it to number fifty-six and is a calling card for the girls who will go on to have a huge hit at the end of the year with Spector's production of "I Love How You Love Me."

Summer 1961: Spector sets up Philles Records with his friend and promotions man Lester Sill. Spector signs New York girl group the Crystals as his first Philles act.

June 28, 1961: Spector begins his first recordings on his Philles label with the Crystals' "There's Nobody Like My Baby."

Cultural Events

April 12, 1961: USSR sends first man into space.

May 1961: Attack on "freedom riders" in Birmingham, Alabama, brings international attention to civil rights movement.

August 1961: Construction begins on the Berlin Wall. The wall becomes the defining symbol of the Cold War. The nuclear arms race between the United States and the USSR escalates.

Phil Spector

Cultural Events

November 1961: The United States increases pressure in Vietnam.

December 1961: The Beach Boys release their first single, "Surfin'."

Spring 1962: Spector begins his successful relationship with Don Kirshner and his Aldon publishing company, where he has access to the latest teen material.

March 1962: Spector releases his next Crystals song, Mann and Weil's "Uptown," which establishes him and the Crystals as the newest pop sound.

March 1962: Bob Dylan records his first records for Columbia Records.

May 1962: Spector records a third single for the Crystals, the controversial "He Hit Me (and It Felt Like a Kiss)."

June 1962: Spector's production of Connie Francis's song "Second Hand Love" hits the top ten.

July 13, 1962: Spector begins recording Gene Pitney's "He's a Rebel." He decides he wants the song for the Crystals and flies to Gold Star to record it. He begins his musical relationship with engineer Larry Levine and musical arranger Jack Nitzsche, who introduces him to the Blossoms, Darlene Wright (Love), and the Wrecking Crew

Phil Spector

musicians, whom Spector uses on nearly all of his Philles Records.

November 3, 1962: Spector has his second number one with "He's a Rebel."

February 1963: Spector marries Annette Merar.

May 26, 1963: Spector begins recording demos with the Ronettes. He soon drops the Crystals to concentrate on making Ronnie Bennett a star. Spector and Ronnie will develop an intimate relationship that fuels their music.

Summer 1963: Records his famous *Christmas Gift for You* album. It is a commercial failure, but it is later seen as a landmark album, which gathers much critical acclaim over the years. By the end of the year Spector has nine singles in the charts, three of which make the top ten.

Cultural Events

October 5, 1962: Sean Connery brings James Bond to the big screen.

October–November 1962: The Cuban missile crisis brings the world close to nuclear war, causing permanent anxiety over nuclear war throughout the 1960s.

January 1963: The Beach Boys' "Surfin' USA" is a smash hit.

Phil Spector

June 8, 1963: "Da Doo Ron Ron" reaches number three in the charts. It is the Crystals' sixth release. The song is followed by "Then He Kissed Me," which enters the charts in August. For this particular single he replaces Love with "La La" Brooks as lead vocalist.

August 24, 1963: Spector begins recording the Walt Disney song "Zip-a-Dee-Doo-Dah" with Bob B. Soxx and the Blue Jeans. With a virtual orchestra of musicians in tow, the record is Spector's first real attempt at his "Wall of Sound."

August 31, 1963: Spector records and releases the iconic "Be My Baby." Spector will record many more singles with the Ronettes over the next two years, including "Baby, I Love You" and "Walking in the Rain."

Cultural Events

August 1963: The civil rights movement escalates after Martin Luther King Jr.'s march on Washington.
Antiracial laws passed in the United States.

November 22, 1963: John F. Kennedy is assassinated. Lyndon B. Johnson succeeds him as president.

Phil Spector

January 24, 1964: Spector flies to England to promote the Ronettes. On his trip he meets the Rolling Stones and their manager, a Phil Spector wannabe, Andrew "Loog" Oldham. Spector helps them record their first big break through a number, a cover of Buddy Holly's "Not Fade Away."

February 1964: Spector meets the Beatles and accompanies them on their first American tour, landing with them at JFK for their momentous reception and the beginning of Beatlemania.

Cultural Events

February 7, 1964: The Beatles touch down at JFK, starting off Beatlemania in the United States. "I Wanna Hold Your Hand" is number one in the United States and Britain.
The Beatles' arrival begins the British Invasion with bands such as the Rolling Stones, Herman's Hermits, and the Animals swarming the American charts.

July 1964: Civil Rights Act is passed ending segregation. Race riots in Rochester, New York.

August 1964: Following the Gulf of Tonkin incident, Johnson administration given a mandate to escalate U.S. military involvement in Vietnam.

Phil Spector

Cultural Events

August 31, 1964: Motown's Supremes release "Where Did Our Love Go," giving them their first number one of a string of eleven number ones over five years.

October 16, 1964: Harold Wilson becomes the first Labour prime minister in nearly fifteen years. Wilson's years in office, 1964–1970, mark a period in British cultural domination, spearheaded by the Beatles, throughout the world and great economic prosperity at home, which leads to the decade being defined as the "swinging sixties."

October 24, 1964: After a series of unsuccessful releases, Spector has his last minor success with the Ronettes' song "Walking in the Rain." Spector loses interest in the group, which will disband by the end of 1965.

Winter 1964: Under pressure from the British groups and Motown, Spector responds by making the "biggest record" of his life: "You've Lost That Lovin' Feelin'," using the white, blue-eyed soul sound of the Righteous Brothers.

Christmas 1964: The reaction to "Lovin' Feelin'" in the United States is initially poor, but soon

Phil Spector

the DJs catch on to it, and it reaches the number one spot in February of the following year. Oldham takes out an ad in the British music press to promote the song over the inferior version by Beatles producer George Martin and Liverpool singer Cilla Black. Spector's version of the song is the longest recorded song to date at 3.50 seconds, changing the notion of pop songs' length and quality.

January 3, 1965: Tom Wolfe's famous article about Phil Spector, entitled "The First Tycoon of Teen," is published in the *New York Herald Tribune*.

Fall/Winter 1965: Spector bankrolls a ten-day theater show for the controversial and troubled comic Lenny Bruce. The gigs are not as successful as was hoped. Bruce would be found dead less than a year later, on August 2, 1966, of a drug overdose.

Cultural Events

February 21, 1965: Assassination of Malcolm X.

July 1965: Johnson sends fifty thousand more troops into Vietnam.

August 1965: Race riots in Watts, California.

October 1965: The first major protests against the Vietnam War as more U.S. citizens are drafted

Phil Spector

Cultural Events

into the war. The draft had increased from three to thirty-three thousand per month.

November 29 and 30, 1965: Spector produces the concert movie *The Big TNT Show*, which was recorded at Hollywood's Moulin Rouge Theatre. The show includes Spector's next production interest Ike and Tina Turner.

Spring 1966: Spector teams up with Ike and Tina Turner, keen to take advantage of the couple's stage show to compete with groups such as the Beatles and the Rolling Stones.
Spector makes a deal to record an album of songs with Tina as the main vehicle.
"River Deep, Mountain High" is the focus of the project, and although it does well in the UK it is buried in the United States for various reasons. Spector goes into retirement disgruntled at the American public's reaction to "River Deep, Mountain High," which he considered the best record of all time. Spector publishes an ad in the trade papers entitled "Benedict Arnold Was Right," commenting on the fickle attitude of the American public toward his music.

May 1966: The Chinese Cultural Revolution is initiated by

Phil Spector

Cultural Events

Chairman Mao in an attempt to destroy any remaining elements of capitalist ideologies in the "communist" system. Many are persecuted in the name of "communism."

May 16, 1966: The Beach Boys release their groundbreaking *Pet Sounds*. Bob Dylan releases his iconic triple *Blonde on Blonde*. The Beatles respond three months later with *Revolver*.

June 1, 1967: The Beatles' *Sgt. Pepper's Lonely Hearts Club Band* is released to both critical and commercial success and transforms pop music, making it as culturally relevant as jazz and classical music.

Summer 1967: "The Summer of Love." The hippie counterculture captures a new spirit of hope, peace, and youthful idealism while opposing old ideologies of capitalism and warfare.

1968: The "year of protests" and revolutions around the world; Belgrade, Moscow, Paris, and Prague were particularly significant.

February 1968: Production on Dennis Hopper's classic cult movie *Easy Rider* begins, with Spector playing the part of a drug dealer called Connection.

Phil Spector	*Cultural Events*
	April 4, 1968: Assassination of Martin Luther King Jr.
April 14, 1968: Spector marries Ronnie Bennett.	
	June 6, 1968: Assassination of Robert Kennedy.
	January/February 1968: Public opinion turns against war in Vietnam.
	November 1968: Richard Nixon is elected president.
	July 3, 1969: Brian Jones of the Rolling Stones is found dead in his swimming pool at the age of twenty-seven.
	July 11, 1969: David Bowie releases "Space Oddity" to accompany the moon landing. It reaches number five in the British charts.
	July 20, 1969: Apollo moon landings.
	August 15–18, 1969: Woodstock festival is both the pinnacle and the end of the counterculture influence.
	December 6, 1969: The death of a Rolling Stones fan at the band's Altamont concert is seen by some as the end of sixties idealism and positivity.
January 1970: Spector comes out of retirement to record John	

Phil Spector

Lennon's single "Instant Karma," from which he is offered the job of mixing the Beatles' chaotic *Let It Be* recordings.

May 8, 1970: The Beatles' *Let It Be* album is released. Despite its commercial and critical success Spector faces a backlash from the British press and public as well as from Paul McCartney over his elaborate remixing of the album.

Summer 1970: Spector records Harrison's *All Things Must Pass* album as well as Harrison's live album *The Concert for Bangladesh* and *Living in the Material World*.

September 1970: Spector coproduces the *John Lennon/ Plastic Ono Band* project.

Spring 1971: Spector records a number of Harrison songs with Ronnie Spector in an effort to reignite her career.

June 1971: Spector coproduces the *Imagine* album with Lennon.

Cultural Events

April 10, 1970: The Beatles announce their split.

September 18, 1970: Legendary guitarist Jimi Hendrix dies of a supposed drug overdose. He is twenty-seven years old.

July 3, 1971: Jim Morrison, the iconic lead vocalist with rock

Phil Spector

Cultural Events

group the Doors, is found dead in
his bath, in Paris, at the age of
twenty-seven.

June 1972: David Bowie's *Ziggy
Stardust* makes an impact in
Britain and the United States.
Glam rock takes hold in Britain.

June 16, 1972: After a turbulent
four years of marriage, Ronnie
files for a divorce.

1973: Spector starts work on
Lennon's *Rock 'n' Roll* album, this
time as sole producer, but the
whole episode turns out to be a
disaster, and Lennon abandons
the project.

January 1, 1973: British prime
minister Ted Heath leads the UK
into the European Economic
Community (EEC), bringing the
idea of a United States of Europe
closer to a reality.

January 15, 1973: Nixon
declares a cease-fire in Vietnam.

December 1973: Hilly Kristal
opens CBGBs in Manhattan's
East Village, which creates a scene
from which the next generation of
influential rock groups emerge.
These include the Ramones,
Blondie, Television, Patti Smith,
and Talking Heads.

August 4, 1974: Nixon resigns
following the Watergate scandal.
He is succeeded by Gerald Ford.

Phil Spector

August 1975: Spector records
fifties pop sensation Dion
DiMucci. The album, *Born to Be
with You*, is influenced primarily
by both Spector and Dion's love
for fifties doo-wop. The album is a
commercial flop, though years
later it gains critical respect.

February 1977: Spector sees the
Ramones play live at the famous
Whisky a Go Go.

June 1977: Spector records
Leonard Cohen's *Death of a
Ladies Man*. The album, released
in 1978, does not do well with the
critics. Cohen is unhappy with the
album.

Cultural Events

1976: Britain falls into another
recession, and punk rock emerges
as a result.

November 26, 1976: The Sex
Pistols release "Anarchy in the
UK," expressing the social
alienation and economic
frustration felt by Britain's youth.
"God Save the Queen" is released
six months later, bringing a new
attitude and immediacy to rock
music not felt since the early
sixties.

January 20, 1977: Jimmy Carter
becomes the thirty-ninth
president of the United States.

August 16, 1977: Elvis Presley is
found dead.

Phil Spector

Cultural Events

February 1978: Blondie makes it big in the UK with their cover of Randy and the Rainbow's "Denise."

May 1, 1979: Spector signs a deal to record the Ramones.

May 4, 1979: Margaret Thatcher becomes the first lady prime minister of Great Britain.

January 1980: The Spector/ Ramones collaboration *End of the Century* is released.
Spector and the Ramones have a hit with "Baby, I Love You." Although the album does better than any of their other recordings, it does not become the great success that the group had hoped.

May 1980: The term *yuppie* is first coined in the press. The yuppie would come to define a major characteristic of Reagan/ Thatcher's capitalist ideologies. On "Black Monday," October 19, 1987, the stock market crashed, making the yuppie virtually extinct overnight.

September 22, 1980: The Iran-Iraq War begins. It rages for eight years, making it the longest conflict of the twentieth century.

December 8, 1980: John Lennon is assassinated. Many view Lennon's death as a symbolic death of rock itself.

Phil Spector   *Cultural Events*

January 20, 1981: Ronald
Reagan begins his presidency.
Relations between the UK and the
United States are encouraged
through the capitalist ideologies of
the Thatcher/Reagan
administrations. Reagan
establishes good relations with the
USSR, particularly during the
USSR's Perestroika and Glasnost
period.

August 1, 1981: MTV is
launched in America and begins
changing the nature of popular
music promotion. The music
video becomes all important.

April 2, 1982: The very
unpopular Falklands War begins
between Britain and Argentina.

November 30, 1982: Michael
Jackson's *Thriller* is released to
global success.

January 18, 1989: Spector
inducted into the Rock and Roll
Hall of Fame.

January 20, 1989: George H. W.
Bush succeeds Reagan as
president of the United States.

November 9, 1989: The fall of
the Berlin Wall. East and West
Europe begin their process of
reunification.

August 2, 1990: Iraq illegally
occupies Kuwait, sparking off the

Phil Spector

Cultural Events

Gulf War. George Bush deploys U.S. forces into Saudi Arabia.

December 1990: The Solidarity-led coalition government in Poland is the first free election in East Europe since the 1940s. It is a significant event that signals the end of "communism" in Eastern Europe.

Christmas Day 1991: Spector's son, Philip Jr., dies of leukemia. Spector is devastated.

January 20, 1993: Bill Clinton becomes president of the United States.

November 1, 1993: The Maastricht Treaty comes into force, by which the EEC becomes the European Union.

June 1995: Spector begins work on Celine Dion's album, but due to disagreements with the singer's management he leaves the project midway through.

1997: Tony Blair becomes prime minister of Britain. With New Labour he ends eighteen years of conservative government and brings to many a sense of hope to Britain. He becomes a strong ally to Bush during the "Invasion of Afghanistan," and soon many feel disillusioned by his false promises. In 2016 the Chilcot report gives a

Phil Spector

Cultural Events

devastating critique of Blair's attitude to the Iraq War. George W. Bush is elected president of the United States.

August 31, 1997: Lady Diana is killed in a car accident.

January 2000: The Internet has become a global phenomena for both commercial and personal use.

September 11, 2001: Millions of people watch on TV the attack and destruction of the World Trade Center in New York City. The incident and TV image create a sense of psychological fear and terror throughout the world.

October 7, 2001: The United States officially launches military operations in Afghanistan.

October 26, 2001: The Patriot Act is passed in the United States to counteract terrorism.

August 2002: Spector begins recordings for the next Starsailor album. The band is not totally convinced that Spector can deliver the goods and agree to record two songs, "Silence Is Easy" and "White Dove" as an "audition." He leaves the project a few months later for personal reasons.

November 20, 2003: Spector is arrested for the murder of the actress Lana Clarkson.

Phil Spector

Cultural Events

July 7, 2005: London bombings increase fear of continued terrorist attacks throughout the Western world.

April 13, 2009: After two trials, the first a mistrial because the jury couldn't reach a decision, Phil Spector is convicted of Clarkson's murder and is sentenced to life in prison.

I

TO KNOW HIM IS TO LOVE HIM

The Formative Years

Harvey Philip Spector was born on December 26, 1939, the second child of Ben and Bertha Spector. His mother would claim that he was actually born on December 25 and joke that she had given birth to the second Jesus (M. Brown, 14).

Spector's parents both came from families of Russian Jews, who had arrived in America from Ukraine in the early twentieth century. His mother, Bertha, was the second daughter born into a family called Spektar or Spektor. She was born in Paris in July 1911, an intermediary place in which the family took residence before finally arriving in America (Ribowsky, 12). Bertha's father westernized his name and became Spector, probably to conceal the family's origins, which he may have felt could have been met with unwelcome prejudice in the new world. Spector's father, Ben, was also born into a Russian family with a similar sounding name to his wife, Spektus or Spkres, and both, intriguingly, had fathers called George. According to Spector biographer Mark Ribowsky, Ben Spector came to America during the "great Russian immigration of the early 1990s," and an immigration officer Americanized their Russian name by spelling it with a *c* instead of a *k* (Ribowsky, 12).

It seems that on arriving in New York both families, members of whom may possibly have been cousins (M. Brown, 14), settled close to each other and mixed socially. Ben and Bertha would officially unite both families through their marriage in 1934 (Thompson, 13). Though Spector would often romanticize his upbringing, claiming he grew up in a Spanish Harlem ghetto (M. Brown, 14), in reality Ben and Bertha settled down in a small brick house in Manor Avenue, in the heart of the once Irish, but at the time Jewish, neighborhood in the Bronx called Soundview. Ribowsky and Spector enthusiast Dave Thompson write that the Spectors lived at 1024 (Ribowsky, 13; Thompson, 13), but Mick Brown, in his comprehensive biography on Spector, gives a different address, writing that they lived at 1027 (M. Brown, 15).

Harvey grew up in a house full of music, where the radio was very popular, as too was the folk music from Mom and Dad's own country, which they would regularly play on their guitars, instilling in the young boy a lifelong fascination for the instrument (Thompson, 15). Although he would suffer with mild asthma throughout his life, Harvey was, by all accounts, a happy, "round-faced, wavy-haired infant with searching eyes" (Ribowsky, 13). His sister, Shirley, who was four years older, was a seemingly beautiful and precocious girl, much admired by the Spectors' extended family of nieces and nephews, and was much more inclined toward the world of glamour and fashion. It became no surprise to the family, therefore, that as a teenager Shirley became a model with a desire to one day be a Hollywood starlet (Ribowsky, 15). Unfortunately, all the attention made her vain, and over time, as her dreams of Hollywood became unrealized, her vanity would turn to anxiety and arrogance, posing an emotional and mental challenge for the whole Spector family.

Both father and mother doted on the young Harvey, and although he was the apple of his mother's eye, Harvey idolized his "ruddy-faced," "handsome," "jovial," and "fun-loving" father, and felt happy and secure in the relatively comfortable family environment, which his father worked hard to provide. Harvey's father had a secure job as an iron-worker in Brooklyn and was, by all accounts, "the picture of American stability" (Ribowsky, 13). Harvey's mother, on the other hand, had a strong and forceful personality, which, coupled with a social ambition, possibly created in her a slightly unhealthy obsession with social status and wealth.

While Bertha Spector lavished attention on her youngest child, she seemed to keep her affections away from her husband whom she instead pushed and thwarted to do better. Whether she did so as a means to create a greater and more opportune life for her children or whether for her own desire to be "respectable," or possibly both, is hard to say. Nevertheless, her determination to improve the family's status, despite their already relative comfort and wealth, pushed Harvey's father to the point of exhaustion, both mentally and emotionally. It is not known if there were underlying emotional issues in Ben's makeup, but it seems he was not fully able to cope with his wife's continuous demands (M. Brown, 16).

DEATH OF A FATHER

On the morning of April 20, 1949, Ben Spector took his own life. He had pulled up at the side of the road a few blocks away from his home; "he drew out a water hose and attached one end to the exhaust pipe, then dangled the other end through the open front window" (Ribowsky, 14). "The cause of death was 'Carbon Monoxide Poisoning—Asphyxia; Suicidal'" (Thompson, 16).

The suicide was regarded by both sides of the family as "a horrible, ugly stigma, a perversion and aberration of the hope and promise that the Spector and Spektor families had brought to America" (Ribowsky, 14). Young Harvey felt the loss of his father deeply, and the episode would have "serious emotional repercussions for him" (Biography Channel).

Spector seems to have carried the loss of his father with him for his whole life, and to a large degree, his father's death has been a very clear cause for his drive and ambition, as well as his deep feelings of insecurity and isolation. His "misery," wrote Ribowsky, "could be measured by his contrasting mood in the rare moments when he spoke of his father" (Ribowsky, 19). Simultaneously, the tragic loss of his father gave him the emotional charge he needed to create his music.

In order to escape the anxiety of her husband's suicide, Bertha moved out to join her uncle in Los Angeles. The Spectors made their new home on South Spaulding Avenue in West Hollywood, and Bertha took a job as a seamstress, traveling the long journey, by bus, to the sweatshop in downtown Los Angeles twice a day (Thompson, 16). After her husband's death Bertha became even more protective of her son. She saw the world as a "dangerous and threatening place," a fear she may have lumbered on her son (M. Brown, 16). Despite, however, these obvious insecurities, Spector always believed he was destined for greatness (M. Brown, 16).

Harvey Spector was now insisting on being called Phil, the move giving him the opportunity to create a new identity—possibly one that would enable him to distance himself from his old life in New York and the emotionally crippling effect of his father's death. The young Phil Spector, who was once extroverted and friendly, was now withdrawn and introverted. He seemed to find solace in his room reading history books or playing his guitar late into the night.

Though most parents in this new neighborhood thought Phil was "weird," he made some close friends at John Burroughs Junior High School, one of which was Marshall Leib (Ribowsky, 16). Marshall was a very different boy to Phil; he was tall, athletic, and outgoing, the very things Phil was not but very much wished he was. Though physically very different, both boys shared a keen interest in music, and Phil, who had a quick mouth and fiery temper, could find himself in difficult situations, which Marshall would often be called upon to sort out, thus making him one of Phil's first bodyguards, an accessory he would later rarely be seen without.

DOMINEERING MOTHER

During Spector's high school years at Fairfax High School, which he entered in 1954 (Thompson, 17), his relationship with his mother became strained, as he, like many teenagers, felt the need to exert his independence. She fussed excessively over his health and his friends, and since he was the only male in the house, she put a lot of pressure on him to be successful. "To Bertha he was still her little boy," and no matter how much he tried, Phil could never seem to cut that cord (Ribowsky, 38). Mixed with all this was the seemingly argumentative nature of the Spector family itself. Phil and his mom would argue about everything, shouting and screaming at each other. "I got phone calls in the middle of the night," said Marshall Leib, "'come over and help!' And I would go over and sort of break the mood that was going on" (Ribowsky, 17).

It was not just through his mother though that all this conflict existed but also with his older sister, whose smothering concerns for him created its own fractious relationship. The atmosphere at home as a result was often bitter. "I didn't see a lot of endearment," Leib commented; "I never really had a feeling of any kind of togetherness" (Ribowsky, 17).

When Spector started to become interested in girls and was going steady with his first girlfriend Donna Kass, his mother and his sister were very jealous and possessive of him. Kass recalls that they acted like jealous lovers, as if they themselves were in love with him, both vying for his attention and deadly antagonistic toward any girl who caught his interest: "I always felt they were in love with him or something. They treated him like he was a god. They protected him, and they wanted to protect him from me" (Thompson, 43).

On another occasion after Phil had some success with his first hit record—"To Know Him Is to Love Him"—Shirley and Bertha accused Donna of interfering in Phil's music career and of getting in the way of his destiny: "They attacked me, not physically but yelling and tormenting me for hours. . . . They accused me of all kinds of things, that I was taking him away and not encouraging him about his music, and he was spending too much time with me and couldn't write" (Ribowsky, 38).

Phil did not seem to have the same feelings about his mother and sister as they did about him. While they smothered him with their love, Spector reacted with little affection toward them, possibly blaming his mother for his father's suicide. Despite the strained relationship, Phil came to depend on his mother and sister's strength and doggedness. In fact it was Bertha and Shirley who initially pushed Spector toward his musical career. While Spector's love of music came from his whole family, it was his mother who encouraged him by buying him a guitar for his bar mitzvah (Biography Channel; Thompson, 18) and letting him stay up all night playing along to the jazz stations on the radio. When he was fifteen they brought him to see Ella Fitzgerald, where he first became aware of jazz guitarist Barney Kessel, Spector's first real musical obsession (Biography Channel).

When a letter he wrote was published in the jazz magazine *Down-Beat* complaining about the overlooked talents of his hero, Barney Kessel, it was Shirley who sought out the guitarist, though not at her brother's request, and convinced Kessel to meet the fifteen-year-old boy who had so eagerly championed his playing.

Spector, being a quiet and polite boy, would probably not have dared to go and meet his idol, but with his sister's encouragement and his mother's tenacious questioning of Kessel on the music business, Spector attained the vital information and encouragement he needed to set out on his chosen path. It was at this meeting that Spector learned it was actually in rock 'n' roll, not jazz, where the most lucrative career was to be sought.

> I [Kessel] remember telling her that if he did have talent, I thought it was a wise move to direct it more into the pop field. . . . You couldn't go out and play jazz on the road anymore; it was all rock 'n' roll. I said he should get into the pop field and write songs and get involved in publishing and maybe work as an apprentice in a record company to find out how to mix sessions and get involved in the multidimensionality of the whole thing. (Ribowsky, 2)

Spector, taking Kessel's advice, began to search out fellow musicians with the intention of forming his own group. Marshall Leib would be Spector's first recruit, but soon another, Michael Spencer, would too become a musical comrade. While Spector had his guitar and his jazz, Spencer was a talented piano player more inclined toward classical music, and it was through Spencer that Spector became familiar with many different types of music. According to Spencer,

> Spector was very quiet, very sensitive, a little mouse-like creature without a lot of confidence—but when Philip was playing music, he had a tremendous aggression. . . . It was perhaps a desire to be independent from his mother. Phil was overly dependent on Bertha when we met, very coddled by her, smothered really. The relationship they had was extremely intense, because they were both very emotional people, and Phil's aggressive personality burst out of there as a way of compensating for being dependent so much of that time. (Ribowsky, 22–23)

WAGNER, JAZZ, AND ROCK 'N' ROLL

Spector would often go to Spencer's house where they would listen to all of Spencer's parents' classical records; this is where he became introduced to his greatest musical inspiration, the German composer Richard Wagner. According to Ribowsky, Michael Spencer's parents had an enormous collection of music ranging from classical to R&B, and Spector would listen to all these records through their "six-foot-high Patrician Electro-Voice speakers" and an amplifier with a time-lag feature that could reverberate any kind of music to make it sound as if it were being played in a concert hall. Seemingly, Spector experimented with this feature on all kinds of music from Sibelius to Gershwin and Wagner. More than any other, Wagner captured and ignited his imagination, and Wagner's music would become the inspiration to Spector's famous Wall of Sound (a term that Rolling Stones manager and Spector admirer Andrew "Loog" Oldham would use to describe Spector's later epic productions, although it had been a term previously coined by Stan Kenton for his own jazz orchestra). In essence, Spector's experiments with the Patrician Electro-Voice speakers at the Spencers' home were his first realizations of his Wall of Sound.

The feeling of acceptance and welcome that he felt in the Spencers' home, along with the music that he experienced there, filled him with a sense of belonging, creating a sanctuary for him away from the anxieties of his family life as well as from the world at large. It is possible that here, not only were the seeds to his Wall of Sound planted but also was planted the need to capture that all-embracing and all-enveloping musical experience in his own music, which would rekindle those happy days spent in the Spencer household, lost in the music of his beloved Wagner.

Though Spector was now well versed in classical music and jazz, in 1956 a new sound, dominated by charismatic young figures such as Elvis Presley and Buddy Holly, burst unapologetically onto the scene, and like all other American and British teenagers Phil Spector "was hooked" (Biography Channel).

With his jazz and classical education, the simpler form of rock 'n' roll was no problem for him to play. He was far ahead of the other kids who had caught the rock 'n' roll bug, and like many of the other teenage boys, Spector wanted to play the latest hits, mainly as a means to attract girls and find social acceptance. Spector recruited many different people into his many and varied musical ventures, picking them from the Fairfax High music club, known as the Barons, and searching for singers with whom he could create doo-wop-type harmony groups, another of Spector's musical favorites. These new singing partners included teenage friends such as Marshall Leib, Steve Price, Donnie Kartoon, Bart Silverman, Harvey Goldstein, and Bruce Johnston, who would later go on to join the Beach Boys (Ribowsky, 24).

Phil was the musical fulcrum in his area, often winning talent competitions and even making an appearance on a local TV program called *Rocket to Stardom* (Ribowsky, 24; Thompson, 28–29) on which he and Marshall Leib performed "In the Still of the Night." It was not before long Spector came across Gold Star Recording Studios, where he put more of Kessel's good advice into practice and became their apprentice.

GOLD STAR

Gold Star, built in 1950, was originally an old dentist's office situated at 6252 Santa Monica Boulevard. It functioned as a studio until 1983, but in 1984 the property was completely destroyed by fire. According to singer Darlene Love, who would sing on many of Spector's classic records with songs such as "He's a Rebel," Gold Star was a "dingy place," which you could only enter through an alley at the back of the studio (Love, 61). Although some hit records, by groups such as the Hi-Lo's and the Four Lads, "white and light" harmony groups, as well as Eddie Cochran and Ritchie Valens, were made there, it was used primarily for songwriters to make demonstration tapes (Kubernik).

The space was unusually small for a recording studio, with a ceiling of only fourteen feet, well under the normal height of most professional studios, and a floor space of thirty-five by twenty-three feet, which meant a tight squeeze for any regular-sized band, though possibly more suitable for the R&B-type combos that were becoming popular and especially for the doo-wop vocal harmony groups that didn't necessarily require musicians and musical instruments that could crowd such a small space.

The studio's small size; the particular equipment, such as the warm and rich sound-producing tube microphones that the studio used; and the dedication of its two owners—Stan Ross and David Gold—made the studio a unique sound-recording environment. In fact it was this very unique recording environment that would play an essential role in the whole Spector sound (Kubernik). "You could literally smell the tubes inside the mixing board as they heated up," explains the Turtles'

Howard Kaylan. "There was a richness to the sound that Western and United, our usual studios, never had. . . . Perhaps we were all reading too much of the Spector legacy into the room, but I don't think so. Our recordings from Gold Star always just sounded better to me" (Kubernik).

One of the key features of Gold Star were the two echo chambers that were designed and built by Ross and Gold, which apparently used to counteract the effect of the low ceiling and the small dimensions of the space. It must have reminded Spector of the sounds he had fallen in love with that offered him an escape from the turmoil of his own family life when he would visit the Spencers' family home and lose himself in the music of Wagner on the heavy reverberated speakers. It is no wonder that the lush sound of Gold Star's echo chambers made it the most attractive of the studios around town to Spector, who would spend more and more of his time there in between studying court reporting at Los Angeles City College, which he had entered in the fall of 1957.

Both Ross and Gold seemed happy enough for Spector to hang around and absorb the atmosphere while listening to his dreams of "making it" in the music business (Ribowsky, 27). Despite being still very young, not quite seventeen, when he began studying the studio techniques of Stan Ross, though still by all accounts shy and polite in company, Spector seemed always confident in his musical ability and his skill at producing a record despite never having done so up to this point. "I saw a lot of growth with Phil very early," claimed Ross. "The day he first walked in I explained to him the studio policy of buying time by the hour and a role of tape. I had to be firm 'cause I didn't want twenty more Phil Spectors coming in" (Kubernik).

He seemed so confident that he could make a great record, a claim not too unusual for him to make since he had already been able to create a "radio sound" from his guitar, which most of the other young musicians around him at the time were fascinated by. Spector's guitar sound, by many reports, was so smooth and enticing that he always had the girls sitting around him at the gigs simply because they were so drawn to the lush "radio sound" coming from his guitar. This would also suggest that Spector not only had a keen ear for melodies and harmonies, and a great guitar-playing gift, which many vouched for (Ribowsky, 11, 22, 24, 50, 65), but also had absorbed the tonal characteristics and colors that different guitar players could get through the technical manipulation of their amp and guitar settings. From this aspect Spector had begun to tune his ears to the sound of instruments in the context of studio production and record making.

With the attainment of this musical and production knowledge, Spector was keen to apply it in an actual studio, and Spector pleaded with Ross and Gold to give him access to the studio when it was not being used. They refused to give him free studio time but made no issue with him making a record for the standard studio fee of $15 per hour, approximately $150 to $200 in today's money. Spector, being an impoverished student from a not particularly well-off family, had not the means to cover the costs. Also it was unlikely he could achieve anything substantial in an hour with the standard time being at least three hours to cut any kind of record at all, which meant $45 would be required. Also there were other studio expenses, which needed to be considered, including $6 for the quarter-inch tape on which the music, in the predigital days of studio production, was recorded.

His always-supportive mother donated $10 toward the venture (Ribowsky, 28), while the rest he got from band members, the ever-faithful Marshall Leib as well as Harvey Goldstein. The final donation came from a young girl called Annette Kleinbard (a friend of Donna Kass), whose strong and moving soprano voice, which according to Ribowsky, she would belt out of her tiny framed body at the Fairfax High talent shows, greatly impressed Spector (Ribowsky, 28). Spector, however, was initially reluctant to use Kleinbard as he was not interested in having girls in his group (Thompson, 24); the trend at the time was that rock 'n' roll was played by males, and girls had to be content with light pop music that the boys didn't take too seriously. However, Phil's ambitions to prove himself in the studio and record a record outdid his pride in this matter, and since she was willing, after some "gentle persuasion" from Phil, to part with $10 (which incidentally she got from her mother), Spector let her on board. Although he did not intend to make her a singing star, this seems to be the angle he fed her in order to get her financial input; instead, Phil used her more as a tool in his drive to becoming a serious and successful creator of music.

It was not Spector's intention to just simply go into the recording studio and record faithfully the sounds of the musicians. Even at this early stage Phil was considering his musical vision; he had been creating sounds and music in his head for some time and was determined to create records that were in themselves artistic creations that merged the musical styles of the time with the technological developments of the age and stretched them to their ultimate capacity to create something altogether unique.

When Spector had raised the sufficient finances, he, Leib, Goldstein, and Kleinbard entered Gold Star Studios on the afternoon of May 20, 1958 (Thompson, 30), and the song he chose to record, with little say from the other three, was his own composition: a harmony-based number entitled "Don't Worry My Little Pet."

DON'T WORRY MY LITTLE PET

The song draws on the West Coast sound of the late fifties, such as Duane Eddy, whose songs "Movin' and a Groovin'" and "Rebel Rouser" made him the new pop sensation at the time Spector was beginning his recording career. Other songs of the time, such as the Silhouettes' "Get a Job," which had been a number one earlier in the year, possibly exerted an influence with regard to the song's pace, as well as the obvious doo-wop elements. The song was also clearly influenced by two of Spector's favorite rock 'n' roll recording artists, the Everly Brothers and Buddy Holly, and though it was not one of Spector's more inspired pieces, it is, by the sheer fact that it was his first ever songwriting attempt, definitely worth commenting on.

Although it is not, by any stretch of the imagination, a well-written song—the melody is weak, the sections are difficult to define, and it lacks significant hooks—lyrically the song is interesting, not from the point of view of capturing well-expressed thoughts or feelings, but because they resonate with a popular mood and theme that young, particularly white, rock 'n' roll performers seemed to relate to. He expressed the feeling of emotional loss and anxiety, which suggests a mood that had entered into the culture of the next generation of post–World War II youths—described by the music critic Bob Stanley as being "deliriously happy one day, desperately sad the next" (Stanley, 112).

The lyric "Don't Worry" suggests a response to the emotional problems experienced by this generation, particularly as it was expressed in songs, such as Elvis's "Heartbreak Hotel"; Ricky Nelson's "Stood Up" and a "Teenager's Romance," which certainly expresses Stanley's sentiment above; and the Everly Brothers' "Bye Bye Love." It can also be seen in the Everly Brothers' song "Problems" (though not released until some months after Spector's song), in which the singer feels overwhelmed by the personal problems, trivial to those not in the throes of adolescence, ultimately stemming from a lack of self-confidence regarding mainly his romantic relationships. Here Spector reassures his subject that any problems will be overcome mainly because his love is strong.

Musically the song blatantly borrows from the opening riff to the Everly Brothers' arrangement of Ray Charles's "This Little Girl of Mine." The melody and vocal delivery is quite similar too, while the rhythm borrows heavily from other Everly Brothers' songs, such as "Wake Up Little Susie" and "Bye Bye Love." However, there is more emphasis, in Spector's song, on the punctuated percussion, pushed further to the front of the mix, as in Buddy Holly's tracks "Peggy Sue" and "Not Fade Away." The cleanness and clarity of the Everly Brothers' recordings, however, are not there; this is not surprising though, considering Spector recorded the song in two hours and it was the first time he had ever recorded his own music in a studio.

From a production point of view the song is a sonic mess. There is little separation between the instruments, while the vocal harmonies (and a significant amount of the lyrics) are virtually incoherent. Spector does, however, capture something of the production style of the Everly Brothers, particularly the reverb on songs such as "Wake Up Little Susie." The Everly Brothers would be a continuous influence on Spector for the next few years; the hook to their song "Should We Tell Him," for example, became the central motif of Spector's "Then He Kissed Me."

"Don't Worry My Little Pet" had incorporated elements of rock 'n' roll and doo-wop harmony mixed with production elements borrowed from the Everly Brothers and as such seems something quite different and new, though the two hours of studio time that Spector had bought were simply not enough to capture the musical ideas he had developed in his mind for it. Despite Stan Ross's engineering skills and Spector's enthusiasm, the track came out muddy and rough sounding.

The song, suggests Brown, "evinced a raw and spontaneous youthful energy"; despite this, however, nobody, except Spector, thought the song was much good. Stan Ross would later dismiss it as "a piece of crap," and even the song's singer, Annette Kleinbard, thought it was "dreadful" (M. Brown, 36). Richard Williams, however, in his book *Phil Spector: Out of His Head*, suggests that although "it is impossible to sort out a lead voice . . . with the benefit of hindsight this curious mixture of folk and commercial R&B and heavy arrangement certainly seems a rehearsal for bigger things to come" (R. Williams, 26–27).

PHIL SPECTOR MAKES A DEAL

Phil, being only seventeen years old, had little real knowledge of the process of getting the song any attention; he didn't know how to get the radio to play it or get it into the shops. In fact, Ribowsky tells us that after cutting an acetate copy of the record, Spector and Leib went into the first record store they saw but were, to their surprise, met with total indifference (Ribowsky, 29).

Although Phil had demonstrated his musical talent and put some of his studio ideas to the test for "Don't Worry My Little Pet," his other talent of knowing who could best help him to achieve his goals was put to greater use. Along with his manipulation of Kleinbard and Goldstein, using them as both musical instruments, as well as financiers for his projects, another person who was dragged into Spector's quest for success was ex–Fairfax High student Donnie Kartoon.

Kartoon lived next door to Lew Bedell, the co-owner of a small record label called Era Records, which Spector was savvy to know about, and he was persuasive enough to get Kartoon to set up a meeting with Bedell. At seventeen, Spector, though shy and reserved when not playing music, at least by the accounts of many who knew him, at the time was not so shy and forthcoming when it came to pushing his music.

Bedell and Herb Newman, Era's other co-owner, listened to Spector's demo enthusiastically and by the end of the meeting had decided to sign the group, which were as yet unnamed, to their label. The label, keen to reap the benefits of the new rock 'n' roll market, signed the four with the consent of their parents but not to a permanent contract. The deal was, in fact, for four songs for "lease of master." In other words the group remained independent of the record company, which would have first rights on four songs to promote and distribute as they saw fit, reaping any profits and paying the four group members a small royalty for each record they sold.

On July 3, 1958, the group signed to Era Records. The contract gave Era "all right, title and interest of what so ever kind" to four recordings along with the "exclusive and perpetual ownership" of them (M. Brown, 37). Effectively this meant Era owned and could do as they pleased with the master recordings of whatever four songs Phil chose to give them.

For their next single Spector decided on two self-penned songs: "Wonderful Lovable You" and "To Know Him Is to Love Him," a song that would ignite Spector's musical career and propel him into the stratosphere of pop stardom.

TO KNOW HIM IS TO LOVE HIM

"To Know Him Is to Love Him" was a song written for the memory of his father, expressing the absolute love Spector felt for him and the yearning he felt at his loss. Though the song was a deep expression of Phil's innermost feelings, feelings that he found difficult to relate unless through the mysterious and indirect language of his music, the song also rang through with the universal appeal of unrequited love and touched the hearts of many teens who seemed, since the beginning of rock 'n' roll, to have developed a more melancholic disposition than that of previous generations. As Ribowsky noted, the song

> was an epiphany of yearning in the placid Eisenhower years. For all its innocence, the song had an undercurrent of sadness and aliena-tion. It swayed back and forth in a hammock-like lull, sounding like a mantra, then given a sudden urgency by a ninth chord that was dark and melancholy in itself. In its inscrutability, the title regained its original implication. (Ribowsky, 34)

The writing of this classic song, which is still a standard of rock 'n' roll compilations, was also a forerunner of the girl group sound that began to make a slight impression a year before with the Chantels' "Maybe." It was the "first girl ballad of its time," remembers Kleinbard. "There was no girl, innocent, white-type voice on songs like that" (Ribowsky, 34; Stras, 33–55). Kleinbard is referring here to the fact that most female voices were more midregistered conversation style and were more developed and mature sounding. These were often trained singers such as Doris Day and Judy Garland.

Kleinbard's untrained voice was high and thin, and as such resonated with the sensibilities of white teenage girls, who according to the fashions and tastes of the time had an inclination toward the melancholic, similar in a way to films of the time that had a definite teen theme, such as James Dean's *Rebel without a Cause* (1955). Kleinbard's confident little "oh" at the end of the bridge after the words "that he was meant for me" is pure New York in content, just the kind of small improvisation that an R&B singer would consider second nature, but the approach is softer and whiter (R. Williams, *Phil Spector*, 25).

Kleinbard's untutored and distinctly girlish voice would strongly appeal to the new social class of teenage girls that was looking for something, distinct from their parents' generation, to call their own. The boys had found it in Elvis and the Everly Brothers, but while the girls had found these male figures along with movie stars, such as Dean, Newman, and Brando, as something to desire, there was no girl's voice for them to feel their own emotions through. Kleinbard, as mentioned above, suggests that she or at least the song "To Know Him Is to Love Him" was the first to directly resonate with its white female audience. As Richard Williams suggests,

> At best the song sounds like a demo, and a particularly hesitant one. But it was the beauty of pop music in 1958. It was such a powerful expression of the new teenage consciousness that flimsiness and naïvety actually made music more appealing, not less. Annette Kleinbard singing "To Know Him Is to Love Him," with Phil Spector and Marshall Leib in support, sounded exactly like the people—immature, unformed, full of tentative romantic hopes and dreams—who would hear and respond to the record when eventually it was heard on the radio. Devoid of calculation, it simply was its audience. (R. Williams, *Phil Spector*, 25)

A few years later another group, the Shirelles, would push this idea of the "girl ballad" further with their hit "Will You Still Love Me Tomorrow," which captured the same feeling and sentiment, though with a more sexual tension to it that would set forth a whole controversy over the sexual curiosity of sixties teenagers. From such a point of view,

Spector's song was pivotal in encouraging and influencing young girls to express themselves musically and emotionally in such a way as this and not to just sit in the background while the boys monopolized the sound and feelings of the new rock 'n' roll genre.

While the song did eventually gain commercial and critical favor, few initially realized its potential, apart from maybe Spector and Harvey Goldstein. Donna Kass thought the song was terrible on first hearing Phil sing it to her over the phone, and Stan Ross, the engineer, thought it relatively insignificant. "I thought it was a good song, but I certainly didn't think that a ballad like that, done the way they'd done it, could be a hit," he said (M. Brown, 38).

Greil Marcus in *The History of Rock 'n' Roll in Ten Songs* saw the song as all but worshiping weakness "as a way of life" (Marcus, 243); for Marcus, it wasn't until Amy Winehouse unlocked it fifty-odd years later that the song finally found the right voice to express Spector's true feelings. "The song," he remarks, "expanded as if, all those years, it had been waiting for this particular singer to be born, and was only now letting out its breath" (Marcus, 250). Marcus, however, misses the point: Spector's recording with the Teddy Bears connected to a new teenage sensibility of the time, a sensibility that was not in the least concerned with vocal excellence but more so with a true expression of teen emotions, which would have been more encapsulated in the untutored and "rough" vocals of a seventeen-year-old, such as Kleinbard.

From a writing point of view, Spector took the basic elements of the doo-wop sound and applied it to the standard pop ballad, though he added another element to the standard arrangement with the use of a minor ninth chord, following its standard tonic-dominant progression of G to D. For the time this was unusual and captured a deep feeling of teen angst and yearning that was not yet present in rock 'n' roll music.

"The melody," suggests Ribowsky, "which would revolve around three-beat repetitions on the words 'know' and 'love,' was abruptly broken midway through by a minor—a ninth chord, which was common in jazz but radical for the straightforward arrangements of early rock 'n' roll" (Ribowsky, 32). Others saw that the song's structure demonstrated

> that Spector had already mastered the kind of harmonic devices which then ruled pop, and in particular the cyclic progression on which most of the black vocal group records, like the Five Satins' "In The Still Of The Night" or the Penguins' "Earth Angel," were

based. . . . In retrospect this record can be seen as the beginning a
the Los Angeles style which Spector himself updated with the Paris
Sisters and which later culminated in the Mamas and the Papas,
whose records were really little more than an updated Teddy Bears
sound based on youthful, clean-cut, heavily arranged harmonies. (R.
Williams, *Phil Spector*, 25)

The song took its title from the headstone on Spector's father's grave
on which the epitaph read "To Know Him Was to Love Him." Spector
woke in the middle of the night with the tune playing in his head, and
the words on the gravestone came flooding out with the melody; the
whole song, bar the middle section, was fully formed. Such an outpour-
ing of emotion would seem to indicate the effect the loss of Spector's
father had on him, often feeling lonely and insecure in the world with
no father figure to look to in his formative years.

This feeling of loss in Spector's life would be the essential element in
his musical journey; he was constantly searching for that "Paradise
Lost," a time when he and his family felt close and unified, not broken
and fractured, smothering and conflicting, as it had become since the
loss of his father. His relationship with his mother, who would spitefully
blame Phil for his father's death (M. Brown, 27), was very difficult, and
as such it was in a sense the losing of two parents—one gone and the
other virtually estranged, at least emotionally.

The other influence of the song seems to have come from Kleinbard's voice, which Spector seemingly fell in love with and was intent
on writing a song to showcase it (Ribowsky, 32). If Spector had told
Kleinbard that he loved her voice and would write a song for her, it is
difficult to say whether he really meant it, since he often charmed
people by saying things that were not exactly true, a fundamental flaw
in his personality. It is probably more the case that Spector had the song
already written, or at least partially written, and knew that Kleinbard's
voice would be ideal for it. Hence Spector was still knowledgeable
enough to know what songs would work with what voices, and his eager-
ness to get into the studio to record it suggests how aware he was of its
commercial potential.

According to Marshall Leib, the song sounds sparse and demo-like
because that was the way Phil Spector wanted it to sound (Ribowsky,
34). This seems an unlikely tale since Phil would certainly have spent
more time on it if he could, but nevertheless the half hour extra given to

the group (now known as the Teddy Bears, after the Elvis song, which topped the charts that week) by engineer Stan Ross was masterfully used, and the resulting sound was an exceptional achievement considering the time constraints.

What was it that made "To Know Him" so successful? Why did it appeal to the American and British public so? Why did groups such as the Beatles, hardened rock 'n' rollers, and contemporary singers, such as Amy Winehouse, cover the song? Brown suggests that, even after fifty years, despite Ross's starkly matter-of-fact description, during that one hour in Gold Star Studios "something quite magical had happened" (M. Brown, 39); the song was about "yearning," and "it carries a palpable premonition of abandonment and loneliness, as if to confirm the melancholic truth that to gain what one most desires is at the same time to know that one day it will inevitably be lost" (M. Brown, 39). For such a reason it probably appealed to sensitive artists, such as Paul McCartney and John Lennon, who both knew the meaning of losing a parent, and who would include it in the set of their early performances. This sense of loss was also deeply felt by many who had lost brothers and fathers only a decade earlier in World War II, while Winehouse's troubled life, which was compounded after her first success in the music industry, also found an emotional resonance with the music of Spector.

When Era finally released the song, it did little in terms of radio airplay until finally a DJ in Minneapolis, who had fallen in love with Kleinbard's voice, gave it constant airplay, finally pushing it into the charts at eighty-eight. This was a high enough position for Lew Bedell to call on his friend Dick Clark and persuade him to give the group a slot on *American Bandstand*. The record finally reached number one in the Billboard charts in the first week of December 1958. After selling over 1.4 million copies, Spector found himself a virtual overnight success and the new golden boy of the music industry in America.

THERE'S NO OTHER

Entrepreneur and Businessman

PHIL SPECTOR: A NEW KIND OF BUSINESSMAN

For Phil Spector the world literally consisted of two different types of people: winners and losers. "Some people are born to win," he once told his protégés the Righteous Brothers, possibly as a subtle means to intimidate them, "and some are born to lose." Phil thought of the world as straightforward black and white, perhaps as a means to make sense of the myriad conflicting emotions he was constantly struggling with. This was the ultimate contradiction with Phil Spector. As the musicologist Alan Betrock well observed,

> Intellectually, to Phil, it was a black-and-white world, clear-cut, one way or another, with nothing in between. Emotionally there was a vast array of colors to be dealt with. Ultimately it was this black-and-white verses color dichotomy that would lead Spector to the creation of records that would not only revolutionize the trends, scope, and technique of popular music, but actually alter the very way we saw, heard and felt sound. (Betrock, 22)

While there were many impresarios in the sixties, such as Beatles' manager Brian Epstein or Led Zeppelin's Peter Grant, who seemed to care about their acts and worked very hard on their behalf, there were a number of others that were determined to make themselves very rich out of their artists. America had its Colonel Tom Parker, for example, whom many felt put his protégé, Elvis Presley, under intolerable pressure, while Britain had individuals such as Larry Parnes, who was seen to exploit young naïve boys for his own gain, or Don Arden, the father of Sharon Osbourne, one of the most notorious and unscrupulous figures in pop music.

Despite the great number of unscrupulous pop impresarios, many within the industry seemed to be particularly angered by how Spector treated his artists, by his disdain for the industry and the total lack of modesty he showed toward his work. Spector was hypocritically viewed as conceited and arrogant; "rather than develop his artist's career," they would claim, "Phil developed himself; rather than serve the artist, the artist served Phil" (M. Brown, 133).

Regardless of how Spector was seen to behave toward his artists, and the music industry in general, he was without doubt one of the first producers of pop music who saw it as something more than just "disposable ephemera" (Biography Channel). In fact, he was one of the first, if not the first, who considered the new sound of pop music as a genuine art form. "I would try to tell the groups, we're doing something very important. They didn't know they were producing art that would change the world. I knew," Spector would often boast (Jayanti). It was for this precise reason that acclaimed writer Tom Wolfe saw Spector as the "first tycoon of teen," while famous music critic Nik Cohn considered Spector "the first of the anarchists/pop music millionaires" (M. Brown, 10). Mick Brown would later describe Spector as "a mercurial and combustible mixture of genius and hustler, a precocious, brilliant and off-the-wall visionary, who would change the face of pop music forever" (M. Brown, 1).

By the age of twenty-one, Harvey Philip Spector had become a wealthy and powerful giant within the fledgling pop music industry. The year 1963 particularly catapulted him into the realm of stardom; he became so famous that up-and-coming artists, with stars in their eyes, were falling over themselves to get him to produce a song for them. A song called "Please, Phil Spector," by the Attack, although not released until 1967, captured in its tongue-in-cheek manner, the essence of Spector's power. Phil Spector was essentially "the man other record company executives wish they were." Former journalist and KFWB DJ Larry McCormick explained that "Phil Spector is liked by few, disliked by many, misunderstood by most, and envied by practically everybody. His recent television appearances on panel shows have displayed to the world an honest, say it like it is, freak. I think he's 'out of sight' . . . 'fantastic,' and remember . . . the 'Freak' will inherit the earth" (Kubernik).

The descriptions, by these writers, of Spector as a man and as a producer are enormously significant. First, the fact that he became a millionaire out of pop music was in itself quite extraordinary, since most pop music of the time revolved around small record labels that really only made significant impact in local areas, particularly in the United States, while Britain and Europe were a virtual no go for pop music. Only big organizations, such as Atlantic, were able to command so much power and hence were able to take control of many markets, such as classical and jazz, which ultimately, however, meant little to the emerging teen audiences. Spector though had begun to realize the potential of the new youth market and more or less single-handedly created a multi-million-dollar record label out of the fact. "He was the first one," declared the legendary DJ Brucie Morrow, "who realized there was going to be a big market" (Biography Channel).

In terms of pop music, Spector had set the template for success, and many young entrepreneurs, who wanted to break into the business, saw Spector as a clear role model. In America, these individuals consisted of Sonny Bono, Nino Tempo, and Jack Nitzsche, while British "hustler" Andrew "Loog" Oldham saw Spector as the true-to-life version of his fictional hero, Johnny Jackson, in Wolf Mankowitz's *Expresso Bongo* (1959).

Cohn's description of Spector as "anarchist" is particularly apt, in the sense that Spector challenged the established attitudes and practices of the music industry, which to him was full of insincere, artless hustlers. Spector disregarded the protocol of business and established his own rules and his own approach to record making, seeing first and foremost that it was an art form. Spector also refused to play second fiddle to anyone, realizing his own abilities and worth, and for this the young up-and-coming musicians, engineers, and impresarios, or "pimpresarios" as Oldham would refer to them, of the music industry, took their cue from him.

He set out reshaping an idea of pop music, giving it a structure and form, as well as helping change its perception as an art form that could rightly compete with already-established musical forms, particularly, folk, jazz, and blues, and encouraged the new breed of musicians to push the boundaries of the pop song, particularly Brian Wilson, the Beatles, the Rolling Stones, and Motown, who together created a pop universe that has nearly equaled the great composers of the classical realm and to which modern music has been entirely indebted since.

Phil Spector took the essence of rock 'n' roll and built it up into an operatic teenage pop idiom, a musical equivalent to his great hero Wagner, "pocket symphonies for the kids," as he liked to call them. Spector created music of fast-paced, explosive color that blended with the new American, and to some extent British, postwar lifestyle of the young, who rejected the bleak world of war, rationing, and black and whiteness of life that had once existed.

This new power wielded by the new attitude of the postwar youth had made it possible for anyone with any sense of know-how to make a fortune from the new youth markets. This is why the liner notes to the *Teddy Bears Sing*, Phil's first album, stated, "The Teddy Bears are a good example of how today's teenagers have a chance to become famous in the record field. . . . In no other field in creative or industrial endeavor can the youngster express himself for so many and reap the lucrative rewards." Most teenagers, at the mercy of the older producers and managers that controlled them, never reaped their "lucrative rewards," something that Spector would, very early on in his career, become extremely aware of.

Spector has been primarily known for his Wall of Sound productions, creating some of the best loved and most successful records of the late 1950s and early 1960s, including "Da Doo Ron Ron," "Be My Baby," and "You've Lost That Lovin' Feelin'." He is also well known for writing other classic hits from the period, including Ben E. King's "Spanish Harlem" and the hugely successful "To Know Him Is to Love Him," which began his music career. However, Spector was also very savvy when it came to the business aspects of the music industry. He established a precedent in the music industry by taking control of all aspects of his music from writing, recording, producing, licensing, and marketing his records to becoming his own PR machine. From this point a significant number of managers and producers, such as Brian Wilson; David Geffen, to whom Spector never warmed (M. Brown, 34); Bruce Springsteen; and possibly even Paul McCartney with his MPL

Communications, owe something of their awareness and approach to the music industry to Spector. One man particularly, the Rolling Stones' manager and producer, Andrew Oldham, was more than just influenced by Spector and modeled his whole attitude not only to record making but also to living, on Spector, even emulating Spector's habit of wearing shades morning, noon, and night:

> Oldham absorbed ideas from Spector, recorded the artists privately by the producer at his own expense and free from interference from others—the mastered tapes were then leased to the record company which manufactured, distributed and marketed the product but had no say in its character or creative evolution and crucially it did not own the copyright—something that had never been proposed before. . . . Such was Decca's terror of losing the next big thing that they complied without a murmur. (Norman, *Mick Jagger*, 99–100)

By the time Oldham left the Stones, however, the music industry was becoming a shark pool, where vast sums of money swelled around men of dubious character (*Music Moguls*).

PHIL SPECTOR GETS BURNED

While the young Spector was adept at coaxing people, such as Annette Kleinbard, into his musical circle and then extracting money from them for his recording projects (Ribowsky, 28–29), he was also savvy enough to use his contacts to get himself introduced to the right people. Phil, unfortunately, had a manipulative side to his character, often using and then discarding friends when it served his means.

Phil's school friend Donnie Kartoon, who was a neighbor of Lew Bedell's, the owner of Era Records, was just one example of Spector's canniness in this regard. Once he was introduced to Bedell, however, Spector tried to elbow Kartoon out of the deal (Ribowsky, 30). Spector also ditched Teddy Bears member Harvey Goldstein (even ousting him out of an *American Bandstand* appearance; M. Brown, 43–44; Ribowsky, 36) after Phil had used Goldstein's $10 for the group's first Gold Star recording.

According to Bedell, Spector had turned from a polite, likable Jewish boy to a virtual monster after the success of "To Know Him Is to

Love Him." And when Spector made greater demands on his first record label, which had generously taken Phil under its wing, Spector didn't think twice, when his demands were not met, about moving from Era to the record company with the most attractive offer (M. Brown, 44).

However, it was from his first record company that Spector would learn, although the hard way, the most effective way to engage with record labels and distributors. Era Records did not directly sign Spector and the Teddy Bears, as may have been the more common thing to do, but instead took out the option to lease the masters of his songs, which meant that Spector could still use the songs and rerecord them with other companies with only that particular recording of the song going to Era Records. Spector and his group were also free to leave the company after the four songs were delivered.

Although Phil became a canny and shrewd businessman, his initial dealings with Era awoke him to the realities of the music industry. Of the 1.4 million copies of "To Know Him Is to Love Him" that were sold, Phil had stood to reap the sum of at least $20,000 ($500,000 in today's money), but Phil came out with little over $3,000 (M. Brown, 50; Betrock, 24–27). Such dealings as this, as well as the payola scandal (DJs getting paid by record companies to play their artists' records) that had shaken the music industry in 1959, just as Phil was beginning to make his mark, made him very suspicious of the industry's business practices. Though, as Betrock points out, he was still in school, he had learned one of the most important lessons of his life. As a result, he became more conscious of having control over every aspect of his music career and set down a new code for himself to follow:

1. Music must be emotional and honest.
2. Music must create a sound on record that no one can copy or "cover."
3. Make sure you get your money.
4. There's never a contract without a loophole. (Betrock, 24–27)

SPECTOR FINDS HIS NICHE

Spector left Era using Bedell's and his differing musical tastes as an excuse. The truth, however, is that Spector had been approached by Lew Chudd of Imperial Records, who offered Spector a better deal of 3 percent on every record, essentially twice what Era was paying him. Spector showed the same savvy and cunning dealing with the older generation as he had done dealing with his peers.

Even in his first studio experiences, while at Era, with "Don't Worry My Little Pet," "Wonderful Lovable You," and "To Know Him Is to Love Him," Spector had been keen on experimenting in the studio, using it as an instrument and an integral part of the overall sound, and when he moved to Imperial he continued experimenting to get the sound he wanted (M. Brown, 48, 49). But all this took time, and just as it had infuriated Bedell and Herb Newman, it began to wear on Lew Chudd at Imperial, who was not used to artists taking as much time in the studio.

While most records were recorded in an afternoon back then, Spector had only recorded six of twelve songs for Imperial in two weeks, costing Imperial money and frustrating everyone involved. As a result Chudd insisted that the remaining six songs be recorded in a day, which essentially meant abandoning Spector's refined and detailed approach, leaving the music, according to the engineer/producer Jimmy Haskell, sounding "sterile" (M. Brown, 49). A little more than a year later, while still only a minor player, Spector spent a total of $14,000 producing four songs for Gene Pitney—the average at the time was $500 per song (Betrock, 27).

Success dwindled for Spector for some time after "To Know Him Is to Love Him," with only the song "Oh Why," which had incidentally caused the rift between Spector and Era, hitting the charts at an unconvincing ninety-eight. For many, particularly those who had little musical understanding or appreciation ("the short-armed fatties," as Spector like to call them [M. Brown, 70]), the music industry existed primarily as a means to make a quick buck, but for Spector it existed for very different reasons. He was not interested in it solely as a means to make money, though it is not entirely fair to say everyone else was; Bedell, for example, had written a number of hits before running his label. But Spector seemed truly to need music to survive the vicissitudes of his life; it was something that was all embracing and important to him, and music was ultimately what he wanted to make, not money. Money, however, allows dreams to come true and goals to be reached, but where Spector was contemptuous with money, sacrificing his as well as company money to achieve his musical dreams, others were penny pinching and frugal, thinking primarily of the bottom line.

When Spector realized that the Teddy Bears were not going to repeat the success of "To Know Him Is to Love Him," he distanced himself from them and essentially allowed the group to become defunct. He would become so detached from the group and the other members that when Annette Kleinbard was in a serious car accident in September 1959, only a short time after the success of "To Know Him Is to Love Him" had waned, spending three months in the hospital having reconstructive surgery, Spector made no attempt to visit her (M. Brown, 50). This was a stark contrast to the year earlier when he wooed her for his own musical success. Now that she was not needed he didn't seem to want to know her.

Seemingly Spector, while thinking over his options and planning his next step along the lines of musical world domination, realized that it was not as a performer that he wanted to dominate the world but as someone in the background, calling the shots, making the decisions, and crafting the music. And through the music, he could reach the hearts and minds of those, mainly teenagers, who listened to him. Spector knew his own limitations, and though "To Know Him Is to Love Him" had shown that he had some talent as a songwriter, Spector struggled to write anything else comparable. He was not a competent lyricist; he could write a tune, but they were never strong enough (M. Brown, 6). Instead of songwriting, Spector chose to focus his attention on production, realizing that the right production could transform a song and make it a hit.

It seems that Phil knew he had an ability and power to attract and mesmerize young people with his music, and this had been ultimately confirmed to him by the success of "To Know Him Is to Love Him." From this point of view Spector began to see himself in terms of the great composers, Mozart, Beethoven, and Wagner, whose very names outshone their greatest musical achievements. Spector too wanted his name to become more famous than his music and so be associated with these giants of world culture. "I wanted," he affirmed, "to be in the background, but I wanted to be important in the background. I wanted to be the focal point. . . . I knew Mozart was more important than his operas. That Beethoven was more important than his music. . . . That's what I wanted to be" (M. Brown, 51). Spector also expressed this view of himself in cinematic terms: "When you see a [Stanley] Kubrick movie," he would say, "you tell me how many names you immediately remember in the cast. One, two? It's the same with Fellini, and that's what I wanted to do when I directed a recording. Singers are instruments. They are tools to be worked with" (Kubernik).

PHIL MEETS LESTER

In order for Spector to achieve his goal of world-renowned record producer, he needed to be in a position of greater control; ultimately to control every aspect of his music and the business decisions that were made surrounding it, he couldn't have the likes of Bedell and Chudd around telling him what and how to record and then deciding if and how it would be promoted or distributed. As luck would have it Spector would soon meet the individual with the right connections to make all this happen for him.

Lester Sill was a "peerless record salesman" (M. Brown, 51), known and well loved throughout the music industry of America's West Coast. It seems that Spector ingratiated himself with Sill, who had met him during the recordings for the *Teddy Bears Sing* album, and seemingly he was impressed by his precociousness in the studio. Sill was also most likely impressed by Spector's youth. Spector was so young he would flower into an even greater producer with time, and his youthfulness meant he would be more in tune with what was happening in the genre of pop and rock 'n' roll and would be able to deliver his music directly to a teen market, with whom he inherently empathized.

Others such as Lew Chudd of Imperial constantly had to find out indirectly, through whatever means, what was fashionable amongst the teenagers in order to manufacture his products. From this point of view, Spector was not a manufacturer of the latest fads, which even the talented Jerry Leiber and Mike Stoller could be accused of doing. (They switched their interest in pure blues and R&B, such as Big Mama Thornton for whom they originally wrote "Hound Dog," to writing for

Elvis Presley, in whom they had no initial interest; nor did they understand him, his music, or his public appeal, but since they were making a lot of money from him they continued to write songs for him [M. Brown, 59].)

Sill was open to the idea of Spector producing records for him and his label Gregmark, which he ran with the producer Lee Hazelwood and whose biggest artist was Duane Eddy. Sill was so charmed by Spector that he brought Spector to the studios to watch Hazelwood in action. Hazelwood resented a young upstart being around and guarded his recording techniques well, but Spector absorbed all he could, particularly the use of echo and tape delay, Eddy's trademark sound, which Spector would later apply to his epic Wall of Sound.

PHIL GETS IN WITH LEIBER AND STOLLER

Since the success of "To Know Him Is to Love Him," Spector had been stuck in a rut, full of ideas yet nothing substantial was coming from them. He had dissolved the Teddy Bears and suggested to Sill that he move from Los Angeles to somewhere more conducive to his temperament, someplace where he was unknown, such as New York, the home of his beloved doo-wop.

New York was becoming a thriving pop music city whose success in this field mostly came from the talented songwriters that occupied New York's Brill Building, located at 1619 Broadway, and its edgier younger brother on 1650 Broadway, which produced mostly rock 'n' roll. The Brill Building was the perfect example of vertical integration, where many aspects of a business merged into each other; in this case it was songwriting, publishing, arranging, recording, and promotion. New York also boasted the big six music labels of rock 'n' roll in the 1950s, including Atlantic, RCA, and Columbia, as well as major publishers such as Hill and Range and the two principal performing rights organizations, ASCAP and BMI. Considering all this, New York really was the place for a young and ambitious music producer such as Phil Spector to be.

Sill, who had helped Leiber and Stoller with their initial success, arranged for Spector to work as an apprentice to rock 'n' roll's guru producers. Leiber and Stoller were simply doing Sill a favor and didn't care either way about Spector being there or not. This was a drastic miscalculation on Leiber and Stoller's part, as it was essentially Spector, and his new breed of artist-impresario types, that would bring the old guard tumbling down; the brash and new youthful attitude that Spector incorporated and that ultimately manifested in the Stones and later the Sex Pistols would propel the new music generation.

Leiber and Stoller were too shortsighted and caught up in their own success to notice a young wannabe like Spector, and little did they realize their fate when he walked into their office as their new apprentice. Of course there was probably little they could do with the turning tide of progress; whether or not they took any notice of Spector, it would probably have not altered the outcome of his success or their ultimate falling out of favor when, by the midsixties, other pop groups, led by Spector and the Beatles, began to dominate the music scene.

Despite this, however, Leiber and Stoller provided Spector with his next important learning experience in terms of business practice. Leiber and Stoller, who through a fortuitous meeting with Sill, a savvy businessman himself (M. Brown, 56–57), had managed to break into the R&B market. Though Leiber and Stoller had a big hit with "Hound Dog," they were burned financially by the record and publishing companies, an incident that pushed them to set up their own Spark label and a publishing company, called Quintet, with Lester Sill as a partner.

Though Spark had had some local success, they were bought out by Atlantic, who kept Leiber and Stoller on as independent writers and record makers. Leiber and Stoller agreed to the deal on the grounds that they were credited as producers, and in this sense the birth of the modern-day record producer was born. Where traditionally the producer would have been Atlantic, who put up the money, Leiber and Stoller turned the notion of producer into what was traditionally the role of the director, someone who would guide and shape the material—be it a play, film, or in this case a piece of music. Their setup as independent producers, under the wing and financial support of a major record label, with all its stature and industry connections, is exactly what Spector needed to be involved in (M. Brown, 58–59).

While in New York, Spector also developed strong contacts with Ahmet Ertegun and Jerry Wexler at Atlantic Records, as well as Paul Case, artists and repertoire (A&R) manager at Hill and Range, and the songwriter Doc Pomus, with whom he collaborated on two songs recorded by Ben E. King: "First Taste of Love" and "Young Boy Blues." It wasn't long before Atlantic CEO Ahmet Ertegun became Spector's new mentor; and Atlantic, the model for his own imagined musical empire. Ertegun offered Spector the chance to be his assistant and produce for Atlantic, and Spector also signed a deal with Hill and Range, who had offered him the chance to write for Elvis Presley's new movie *Blue Hawaii* (although this never actually materialized into anything).

When Leiber and Stoller found out about his other deals, they were fuming, more so because Spector went behind their backs, taking with him all the tricks they had shared. Spector believed (though wrongly it would later transpire) that they would all accommodate him, but essentially he didn't seem to care who he upset; he seemed to be only interested in how he could make his impact on the industry, thus gaining a nasty reputation, among many, for being unethical and dishonest, simply out for what he could get (M. Brown, 74). When Spector finally walked out on his contract with Leiber and Stoller, claiming he was not of legal age when he had originally signed with them, the two producers couldn't quite believe his arrogance.

CORRINA CORRINA

It had, however, been due to Leiber and Stoller that Spector got his first big studio break, after they passed pop singer Ray Peterson's cover of "Corrina Corrina" on to him to record. Peterson had had a big hit earlier that year with "Tell Laura I Love Her," cowritten by Jeff Barry, who would, within the next two years, become one of Spector's principal songwriters. It was the perfect opportunity for Spector to make an impression with an already-established artist but this time as a producer.

"Corrina Corrina" (incidentally, also known as "Corinna, Corinna" and "Corinne Corrina") was a standard country blues song, with a traditional twelve-bar structure, first recorded in 1928, on Brunswick label, by Bo Carter. Many artists have covered the song, but it was the Collins Kids, a rockabilly brother and sister duo—"Lorrie" and "Larry" Collins—who had made it popular, with their crazy rock 'n' roll version, which was televised on the Grand Ole Opry in 1956. Bob Dylan would also later devise an alternate folk version for his 1962 *Freewheelin'* album.

The Spector/Peterson version was mostly inspired by Big Joe Turner's 1956 boogie woogie/jump blues hybrid recording, and followed the trend of white artists covering successful R&B artists but for a specifically white audience. Turner's hybrid style, with its walking bass lines and punctuated brass sections, had strongly influenced the birth of rock 'n' roll, particularly his 1954 hit "Shake, Rattle 'n' Roll," and his particular version of "Corrina Corrina" was much more upbeat and vibrant than Spector's. Turner's version also had a positivity that Spector's version deliberately lacked.

The positivity of the Turner version possibly reflected the more positive mentality of the economic boom in the United States following World War II, while also reflecting the newfound sense of purpose, opportunity, and equality that had been gained by the African American communities after the war.

While Spector's version certainly lacked the grit and muscle of Turner's version, Spector had produced it for a white audience whose sensibility, for the time, starkly contrasted with the black audience that Turner's was aimed at. The Spector/Peterson version was much less vibrant simply because it reflected, either consciously or unconsciously, the deep, but mostly unconscious, melancholia of a white, middle-class consumer culture, a melancholy not experienced or expressed in the race music of the time.

After the war, whites appeared to suffer from the emptiness of consumerism, the threat of wide-scale nuclear war, and a greater sense of expectation that postwar society had placed on them. For these reasons, the morbidity of the "death disc," a specific genre of pop music inspired predominantly by the tragic lives of modern American heroes such as James Dean that typically ended with the melodramatic death of the song's protagonist, resonated strongly with a young white audience. Peterson's previous single, "Tell Laura I Love Her," fit into the genre, while some of the early white rock 'n' roll songs, such as "Corrina Corrina," with their subdued and almost anemic sound (at least compared to the race music of the period), though not specifically in the "death disc" genre, were the product of the same feeling of melancholia. In many ways the Spector/Peterson production is more similar to the original Bo Carter 1928 version (a period in which America, particularly white America, was on the brink of depression) but with a more lavish and sophisticated production than both the original and the Turner version.

The song went to number nine, giving Spector his biggest hit since "To Know Him." During this same period he cowrote "Spanish Harlem" for Ben E. King, which also went to number nine. Spector was beginning to have an impact. His work with Leiber helped him more to understand the craft of songwriting, particularly in the pop idiom (M. Brown, 66), while his experiences in the studio were greatly helping him to develop his skill as a producer. Although it took Spector some time to find his feet in the studio, with the success of "Corrina Corrina" he was presented with more and more opportunities to make the type of records he really wanted to make.

"Corrina Corrina" was not so much tailored for the teen market, as would be his later Crystals and Ronettes records, but for a slightly more general adult-orientated audience. From a certain point of view, "Corrina Corrina" is an interesting song that demonstrates Spector's early attempts to create his musical vision, as well as showing that given the right material he could produce something of quality. His approach in this occasion was to use strings, which he would do for the first time (Thompson, 58), as well as the studio trickery he had absorbed from Leiber and Stoller.

Leiber and Stoller had most likely passed the Peterson project on to Spector because they didn't like making white music (even though they themselves were white). They had a greater love for "race music" and wanted to make R&B records, hence their initial reluctance to have anything to do with Elvis. "We don't go for that white bread trash. We wrote for black people—we were race record makers," said Leiber (M. Brown, 59). Spector, however, was as keen to write for a white audience as he had obviously done for the Teddy Bears and was happy to prove himself with whatever material he was given.

With the success of "Corrina Corrina" (and "Spanish Harlem"), Spector's confidence soared, producing in him a new sense of brashness that the old guard didn't have or understand, and from that time on "he never doubted himself ever" (M. Brown, 76). According to Jerry Wexler, Spector didn't seem to care who you were; he spoke his mind, right or wrong, about music, even insulting the very popular and very successful Bobby Darin, when he played some new songs to Ertegun while

Spector was present. Such an attitude would soon become the attitude of the new modernist culture that groups such as the Rolling Stones, and their Spector-modeled manager "Loog" Oldham would adopt and represent.

ALDON MUSIC AND PHILLES RECORDS

While in New York, Spector realized he needed access to the Aldon Music publishing company, situated at 1650 Broadway, where the most relevant songwriters of the time were emerging. Spector ingratiated himself in to the Aldon circle, where Don Kirshner, the company's founder and owner, realized his talent as a producer. Although Kirshner found Spector to be very charming, he was savvy to the darker side of his character. "Philly," recalled Kirshner, "was a user and pretty manipulative." Spector's relationship with Kirshner and Aldon proved to be less a partnership based on mutual trust and respect and more a "marriage of convenience" from which Spector could mine the wealth of talent now at his disposal, while it would provide Kirshner with an "unbroken stream of royalty payments for years to come" (M. Brown, 83).

His first song from Aldon, "I Love How You Love Me," which he recorded with the Paris Sisters, was to be Spector's first attempt to produce a song as an independent producer working under his own initiative. Before this, he either was under pressure from the record company or had had the song given to him, but this time he chose the material, he chose the studio in which to work (Gold Star), he chose the group, and he could take as much time as he pleased getting it all right. With the success of the song and with Lester Sill now partner-less (after Lee Hazelwood had become antagonized by Spector, possibly seeing him as a real threat as a producer and as someone that had more sway over Sill than he himself had [M. Brown, 86]), Sill approached Spector with the idea of going into partnership. This was the opportunity Spector had been waiting for, the opportunity to free himself from the likes of Leiber and Stoller, Atlantic, Lew Chudd, Bedell, and Newman and have control over his own business affairs, over his own music, and ultimately over his own destiny.

Spector had ultimately refused to bow down to anyone in the music industry, and though he was often accused of being manipulative, which he most certainly was, Phil also had a tremendous belief in his talents, if not necessarily in himself. He didn't relish the use of "promotion" money, which lined a variety of pockets; he didn't enjoy being dependent on publishing houses for new song material; and he didn't even feel the need to spend money on trade advertisements for his records. "I felt if a guy doesn't like a record, that's it, you don't take him to dinner, you don't send him something in the mail. If he doesn't like it that's the way it is" (Betrock, 31). Even though this attitude won him many admirers, it also made him many enemies, as "Spector was rocking the boat, and the music industry captains and their crews, already safely on board, didn't enjoy having their ride disturbed" (Betrock, 31).

Spector's new collaboration was to be called Philles Records; again Spector showed his business and marketing savvy by having the label's name reflect his own name more than his partners. Meanwhile his emotional dependence on his mother was reflected in the name of his new publishing company, Mother Bertha Music, which had been set up in tandem with his record label to control all his publishing rights.

As soon as his label, with Sill, was established, Spector wasted no time in scouting for new talent. He settled on a black girl group from New York called the Crystals. Spector probably made this decision based on the fact that his two biggest chart successes to date, "To Know Him Is to Love Him" and the Paris Sisters' "I Love How You Love Me," were essentially part of the burgeoning girl group sound, which had been sparked off a few years earlier with the Chantels and which was becoming increasingly more popular with the success of the Shirelles, whose song "Will You Still Love Me Tomorrow" had made them the hottest group around. Since he was hugely enamored with black artists and the sound of their voices, and the added bonus of the group having a great original song called "There's No Other (Like My Baby)," the Crystals thus seemed the logical choice.

When Spector signed the Crystals, however, he was in a dilemma as they were about to sign to Hill and Range's publishing company Big Top. In order to have control over the song's publishing he needed to move quickly, but the deal with Sill, who was looking after the financial side of the business, had not yet been finalized and Spector had no money with which to sign the group. Instead of losing the group to Big

Top he sought out independent financing, namely, with a woman called Helen Noga, a bolshie woman, who had been managing the mixed-race singer Johnny Mathis and successfully running jazz clubs in San Francisco. Noga had ruffled a lot of feathers when she challenged the colored bar imposed on black artists in Las Vegas, which had made it difficult for her own client to achieve greater success. While others were afraid to challenge the establishment, which they feared would cause more problems for black artists, Noga stood up for her artists. Spector was attracted to her gutsiness, and Noga, obviously seeing something similar in the young Spector, who had been introduced to her through his connections at Hill and Range a few years earlier, agreed to finance the record.

Hill and Range were furious with Spector for poaching their group, particularly when he had spent weeks rehearsing the girls in their offices while they were still under contract to them. Such manipulation and sheer disregard for those who had backed him meant little to Spector, if it meant he could make a great record. As Brown comments, he had no qualms about burning relationships if the occasion demanded it (M. Brown, 93), or as Doc Pomus so pertinently put it, "He knew what the game was, and he played it. Every businessman is your best friend until they've sucked you dry of whatever they want. Phil just got to them before they got to him, and they didn't like it one little bit. And I must admit, not a lot of people felt especially sorry for them when it happened" (M. Brown, 93). With the success of "There's No Other" it seems that Helen Noga also got burned with zero return on her investment (M. Brown, 99).

In the meantime, Spector negotiated deals with other labels, such as Liberty, where he was given a year's salary of $25,000 to scout and produce records, while still free to record for Philles, a seemingly unusual deal since surely Spector would be more intent on finding the best material for his own label than for Liberty, but Spector was in great demand and his business acumen was such that he could negotiate such deals.

In truth, Spector did little for Liberty, producing essentially only three singles, mainly junk. More significant, however, was that Spector's relationship with his new partner Lester Sill was becoming strained. Spector was keen to dissolve the partnership, feeling money was being wasted, mostly by Sill's "insignificant" productions, which

Spector saw as a blemish on the label. Spector felt, artistically and commercially, that "every record Philles releases should be a hit. If it's not a hit, why bother to put it out? If I don't have the right song, I'll just wait for one to come along" (Betrock, 31, 32, 35). To Spector, the supposed artistic head of Philles, this was also seen as a personal affront (Betrock, 31). Spector also wasn't seeing the kind of money he should have been making by working for both Philles and as a freelance producer. He had by this stage only one hit on Philles, and as a freelance producer he merely got a fee for his work; if any royalties were due him he had to wait for months to get them and only then if he happened to be lucky enough (Betrock, 31).

Spector approached the label's third partner, a silent partner, Harold Lipsius and Harry Finfer, and together they put pressure on Sill to settle with Spector the other third of the partnership. Exasperated by Spector's dealings and not totally as committed to conquering the world through music as Spector was, Sill sold his interest in the company for a paltry fraction of its potential value ($60,000). Spector felt he no longer needed Lester Sill, so "Sill," as one of Spector's musical collaborators put it, "got the knife in the back" (Biography Channel).

The first two Crystals records, "There's No Other (Like My Baby)" and "Uptown," firmly established his fledgling independent record label, but when his third release, "He's a Rebel," reached number one, with a sound so different than anything before it, coupled with the social context of the song and its very definite teen attitude tailored precisely for a teen audience, Spector's destiny as pop's maestro was definitely beginning to unfold.

While "He's a Rebel" had grabbed the pop music industry by the scruff of the neck and made everyone stand up and take notice of the young "punk" Phil Spector, his next few Philles releases, two singles with the Crystals and his following one with the Ronettes, catapulted Spector into the realm of mega-stardom. With just a small independent label behind him, Spector chose to take the established music industry on and play by his own rules. What made it all the more impressive was that Spector was only twenty-two. Spector was now fully in control, of not only Philles Records but also his own destiny as well as the destiny of many others that came to record and work at Philles. Ultimately, Spector was in control of the sound of his records, and because he made the sound and the sound was what sold, Spector became one of pop music's first star producers.

3

TOMORROW'S SOUND TODAY
Technical Wizard and Musical Visionary

SPECTOR THE PRODUCER

While rock 'n' roll proved to have an enduring influence on Anglo-American culture, its initial impact, in 1956, was relatively short lived. It wasn't until the Beatles, and many of the other British bands that emerged in the first half of the sixties, revitalizing and expanding its first impulse, that the original fervor of rock 'n' roll was reawakened. However, the gap left between these two distinct periods allowed a space for individuals to come in and construct a new musical language, incorporating elements of a variety of musical devices from jazz to blues and rock 'n' roll; these themes reflected the new youth culture, along with the sonic enhancement of studio techniques and trickery. It was between the periods of Elvis and the Beatles that a very particular era developed, "an era when the hit single became a highly crafted work of art, an era of a new genius in rock—the producer" (*Rock and Roll: In the Groove*). It was this era that essentially belonged to Phil Spector, arguably the most significant producer of the early sixties.

Although there were many different producers with different styles and approaches to making a record, onetime journalist-turned-producer Jerry Wexler reduced the style and approach to two clearly distinct categories: those who simply documented the raw sound of an artist with no embellishments, such as Leonard Chess, and those, such as

Jerry Leiber and Mike Stoller or later Motown, that were "the servant of the project," whose function was to couple the right song with the right artist and find the right musicians, studio, and so forth, to bring out the potential of both the song and the singer. Spector, however, in Wexler's view, fit into a totally separate category, all on his own: "the producer as star, as artist, as unifying force" (M. Brown, 133).

There is a far-reaching myth that Spector turned to gold everything he touched and did so from the first moment he walked into a recording studio at the age of seventeen, as this comment from a biography of Spector suggests: "He bought all the sessions he could at Gold Star [and] stacked all the vocals to make it sound bigger than ever before" (Biography Channel). Yet it is not true that Spector produced magic from the start. Though Spector certainly displayed some talent as a producer, along with a vision of how popular music could be advanced, it is only in hindsight, easy to claim, that Spector's first recordings, "To Know Him Is to Love Him" and "Don't Worry My Little Pet," demonstrate his prodigious talent as a record producer.

It is probably more accurate to say that Spector early on recognized the potential of the studio and, with a tremendous desire to achieve fame and success, he explored the possibilities of the studio unlike anyone before, establishing new and innovative techniques to record sound and music. By so doing Spector was able to conquer the world and ultimately prove himself to the many people he felt had dismissed him as wired, unusual, and insignificant.

Though some felt Spector was not overly convincing in the studio (R. Williams, *Phil Spector*, 88–89), most people felt Spector had from early on a vision of his music enhanced by the aid of the studio. And although he certainly managed to capture something magical in "To Know Him" it was partly Annette Kleinbard's mesmerizing voice, along with important connections and luck, that managed to make the song the commercial success it was. Spector produced a great many songs before he finally established his own Philles label, which gave him the financial backing, as well as the artistic control, to create his famous Wall of Sound. Some songs deserving of mention that helped Spector develop his musical masterpieces and that are significant records in themselves are as follows: Connie Francis's "Second Hand Love"; Billy Storm's "When You Dance"; Curtis Lee's "Pretty Little Angel Eyes" and "Under the Moon of Love"; and Gene Pitney's "Dream for Sale."

Other tracks worth mentioning, although not for their greatness, are the Top Notes' "Twist and Shout" and the Castle Kings' "You Can Get Him Frankenstein," which really show how terrible Spector could be when his ego became the focus of the project rather than the song.

THE PARIS SISTERS

When Lester Sill asked Phil to record an act he had recently signed to his Gregmark label, Spector although obliging, considering the generosity Sill had shown him, thought little would come of the Paris Sisters' less-than-modern sound. However, on reflection Spector thought that he could reinvent the group, and instead of focusing on their 1950s-style harmonies, he reinvented them in the vein of the Teddy Bears, highlighting Priscilla Paris's "breathy" voice, which had a similar quality to that of Kleinbard (Ribowsky, 79).

Although the other sisters resented being pushed into the background (Ribowsky, 79), the success of Spector's decision to reorganize the trio, in the way he did, turned out to be more than justified. If the trend for music needed to appeal to the emotional concerns of teenagers, then there was simply no room for the outdated 1950s bebop harmonies the Paris Sisters had borrowed from groups such as the Andrew Sisters. Spector's revised arrangements and productions created a much more intimate and sensitive setting, evoking teen feelings and yearnings, while Priscilla whispered her emotional concerns and desires to her listening teen audience, who responded appropriately.

The first song that the group recorded, "Be My Boy," was a Spector-penned song, which he had previously written for Ray Peterson, then titled "Be My Girl." Although not a surefire hit by any means, its simplicity allowed Spector to apply the soft, intimate production and keep a simple emotional theme that could easily be grasped by its intended listener. Spector, according to his friend Michael Spencer, saw the recording of the song as "an aural oral job" (M. Brown, 69); the sonic suggestiveness of such would certainly have titillated a teen market, while his master stroke of pushing Priscilla's very intimate vocal to the front would have seduced the teen market even more. Lyrically the song focused on sentiments that resonated strongly with popular music at the time, simple words of devotion and fidelity. There was a pleading quality to the song that hinted at a teenage yearning, while Spector's arrangement was designed to tug even more at the emotional heart-strings of teenagers as opposed to the more adult-oriented material that the Paris Sisters had been accustomed. The song, however, had not captured the same sentiment that his Teddy Bears' hit had done a few years earlier, but still to everyone's surprise it reached number fifty-six in May 1961.

Considering the sonic textures that Spector first designed for the Paris Sisters, it became a style that he would use to transform their next few singles into hits. As well as recrafting the Paris Sisters' overall style into a more credibly artistic and commercial sound, the particular sonic textures created by Spector for "Be My Boy" would also prove to have an influence on other artists of the time, including the strikingly similar sound of Jane Birkin's "Je t'aime . . . moi non plus," as well as a number of Brian Wilson's earlier love songs with the Beach Boys; songs such as "In My Room" and "Surfer Girl," a song that although it shares similar-ities to Dion and the Belmonts' "When You Wish Upon a Star," owes a great deal not just to the sound of Spector's song but also to the song's overall arrangement and theme.

The B-side, "I'll Be Crying Tomorrow," though much less intimate than its A-side, still captured a more contemporary sound than did the group's pre-Spector records. Spector's production, though less individ-ualistic here, had much of the Shirelles' feel about it, complete with the sound of a music box, which created a beautifully subtle effect that superbly married itself to the very teen lyrics that described a young girl's coming of age—"Tonight I'll let you go and never let you know that I'll be crying tomorrow"—while Spector again made excellent use of the sisters' impeccable harmonizing abilities. Spector's real success with the Paris Sisters came, however, with his next production for them, employing the same style as "Be My Boy" but this time to a song that was more expertly crafted.

I LOVE HOW YOU LOVE ME

When Spector heard Barry Mann's song "I Love How You Love Me" (cowritten by Larry Kolber) while visiting the Aldon group, he immedi-ately realized its hit potential, even after only hearing a rough guitar-voice recording, and convinced Don Kirhsner that it was perfect for the Paris Sisters. Spector's vision as an interpreter for teen music was perfectly displayed with this song as both Mann and Kolber had envisioned the song as a fast, upbeat, positive expression of teen love. Spector, however, heard it differently. He recognized it fitting perfectly into the style that made a success of "To Know Him Is to Love Him," incorporating an overwhelming expression of grief and loss into it, "more befitting a prayer than a song" (M. Brown, 84). Once again Spector produced a sensibility that spoke more directly to the emotional concerns of the teen market at the time.

He flew out to Los Angeles and hooked up with arranger Hank Levine, and together the two wrote and rewrote the string parts, making revisions for many hours until they were satisfied. He worked on the Paris Sisters' vocals over and over again, first coaxing Priscilla into a sultry and believable lead, and then blending in the numerous backup vocal parts. "This extensive pre-production rehearsal [was] itself an innovation for the time" (Betrock, 28).

Although the recording went much smoother than was usual for a Spector recording, "this time it was to be the mixing, not the recording, that would test everyone's endurance and convictions" (Betrock, 28). He obsessed over his first fully realized record, mixing and remixing, listening and relistening, over and over until he was certain it was right. "I've never seen anyone more meticulous about mixing, about recording or mastering than Phil, of all the producers I've worked with," said Lester Sill. "And it was really part of him, he became part of what he was doing . . . his whole life was in it" (M. Brown, 85). "I Love How You Love Me" cracked the U.S. top five, galvanized by Priscilla's intimate lead and Spector's atypically restrained production (Ankeny) in October 1961, and stayed in the top twenty for two months. The song sold over a million copies and was, as Alan Betrock noted, a vindication of everything he had struggled for:

> Left to his own devices, in full control of the material, arrangement, musicians, and production, he alone would bear the responsibilities if a costly project failed, and likewise felt that only he should get the credit and the benefits that entailed if it were a success. "I Love How You Love Me" was unlike anything else then being done. It absolutely convinced Spector that he could do it all. What remained was to prove it to the rest of the world. (Betrock, 28–29).

Even though the record was a huge hit for Spector in the States, he was not yet making any significant impact in the UK, where lesser musicians of the time, such as Jimmy Crawford, were sadly outdoing him. Crawford would record a substandard version of this particular song, which stayed in the UK charts for ten weeks and was probably the first time John Lennon, who was hugely inspired by the song for many of his most tender compositions, had heard it. Despite Crawford's greater success with the song in the UK, it is clear to see, by comparing the two versions, that Spector was far more progressive and adventurous as a producer than most of his contemporaries, even at this early stage of his career.

After problems arose among Sill, Spector, and the sisters, Spector walked away from the project and Sill was left with no choice but to let the girls go. The sisters failed to have any success after leaving Gregmark, since no one wanted to have anything to do with them, and as testimony to Spector's abilities Sill claimed, "I loved the Paris Sisters but I don't think anyone could have made hits with 'em but Phil" (Ribowsky, 106). However, in 1966 they signed to Reprise, which paired them with Spector's arranger Jack Nitzsche and production partner Jimmy Bowen. Though the work, released in 1967 as *Everything under the Sun!!!* did not prove to be a commercial success, the artistic success of the project was easily on a par to anything the sisters had done with Spector, though mostly continuing with Spector's reworking of their style. The album "remains an unsung classic of the waning girl group era, featuring several original songs written by Priscilla herself" (Ankeny), thus proving, at least for some, Sill's estimation that the Paris Sisters were nothing without Spector to be wrong.

Spector's collaboration with the Paris Sisters lasted for a mere five singles (a projected album collapsed under mysterious circumstances), and though they were not the magnum opus of Spector's sound, "the delicate layers of keyboards and strings point towards the ambition of his later masterpieces" (Deming). The sound Spector created for this previously outdated female harmony group can be found in modern female singers, who also adopted a sultry, soft, intimate vocal, for instance, Sandy Posey ("Miss Lonely"), Stina Nordenstam, Nina Persson (the Cardigans), Harriet Wheeler (the Sundays), and Nouvelle Vague.

BUILDING THE WALL OF SOUND

Though "Corrina Corrina" and "I Love How You Love Me" proved Spector was not just a flash in the pan, it was the discovery of a young, black New York girl group, the Crystals, that gave Spector the blank canvas on which to develop his production skills and in doing so helped create some of the greatest and most influential songs in the genre of pop music.

The group was not just a replica of the early girl group sound of the Chantels and the Shirelles but also an experiment that allowed Spector to develop his particular sonic productions culminating in his formidable, and still to this day much-copied, Wall of Sound. "In their raw and untutored innocence, the group offered a tabula rasa on which he could stamp his own identity as a producer. They even brought with them a tailor-made song, 'There's No Other Like My Baby'" (M. Brown, 89).

"There's No Other" was modeled by its creator, Leroy Bates, on the gospel tradition of "There's No Other Like My Jesus" (R. Williams, *Phil Spector*, 55), which Spector captured expertly in his production on the song. Mick Brown comments that "from the opening bars of its spoken introduction, Spector honored the song's antecedents; Spector's storefront church piano chords and the chiming truck-stop guitar riffs combined beautifully with a soaring string arrangement to give the song an almost sanctified feel" (M. Brown, 91). Despite Phil's refusal to play the music industry's game of paying for airplay, the song reached number thirteen, convincing him that there was raw potential with his new group (Betrock, 32).

With his next Crystals production, "Uptown," Spector displayed the real potential of his genius, giving the first indication that rock 'n' roll could be so much more than just fickle entertainment. It could be an art form in itself, a vehicle for social commentary, and a modern musical form that could appeal equally to feelings and intellect. In fact, in terms of the "teen idol fodder" that was dominating the charts at the time, Spector's approach was revolutionary, even a "revelation" (Betrock, 32).

The lyrics and internal rhymes are stunning, the visual imagery is breathtaking, and the vocal phrasing alternates beautifully between descent and ascent. Spector complements it with a tremendously innovative arrangement. There's a downbeat pizzicato musical setting and tone to the "downtown" verses, and a completely different uplifting

quality to the "uptown" sections. With the complex string arrangements, background vocals, castanets, and mandolins blended together
into a three-dimensional mural (Betrock, 32).

For Spector, "Uptown" clearly represented his desire to break free
of the creative and economic shackles holding him down and the need
to be in command of his future (Betrock, 32). Due to the song's success,
Spector took another Barry Mann/ Cynthia Weil song, "Broadway,"
which he attempted to record with the Crystals but was not entirely
happy with its result and held off releasing it as a single. On listening to
the song, which Spector finally released as an album track, one can hear
how Spector's usual polish in the mix was not like his other hits; as such,
the song gives an indication as to the perfection that Phil would seek
and that his extensive listening and relistening was not just a mania that
had no artistic purpose. Spector didn't release the track because,
though good, it was not good enough for his perfectionism. Leiber and
Stoller, however, seeing its potential, recorded it with the Drifters. By
now, the shoe was firmly on the other foot, with Leiber and Stoller
following in Spector's footsteps—just one significant indication of Spector's growing creative influence.

The even bigger success of Spector's next single, "He's a Rebel," was
to become a major milestone in Spector's career, establishing him as a
real tour de force within the industry. When recording the song, Spector had a clear vision of how he wanted to make it a bigger sound than
had ever been recorded before, at least in pop music, attempting his
Wagnerian approach for the first time—his ambitions for the song were
grandiose. Spector employed two guitarists, two bass players, and two
sax players for the session, essentially doubling the number of players
used on most recordings. The mix of all these instruments was then
polished off with a heavy, full-throttle vocal by gospel singer Darlene
Love (then Wright); her full-on gospel voice sounds as if she is praising
the Lord in church, contrasting with the sweet teen voices that had
often been used to capture the essence of teen sensibilities. Though
Wright thought the song was just another throwaway piece of pop, she
was surprised when Spector asked her to use the full force of her lower
voice, "the righteous indignation and in-your-face testimony that I usually saved for church" (M. Brown, 104).

With the follow-up, "Zip-a-Dee-Doo-Dah," a song that some claim
was the first to use a distorted lead guitar on a hit record (Kubernik), he

stretched his orchestra of pop musicians: three guitarists, three bass players, two sax players, a drummer, a percussionist, and two piano players.

Spector's approach was not to begin with the drums and bass, a standard practice still used today in multitrack recording, but instead to start with the guitars, sometimes up to as many as five guitars playing the same chords over and over again, creating a wash of sound. "Start with the guitars, then blend everything into the guitars, that was the basis of the whole rhythm section, the guitars. Phil was unique in that," says Spector's onetime engineer, Larry Levine (M. Brown, 114–15).

Though mostly virtuosos, Spector didn't want virtuosity or individualism amongst the playing, just a consistent sound of all the instruments overlapping and chorusing each other (a technique more easily produced today by effects). "It was basically a formula," explained Spector's songwriting partner, Jeff Barry (R. Williams, "Other Side"). Spector also claimed as much: "I was looking for a sound that could produce fifteen hit records and more. I imagined a sound so strong that if the material was not the greatest, the sound would carry the record. It was a case of augmenting, augmenting, augmenting. It all fitted like a jigsaw" (M. Brown, 114). He would have the players play and play for hours, wearing many of them out and sometimes causing their fingers to bleed; he would adjust mics and levels until the whole sound was balanced just the way he wanted and then record; usually only one or two takes was all that was needed, once the blend was right (M. Brown, 114).

Though Phil was notorious for exasperating some of his coworkers, according to Stan Ross, "he served the song. . . . He was always open-minded. He was very emotional about his records. He felt that this was like his life. They were his children." Jack Nitzsche remarked that "Phil was on his game all the time" and would spend hours with the singers to get the vocals right" (Kubernik). He knew his calling was to write and produce music—the records would be the art, which would carry the song and the singer (even if they were not great). Every artist could be replaced because it was the record that was important not the singer (Jayanti). Spector worked through the night into the early hours of the morning, having all the best musicians around him, the Wrecking Crew, as Spector's drummer Hal Blaine would name them, available for them to be employed when he needed them.

The drums were the final piece of the jigsaw puzzle pulling together all the elements of Spector's approach. Sometimes he would arrive early to the studio to experiment with the drum sound, stuffing blankets and bricks into the bass drum to get the sound he wanted. Phil would often take away Hal Blaine's cymbals again to stop the emphasis on certain parts of the sound and to avoid the cliché of other styles and records; all Spector wanted was the throbbing, pulsating rhythm section. He would then add percussion, often more percussionists than other musicians. Sessions were by union rules at the time, not to extend three hours, but Spector would only just start recording by then, going into double pay over the three hours and making the sessions very costly (M. Brown, 115–16).

Spector loved Gold Star because it was small, and when packed with musicians the sound had little room to move about, keeping everything contained, condensed, and formidable. There was no separation between the instruments, so sounds would spill into each other, and when all these sounds were mixed and blended right, they would be recorded onto a single mono track compressing the overall sound even more (Kubernik). According to the Wrecking Crew's Don Randi, Spector really understood tonality, and he used Gold Star to allow the harmonics that the studio created in the sound to blend. "All those harmonics rising," claimed Randi, "were part of the Wall of Sound . . . the songs in themselves were films. And especially in Phil's case, he knew how to write them and how to produce them" (Kubernik). "The Wall of Sound," said Ronnie Spector, "was just a reflection of Phil's personality, which was very extravagant . . . he didn't have any use for a record unless it was ten times bigger than life. Phil was one guy who believed more is more" (Spector, 107).

The final test was to listen to the song in the car radio. This was a special consideration, as most producers simply took the record as it was, but Spector wanted to make sure the sound he created in the studio would translate exactly to how the kids would experience it, most usually on the car radio as they cruised the streets in search of excitement and adventure, and more often than not to the soundtrack of Phil Spector's larger-than-life productions. Once the song sounded as thrilling on the small car-radio speaker as it had in the studio, it passed the test and was ready to be mastered and sent to the pressing plant. If not, Spector would descend once again to the dark studio room of Gold Star to remix and rebalance the whole sound. "Everything was in limbo," Spector would claim, "until the last dab of paint" (Jayanti).

What was interesting about the Wall of Sound was its attempt to hide the building blocks of the song, particularly the chords and their shifting from one to the other; instead, with all the instruments awash together in this thickness of sound, usually only the vocal stood out on its own. The listeners would not constantly have their attention drawn to the changing chords, but instead these were inaudible and the listeners would become enveloped in the overall sound. The words would relate a story they could lose themselves in, usually a story that directly expressed something of their own life experiences. The Wall of Sound did not, however, come fully formed but was an evolutionary process and one that can clearly be observed developing over the six months between "He's a Rebel" and "Today I Met the Boy I'm Going to Marry."

Jerry Wexler would later describe Spector's production style as an "intaglio," an intricate design carved by a single hand into the surface of a stone.

> I respect Phil. He could do it all. The song and the recording existed in his brain. Phil's records were made in his head before he even entered the recording studio. When Phil went into the studio, it came out of him, like Minerva coming out of Jupiter's head. Every instrument had its role to play, and it was all prefigured. The singer was just one tile in this intaglio. . . . How could I later argue with the results. (Jayanti)

THE WALL OF SOUND: DA DOO RON RON, THEN HE KISSED ME, BE MY BABY, AND A CHRISTMAS GIFT FOR YOU

In early 1963 Phil had clearly mastered his studio techniques and began to create his true sonic masterpieces. "Da Doo Ron Ron" (recorded March 1963, released April 1963) was not the climax of Spector's elaborate Wall of Sound. Written to be a "silly answer" to Duke Ellington's "If You Ain't Got That Swing" (Jayanti), it was the first real defining moment of his legendary sound, establishing new heights in the recording of pop music. Mark Ribowsky described the sound as "mixed with savage-sounding horns and overheated castanets; it was 'Uptown' stirred into a frenzy and ablaze with spirit . . . the wad of rhythm forming a suggestion of awesome power while still preserving the intimacy of the vocal through a radio speaker, and remaining recognizable as rock 'n' roll" (Ribowsky, 148). Meanwhile, Brown called it the most "irrepressibly exhilarating song that Spector ever recorded" (M. Brown, 130).

Usually, Darlene Love was the voice Spector preferred to use, simply because of its strength, but in this instance Spector decided her voice was too mature, too worldly, possibly because she had had a wealth of experience behind her even though she was still only twenty-two at the time. Spector decided to use the Crystals' voices for the song and to put it out under their name. The younger girls were exactly the right medium to express notions of teenage love and innocence to the song's intended audience (i.e., white, teenage girls).

Spector didn't use the groups' usual lead vocalist, Barbara Alston, however; instead, his intuition led him to make use of the groups' newest member, the fifteen-year-old "La La" Brooks. Brooks had a good strong voice, but it had a particular quality of youthful innocence to it as well, and for this reason Spector could combine power and projection with a certain teen innocence, creating a vocal that "is a gust of sheer, heart lifting, love struck joy" (M. Brown, 130). Even the song's "silly" title and chorus refrain made sense on the lips of the young Brooks. It "sounded so funny on my tongue," she remembered, "but me being a kid, it sounded kind of cute, it fit right into my age and character. And I think that was why it came out so good" (M. Brown, 130). Spector's gift for matching the right voice with the right song was perfectly demonstrated here.

For Brooks the song was "the most exciting moment of my life" (M. Brown, 131), but for the rest of the group it signaled just how superfluous they were in Spector's Napoleonic plan for global dominance of the music industry. As for Darlene Love, she too quickly realized that she was not indispensable and that Spector had no loyalty toward her, or indeed anyone, making her future seem insecure and unstable. According to Brooks, "Phil was a perfectionist all the way, and he didn't care if people's feelings got hurt. It wasn't about feelings, it was about Phil. And who ever could pull it off, that's who he would use. He didn't give a damn" (M. Brown, 131). "Da Doo Ron Ron" entered the top forty in the second week of May 1963 and eventually reached number three.

If "Da Doo Ron Ron" set the bar of record production in 1963, "Then He Kissed Me," released only two months later (July 1963), pushed the boundaries of pop music to its utmost limit and captured even more the romance of teen innocence. It had a simple, chiming opening guitar riff and castanets, using a variation on the Baion rhythm; and Jack Nitzsche's string arrangement, as well as a full choir of background vocals, all enriched "La La" Brooks's thrilling lead. Brooks sang the song, about the thrill and excitement of a young girl's first kiss, when she was only fifteen and had never in fact been kissed herself. The sentiment of the thrill of being kissed for the first time hung on Brooks's lips, anticipating the very moment.

Spector's friend, mentor, and onetime songwriting partner Doc Pomus would described the song as "this great wall of enormous sound and somehow through it all there was this lovely romantic, sentimental innocence" (M. Brown, 131–32). It was precisely because of Spector's thrilling productions on these records that gloriously captured the feeling of teen romance and innocence that musicologist and girl groups enthusiast John Clemente sees the Crystals as representing the "voice of teen radio at its height" (Clemente, 81). However, while the Crystals were at the height of their success, dominating pop charts with three breathtaking records and providing Spector with a vehicle to enable him to achieve the success he had sought for so long, he suddenly abandoned them and moved his attention to another girl group.

The Ronettes were formed in New York in 1959, when their grandmother entered them in a talent competition at the Apollo Theater. At this point the group were known as the Darling Sisters and consisted of three girls, sisters Veronica (who later became Ronnie Spector after her marriage to Phil Spector) and Estelle Bennett, and their cousin Nedra Talley. From the moment they met, Spector was smitten by both Veronica's voice and her sultry looks. Ronnie's voice was the last brick to his Wall of Sound. "He knew from the second he heard me that my voice was exactly what he needed to fill in the center of this enormous sound" (Spector, 52). The tough but beautiful look of the girls, with their big, beehive hairdos and heavy eyeliner, was something Spector knew he could also build a successful image around.

Spector recorded two songs with the girls, "Why Don't They Let Us Fall in Love" and "Be My Baby," though some, including the songs' writers, thought it was "Why Don't They Let Us Fall in Love" that was the surefire hit and not "Be My Baby" (Betrock, 133). However, Spector must again be praised here for his knowledge of hit-making potential; he considered the latter to have the more commercial appeal and even reassured Veronica's mother that the girls would have their first number one with the song (Betrock, 131). Spector was ultimately correct in his decision, and "Be My Baby" became the Ronettes' biggest hit, one of Spector's biggest hits, and probably the most iconic of all his recordings; the opening drumbeat and the final coda of lavish strings and wailing vocals have been some of the most copied ideas in pop music since. The song has highlighted numerous pieces of cinema, particularly film director Martin Scorsese's opening to his cult classic *Mean Streets* (1973), while pop groups as diverse as the Beach Boys to the Jesus and Mary Chain have cited it as a major frame of reference for their own productions. The song has been considered one of the best songs of the 1960s by *Pitchfork Media*, *NME*, and *Time*. In 2004, *Rolling Stone* ranked the song twenty-two in its list of "The 500 Greatest Songs of All Time," describing it as the "Rosetta stone for studio pioneers such as the Beatles and Brian Wilson."

The opening two bars of the song show the sheer scale of the track as if a "pocket symphony" of Wagnerian proportions were being created. "Phil was always looking for a new rule to break," observed Ronnie Spector; "he wasn't afraid to try anything" (Spector, 107). The drums on this song are typically big for a Phil Spector production, and the drum sounds are, to quote Jacqueline Warwick, writer of *Girl Groups, Girl Culture*, "a depiction of the sensations of the heart-stopping love at first sight . . . and might conjure an uneven heart thumping followed by a gasp or sharply indrawn breath" (Warwick, *Girl Groups*, 125–26).

For many, the impetus of rock 'n' roll had come with Elvis, whom teenagers of the 1950s saw as a new "messiah" of popular culture (*The Beatles Anthology*), but from a musical point of view it was Spector's productions of "Da Doo Ron Ron," "Then He Kissed Me," and particularly "Be My Baby" that showed this new breed what could be achieved on a pop record. "With Phil as our inspiration," wrote Ronnie Spector, "we'd try to push ourselves as hard as he pushed himself" (Spector, 107).

Spector made pop music such a major commercial success that he was able to turn it into the ultimate commercial product by inventing the Christmas pop song; on November 22, 1963, he released an album of Christmas songs as *A Christmas Gift for You from Phil Spector*. Even though eleven of the twelve composers of the Christmas songs wrote thank-you letters for Spector's production of their songs (Jayanti), the album did not become the initial success he thought it would be. The record, however, has since been revised as a virtual pop classic, making 142 on *Rolling Stone*'s list of the best five hundred albums of all time; being included in Robert Dimery and Michael Lydon's *1001 Albums You Must Hear before You Die* in 2010; and being Brian Wilson's favorite album of all time (DeMartin). The general public was, unfortunately, not quite ready for it and possibly saw it more as a novelty record that attempted to take advantage of Christmas as a crude marketing opportunity. Unfortunately, a tragic event that Spector could not possibly have anticipated took place on the same day as the album's release.

President John F. Kennedy's assassination would send the country into a deep mourning that would last for the next three months. Pop music and certainly Phil Spector's "novelty" Christmas record was the last thing on people's minds, as the sudden and brutal killing of such a young and promising leader cast a dark cloud over the psyche of a whole nation. There is no doubt that Kennedy's assassination affected the sale of Spector's quirky but innovative Christmas album more than anything else, and certainly the album's arranger, Jack Nitzsche, felt as much: "The album never really took off. I think some of that had to do with the world after the Kennedy assassination. It affected the public. No one wanted to celebrate Christmas in December 1963" (Kubernik). Darlene Love suggests a similar reason, feeling that the death of Kennedy had badly damaged the nation's psyche and that people didn't feel like celebrating Christmas in 1963 (Love, 100). In order to heal themselves, Love believed, the American public, particularly the younger generation, distracted themselves with the sounds that were making themselves heard across the Atlantic (Love, 101). With the distraction of these new sounds Spector's music no longer appealed to the American public as much, and as Spector withdrew his Christmas album from the shops, realizing it was not an appropriate time for its release, he also began to withdraw himself more and more from public life, possibly fearful of the challenges that the new British groups were posing.

PHIL SPECTOR: THE MODERN WAGNER—INNOVATOR, PRODUCER, ALCHEMIST

The 1960s brought about extreme social change and a great flourishing of artistic movements. It had, by and large, a strong connection to both the German and British Romantic movement of the eighteenth and nineteenth centuries, with which it shared an interest with Eastern philosophy, an emphasis on imagination, drug experimentation, sensuality, the occult, and a strong focus on the individual and the challenge of conventional structures and laws. It is therefore from such a perspective of some interest to explore Phil Spector's connection to his great idol the Romantic composer Richard Wagner; many saw Spector as being a similar kind of figure (despite Wagner's overt anti-Semitism and Spector's obvious Jewish background) for the pop culture of the 1960s.

While there has often been too big a deal made out of the Wagnerian influence on Spector's music, something the world of classical music certainly dismisses outright (Lambert), it is worth considering Richard Williams's comment that "Spector's finest records—those tumultuous epics that attracted comparisons with Wagner—gave a generation of adolescents a soundtrack to their lives" (R. Williams, "Other Side"). And then there's Brown's comment that "he made records of a hitherto unconceived grandeur and majesty, elevating the themes of teenage love and heartache to the epic proportions of Wagnerian opera—little symphonies for the kids—the clamorous joyous noise of a small tyrant unleashing his vision, his revenge on the world" (M. Brown, 1).

Wagner's bombastic musical creations are seen in the context of German nationalism and large-scale opera, drama, and political changes that were taking place during Wagner's time. Spector's "tumultuous epics" are not to be considered on the same basis as Wagner's operas in the specific period of German history but more in terms of the "generation of adolescents" for whom they were created. In other words, they were created for a period in which different sensibilities and different cultural forces brought about different artistic achievements, serving different ends. While Wagner is considering the whole German nation and its mission in nineteenth-century Europe, Spector's mission is fo-cused on a narrow, though new and significant, socioeconomic group, which after the Second World War would be the first representatives of our modern consumer culture, a culture that was first to experience the notion of extreme individualism. The significance of rock 'n' roll to unleash this new socioeconomic class was what was most important in Spector's time and ultimately where the zeitgeist was moving. Some of the most culturally significant individuals of the time were practically teenagers themselves: Marlon Brando, James Dean, Elvis, the Beatles, the Rolling Stones, Brian Wilson, Bob Dylan, and of course, Phil Spec-tor.

Spector was keenly aware of the mission that lay out before him, absolutely assured that he was making much more than just pop music. Like Wagner, and mostly encouraged by him and his music, Spector had a great ambition to raise the pop record to an epic form. In many ways this seems to be Spector's greatest ambition and at the same time his greatest achievement, which though for some it made ridiculous the simplicity of pop music, for many others it opened up the possibilities of the recording studio and the pop record. He was obsessed by Wagner, "the totality of it—the power and he held it up as a model for him," said his friend Michael Spencer. The Wall of Sound was an attempt to create a "Wagnerian drama and grandeur" (Biography Channel).

It is significant that Wagner and Spector shared a similar attitude and magnetism; the following description of Wagner by his enemy Han-slick is relayed by Bryan Magee in his short book on the composer: "He exercised an incomprehensible magic in order to make friends, and to retain them; the hypnotic power that he everywhere exerted, not mere-ly by his music but by his personality, overbearing all opposition and bending everyone to his will, is enough to stamp him as one of the most remarkable of phenomena, a marvel of energy and endowment" (Mag-ee, 49). While Spector also seemed to have no conscience to use people for his own ends, he too seemed to have about him an aura that could mesmerize, charm, and beguile nearly anyone with whom he came into contact, including talented and intelligent individuals such as Gerry Goffin and Carole King, Jack Nitzsche, Brian Wilson, and even John Lennon, who seemed to defer his own "genius" to that of Spector's (R. Williams, "Other Side"). Individuals with great business acumen as well as master hustlers such as Spector, as well as Andrew "Loog" Oldham, were all seduced by Spector's genius and charm.

His onetime assistant and protégé, Nino Tempo, said, "Between the wires and the booth Phil got magic—he caught lightening time and time again" (Biography Channel), while others saw Spector as an alchemist, who with his great power "alchemized" songs into hits (M. Brown, 9), "turned vinyl into gold," and "revolutionized the sound of rock 'n' roll" (Biography Channel). Words such as "magic," "lightning," "art," "grandeur," "majesty," "epic," and "visionary" were often used in relation to Spector and suggests that for many, though certainly not for all, Spector had conjured, with Merlin-like sorcery, something completely otherworldly, almost magical, with his productions—as had Wagner.

Beyond just their character, both shared a similar vision of their art. Wagner had a vision of *Gesamtkunstwerk*, "total artwork," which was "to adhere to classic Greek principals [sic] of integrating music, drama, text, design, and movement into a one fluid piece of work that assured the genuine admiration of almost any audience" (Musicneverdies). Though Spector's attitude was not necessarily to incorporate all the elements of the arts into one ultimate experience, Spector was ultimately aware of the presentation of his groups and was aware that their image, particularly in the case of the Ronettes, was strong enough for them to have a visual impact on the necessary TV promotion that his acts would need. Spector was also keenly aware of the stage presence and theatrical elements of the acts and how they needed to be strong enough for them to carry a hit song; this is why, according to his own claims, he chose to work with Ike and Tina Turner, because they had an act, they had a revue, and they had a visual and dramatic element that would go hand in hand with his productions. Something he felt was essential to compete with the Beatles (Jayanti), who had similarly integrated all the elements of total art, in the sense that they wrote the music and lyrics, performed, recorded, and conceived the artwork to their albums, and later on their music videos and films.

Along with Spector's awareness of these aspects of the music industry, he was in many senses, like Wagner, determined to integrate all aspects of the music business by owning and controlling every aspect of it, from choosing the songs, words, and music to arranging, producing, and choosing the appropriate singers for the songs and choosing which songs to be released as singles. He also controlled the publishing of his songs as well as the recordings. In these two senses Spector resembled Wagner in attempting to integrate many aspects of the music and record-making industries, and ultimately gaining personal control over them both. From the point of view of the creation of his records, Spector looked to Wagner to deepen his approach to music making, particularly Wagner's "invisible wall of sound" (G. Brown).

Perhaps it was Spector's egomania that had encouraged him to make huge records, as some, such as the critic Albert Goldman, would suggest (*Phil Spector: He's a Rebel*). And perhaps Spector's habit of seeing himself in terms of great artists such as Wagner, Beethoven, and Leonardo De Vinci (Jayanti) along with the encouragement of those around him caused him to push the boundaries of the soundscape and produce bigger and more dramatic works. Though lacking subtlety, Spector had done something that gave pop music credibility, by making it epic.

LEGACY OF THE SPECTOR SOUND

Not everyone was impressed with Spector's music; Beatles producer George Martin, for example, would criticize his work on the Beatles *Let It Be* album, while Jerry Wexler referred to it as a "fascinating treacle" and a "muted roar," which he didn't much care for (M. Brown, 133). Nevertheless, he was considered highly by many sixties and postsixties artists as diverse as Brian Wilson, Leonard Cohen, and Joey Ramone.

The Spector sound also contributed to embellishing the whole musical landscape that began to develop after 1964 and influenced albums such as *Pet Sounds, Sgt. Pepper's Lonely Hearts Club Band*, and the psychedelic movement in general. Eighties indie groups such as the Jesus and Mary Chain (their album *Psychocandy* opens with a reference to Hal Blaine's drum part on "Be My Baby"), Teenage Fan Club, and the Cocteau Twins, as well as present-day "noise pop" bands such as the Raveonettes and the Dum Dum Girls, owe a debt to Spector's music-making approach. "There is a Phil Spector sound [and] everyone knows what it is. It is still regarded as one of the most seminal, dramatic, important creations in the history of pop music," said *Rolling Stones'* Anthony DeCurtis (Biography Channel). The musician and producer David Kessel, the son of Spector's hero Barney Kessel, suggests that the

modern-day use of studio "plug-in" effects used by the current generation of producers is actually a means of "accessing Phil Spector with the
touch of a button." The music of Phil Spector, Kessel claims, "holds up
so well because it's that great and that deep in our social consciousness"
(Kubernik).

4

POCKET SYMPHONIES FOR THE KIDS

Teenagers

MUSIC FOR AN EMOTIONAL GENERATION

"Spector's beat," Binia Tymieniecka's documentary *Phil Spector: He's a Rebel* aptly stated, "is closely tuned to teen desire," and Phil Spector suggested as much about himself and his music, claiming, "I myself have a tremendous yearning, a yearning to be respected, a yearning to be accepted. I see this in the teenagers. A yearning to do things, to be someone, to be important and to be recognized . . . it is an emotional music for an emotional generation" (*Phil Spector: He's a Rebel*).

With his Wall of Sound, Spector created for the teenager a space to retreat to when they felt the world didn't understand them, and possibly his own Wagnerian-type fantasy world into which he himself would retreat when he too needed solace. Although he had been encouraged by Barney Kessel to follow a career in rock 'n' roll as a more viable means to earn a living, Spector seemed naturally to gravitate toward this new sound that spoke directly not just to him but also to all the teenagers of his generation.

Spector's early attempts at forming bands naturally included the more popular rock 'n' roll records of the day, while the sounds of the early girl groups, such as the Chantels, would also exert an influence on the young Spector. Both rock 'n' roll and the teen pop of the early girl groups formed a much stronger connection with teen audiences than did the bland adult-oriented music of the older generation. Jeff Barry put it well when he said, "Nobody was really creating music especially for teenagers, because they didn't have money. Then in the fifties they started to have disposable income. . . . And then young adults like myself—I was nineteen and starting to write—started to create music for young people. And that is the beginning of pop rock" (Emerson, 148). Robert Shelton would echo these sentiments in his article on Bob Dylan. "Where," he inquired, "was pop music 20 years ago? With Dinah Shore singing 'Buttons and Bows' or Kay Kyser singing 'I've Got Spurs That Jingle Jangle Jingle' and 'Ole Buttermilk Sky?'" (Savage, viii).

Although Spector's earlier songs, such as "Don't Worry My Little Pet," had attempted to capture the teen sensibilities of Buddy Holly and the Everly Brothers, his first successful record, "To Know Him Is to Love Him," was deliberately and directly tuned to teenage feelings. While the song's inspiration originated from a deep subconscious expression of his father's death, the fact that Spector and his bandmates were only teenagers themselves meant that their treatment of his artistic idea would more than likely resonate with the feelings of their own social group. Spector realized that the song would best suit a female voice and would similarly benefit from a stylizing similar to the Chantels' "Maybe." Kleinbard's untutored teenage soprano gave it the same appeal to a teen audience that the Chantels' lead singer, Arlene Smith, had done, touching an emotional need in the teenagers of the time and, in this sense, tailoring it for such a market.

Ultimately Spector had used this ballad-cum–funeral dirge to both express the emotional loss of his father and simultaneously disguise it as a love song with a highly emotional teenage sensibility. The Chantels had similarly expressed deep, almost religious, feelings inspired by their church upbringing, with an emotional perspective that directly related to the mood and feelings of teenagers at the time. Not only "Maybe" but also other songs, such as "The Plea," fused religious devotion with the feelings of confused adolescent emotions, which expressed a similar fervor that teenagers had begun to experience during the first stirrings of their inner emotional life.

Another song with the same sensibility, "I Love How You Love Me," followed the same pattern as "To Know Him . . . ," which again Spector deliberately fashioned to appeal to the same market. It seems though that Spector's decision here was more instinctive than calculated, as the original had intended to be faster than Spector's final production (M. Brown, 84). Spector once again tuned his artistic radar to that of teen desire, creating a world of romantic yearning that the youth of the day so desperately identified with.

These two songs, as well as other Paris Sisters releases, such as "Be My Boy" and "He Knows I Love Him Too Much," established a voice for teenagers, who would begin to experience the world as separate entities from their parents, and for the first time teenagers had their newfound feelings and ideals expressed for them in a musical form. Spector's recording approach, though seemingly "chaotic and unplanned" (Ribowsky, 93), was an attempt to capture on record the feelings and ideals of a new generation. For some, such as Mark Ribowsky, Spector's music was, though "chaotic and unplanned," also delicately balanced and sensitively attuned to teen emotions, transcending the mundane and elevating his music (and his listeners' experience of it) to a place altogether otherworldly. Spector, Ribowsky claims,

> was working on a higher plane: it wasn't melody but the blend and balance of that image that consumed him. Thus even though the rhythm section would be barely discernible in "I Love How You Love Me," buried by eight violins and the sugar plum voices of the Paris Sisters, it would be that way precisely because drum, bass and guitar merged into a "feel" rather than separating into select instrumental noises. The balance of a Spector song was diaphanously sensitive; it could happen at any moment. (Ribowsky, 93)

This blend of sounds that would emotionally explode at any moment seemed to best capture the "diaphanously sensitive" emotional world of the teenager, a world delicately balanced between the polarities of excitement and despair, experience and innocence, family and individual, authority and freedom, self and other, and inner feelings and outer reality.

While Elvis, Buddy Holly, Jerry Lee Lewis, and the Everly Brothers represented the feelings and ideals of white teenage boys, Chuck Berry and Little Richard projected the ideals of young African American boys, and the Chantels, and later the Shirelles, represented an African American girl's worldview, it was Spector's early songs that captured the spirit of the white female teenager, particularly concerning their main occupation of teen romance.

Although songs such as "To Know Him Is to Love Him" and "I Love How You Love Me" present a more passive female in a musical style that was less imposing and arresting than some of his later productions with the girl group acts, they also gave a voice to the young, white teen girls that had simultaneously been affected by the sensibilities of the Shirelles' "Will You Still Love Me Tomorrow." "Tomorrow" had essentially been written by a young woman (Carole King) of white, middle-class American values (and her white middle-class American boyfriend [Gerry Goffin]); King was a woman who had a keen insight into not just the emotional desires of young females but also the whole emotional values of the post–World War II youth culture. But the Paris Sisters' "I Love How You Love Me" and the feeling and ambience Spector created around the lyric gave the young, white teen girl a visual, as well as a musical, representation of her feelings.

The vocal delivery of the Paris Sisters, particularly in the manner in which Spector produced them, corresponded to the sensibilities of what Jacqueline Warwick termed the "angst of white suburban girlhood" (Warwick, *Girl Groups*, 72). The Shirelles, who had also been treated with a white sensibility by their producer Luther Dixon, though not all their songs were in this vein, were African American girls; and though they connected with white teen sensibilities (S. Douglas, *Where the Girls Are*, 83–99), visually they were not able to represent directly white female teenagers of the period, so the Paris Sisters and Annette Kleinbard momentarily filled this space.

As well as encapsulating the feelings of middle-class, white American teenage girls, it is significant to point out that these songs also resonated with the more feminine side of the 1950s and early 1960s white, male teenager. John Lennon and the other Beatles, for example, had obviously connected emotionally with Spector's lovelorn sentiments of "To Know Him" by featuring it in their live sets in Hamburg and Liverpool, as well as recording it at the BBC. Lennon also went on to record a solo version of "I Love How You Love Me," and according to Spector, Lennon's "Happy Xmas (War Is Over)" was strongly reminiscent of its melody (Du Noyer, *John Lennon*, 536). Despite his outwardly machismo personality, it's quite obvious that, though often hidden and quite guarded, Lennon's feminine sensitivity resonated strongly with songs of this type; his own songs, particularly in the early days of the Beatles, displayed a very similar sentiment to the white teen ballads of these Spector songs, particularly songs like "Do You Want to Know a Secret," "This Boy," and "If I Fell." With Brian Wilson it is also evident that Spector's white female ballads touched the American male psyche as Wilson responded with a whole series of heartrending compositions, particularly songs such as "In My Room," "Don't Worry Baby," and "Surfer Girl."

Wilson became particularly affected by Spector's sound, while the Beatles were completely immersed in the girl group sound and the Brill Building writing style that Spector's productions transformed into an endless string of hits. It is for these reasons, as Susan Douglas points out, that both Wilson and the Beatles were, as a result, able to blend the male machismo attitude of 1950s rock 'n' roll with a softer feminine quality, thus making them more accessible to both male and female audiences. As well, they endorsed the feelings and attitudes of female singers, which again reinforced more positive attitudes in the girls of the 1960s and allowed them to feel more confident and express their personal thoughts and emotions more readily (S. Douglas, *Where the Girls Are*, 96, 116–17).

THE BEGINNING OF THE GIRL GROUP SOUND

While Spector's most illustrious period was with his girl group acts of the early to mid-1960s—the Crystals, the Ronettes, and Darlene Love—in which his massive Wall of Sound productions established the genre as a real artistic phenomenon in its own right, Spector had made earlier attempts, with the Paris Sisters, to attune to the teen sensibilities of the early girl groups such as the Shirelles.

"All through the Night" (1961), the backup single to "I Love How You Love Me," a buoyant, up-tempo "la-la-la teen tune," captured the high-spirited joys of teenage zest and wonder. The girl fantasizes over what will happen on her first date with her boyfriend, a theme that ran through the emotional center of many young girls' lives, particularly for the time, when little was seen or discussed in matters of sex and romance; this was a time when ideas of how love and romance unfolds between two young people was more imagined and whispered about.

While the lyrics were full of wonder and anticipation, echoing the inner desires of the listener, the upbeat tempo, the handclaps, and the sing-along backing vocals made it a perfect party song in what was becoming a tradition of the girl group genre. Even though this song was a perfect contrast to the sultry, intimate, more concentrated, minimalistic, smoother, and lighter arrangement of "I Love How You Love Me," it "may have served as insurance should the public reject a second ballad" (Kirby).

Both these songs were indicative of Spector's ability to capture very specific moods that would strongly resonate with the various emotional experiences of his intended audience. Spector's great gift in many ways was to blend the right sound and rhythm to a song's lyrical theme. Alan Betrock expressed Spector's ability to do this when he wrote that Spector "realized early on that lyrics must paint a visual picture and relate a concise universal story. By sound and lyric Spector felt that the listener should be transported to a place where visual imagery and youthful emotions would mesh together in a warm, understanding fantasy world" (Betrock, 30).

"All through the Night" captured a greater sense of teenage joy and was one of the first real attempts by Spector to capture such a sound. The song explores the joy and wonder of a girl's first date: "I dream about my first date with you. . . . I wonder will you like me as much as I like you"—a sentiment that was later recaptured for many of Spector's other girl group songs such as "I Wonder," "Walking in the Rain," and "He's Sure the Boy I Love."

"Let Me Be the One," another song by Larry Kolber and Barry Mann, tried to capture the feeling of "To Know Him" and "I Love How You Love Me," but it was too formulaic. Such an attitude might suggest that Spector could easily be as calculating and ingenuous as those he often accused of being in the industry simply for the money and not the art, and it was most likely for this reason that the song only reached number eighty-seven. While "Let Me Be the One" suggested formula, following the success of the other Spector productions for the Paris Sisters, the flip side "What Am I to Do" (March 1962), written with Doc Pomus, was more imaginative, more attuned to the teen sensibilities of their previous successes, and may have possibly been a better choice for a single. The song also shares a strong similarity in its feel, production, and harmonic and melodic phrasing, though with a slower tempo, to the Marvelettes' "I Think I Can Change You," written by Smokey Robinson and released by Motown a few months after Spector's song hit the charts (a possible indication of Spector's influence on the formative years of Motown).

Even before the split with the Paris Sisters, Spector had already moved on and was recording the Chantels' lead singer Arlene Smith, who was now a solo artist. Such a move might indicate that Spector saw his real talent as bringing the raw energy of girl singers and producing the right sounds and textures around their voices. The Chantels had impressed him, and in this sense Spector may have felt his production approach with Smith's vocal would have been a winning combination. Interestingly Spector took his recent Paris Sisters' record "He Knows I Love Him Too Much" and created a bigger production around Smith's vocal, but Spector overshot the mark; instead of producing the tender and emotive records of the Paris Sisters or the yearning cries of the Chantels, for whom Smith's voice did so much to create, Spector had transformed Smith into a third-rate cabaret act. He had tried to transform the simple pop song into a Leonard Bernstein–type number stylized on the Latin sounds of *West Side Story*. Smith herself recognized the clumsiness of Spector's work with her and felt the record was "a stock arrangement and the attention wasn't focused on me. It was lost at the bottom of a big orchestra mix, and it didn't work" (Ribowsky, 107). A second Spector-Smith production, "Love Love Love," was another failed attempt by Spector to sound like Bernstein and again lacked the youthful romanticism of the Paris Sisters, sounding more like something produced for an adult mainstream market, which teenagers had managed at this stage to completely free themselves from.

Other Spector songs of the time included "Every Breath I Take" and Sammy Turner's "Raincoat in the River," with lyrics about throwing raincoats and umbrellas in the river—not necessarily the language of teenagers. As well, there were songs such as the Spector Three's "I Really Do," which echoed much of the Everly Brothers' compositional and production style (the Spector Three was an outfit Spector had cobbled together while uncertain where to go next after he disbanded the Teddy Bears). And there was "I Know Why" as well as the simple rock 'n' roll instrumentals such as "Willy Boy." All these songs had a flavor of teen but were trite and lacked any real substance that could reflect genuine feelings that teenagers could relate to.

In order to continue to connect to the youth market, Spector intrinsically knew he would have to search out the right songs and the right singers. Instead of seeking out more experienced singers like the Paris Sisters, Spector instead preferred to work with the young, naïve, but idealistic new group he had discovered—the Crystals. The Crystals were deeply inspired by the Chantels and especially the more cutting-edge Shirelles, whose use of strings placed them and their song "Tomorrow" into a "more definitively pop space" (Keenan, 43), while their lyrics of sexual intimacy, though controversial, were more reflective of the modern teenager's mind-set. The Shirelles' heroine wasn't a young housewife but a teenage girl, and so the song "positioned the Shirelles as something new—neither the young housewife nor the experienced R&B singer" (Keenan, 43).

In terms of songwriters, Spector found exactly what he needed at Don Kishner's Aldon Music, where, brimming with the youthful energy and joy of the time, the best young songwriters from New York, the energetic and edgy city that had its finger on the pulse of youth culture, were situated. Here he found the young and idealistic writing teams of Ellie Greenwich and Jeff Barry, Barry Mann and Cynthia Weil, and Gerry Goffin and Carole King, from whom the best of his teenage music came. He knew that to "broach the teenage market he needed songwriters who understood the dreams and anguish of being teenagers themselves" and that their songs "shaped and reflected the conservative dreams and aspirations of most American teenagers, with their time honored themes of infatuation and heartbreak, summer romances, the first kiss, dreams of wedding bells and living happily ever after" (M. Brown, 81–82).

CAROLE KING AND GERRY GOFFIN, BARRY MANN AND CYNTHIA WEIL, JACK NITZSCHE AND HE'S A REBEL

After "I Love How You Love Me" reached number five on the charts, Spector had to produce a follow-up, "He Knows I Love Him Too Much," this time from another young songwriting partnership, that of Goffin and King, who had written "Will You Still Love Me Tomorrow" for the Shirelles. Goffin and King had been particularly impressed with Spector when they met him on his first visit to New York. In fact, according to Ribowsky, the couple saw the unorthodox Spector as some kind of modern-day oracle. "He would play us records he loved," said

Goffin. "He was very much in tune with what was happening" (Ribow-sky, 105).

However, Spector's first recording for his new group, the Crystals, came not from this pool of talented young songwriters but from a middle-aged man who was managing the group and had a song based on a Negro spiritual tune; still, Spector used all these elements to create a record that resonated with teen desire on a nearly religious level. The second of their songs was penned by Cynthia Weil, from Aldon's stable of teen writers. Weil's "Uptown" was a song that attempted to create a world of secure fantasy, allowing its listener escape from the harsh world of reality.

Weil conceived the song after seeing a young African American pushing a cartload of clothes through New York's Garment District. The lyric was written from the point of view of the girl whose boyfriend may be "a little man" by day "lost in an angry land" but who is transformed each evening by her love and devotion. In keeping with the cinematic quality of Weil's lyrics, her writing-partner-cum-husband, Barry Mann, wrote a melody that very much characterized the style of *West Side Story*.

Don Kirshner, dubbed "the man with the golden ear" due to his uncanny ability to instantly recognize a potential hit record, encouraged Spector's partnerships with his stable of writers, realizing early on that Spector's true talent lay in effectively interpreting songs in a manner that would strongly resonate with teenagers. The strong connection with its young market, which could easily relate to feeling "small" in an adult world while simultaneously feeling like a king when they could immerse themselves in the fantasy world of teen music and movies, made sure the song entered the top one hundred at eighty. While Weil's inspiration was drawn from the black American, Spector's production, with its Spanish guitar and castanets inspired by his cowritten hit "Spanish Harlem," gave it a Latin feel, making the song more identifiable with the Latin community.

Spector attempted to repeat the success of "Uptown" with "On Broadway," another Mann/Weil song, which was shaped with a similar social conscience "playing on the themes of urban dreams and tribulations" as it sketched out the story of a "small town girl dreaming of fame and success among the glittering lights of the great white way" (M. Brown, 96). Spector, however, was dissatisfied with the results and never issued the song as a single for the Crystals. It wasn't too long though before Spector had found another potential hit, again with a similar theme of alienation and disenfranchisement: "another tribute to a teen dream, this one from the wrong side of the tracks," as Darlene Love would describe it (M. Brown, 104).

"He's a Rebel" would become the Crystals' third single and Spector's real mega-leap into both the charts and the hearts and minds of teenagers—a huge leap into the fantasy world of teenagers reared on the latest teenage Hollywood movies. Inspired by Marlon Brandon's teen classic *The Wild One* (1953), Gene Pitney wrote the song paralleling the theme of the social misfit rebel with a similar romanticized notion that resonated with the teen audience of the time. Spector had heard the singer Vikki Carr recording Pitney's original song while visiting the Hill and Range office and decided it was too good not take it for himself. In a frenzy to get it recorded, before Carr could get her version out, Spector flew to Los Angeles to start recording immediately with his new act.

Spector's usual engineer, Stan Ross, was not available for the sessions, so he had to work with Ross's nephew, Larry Levine. Spector's new business partner, Lester Sill, recommended Jack Nitzsche, another young musical innovator attuned to teen emotions, who had just been working for Lee Hazelwood, to work as Spector's arranger (Betrock, 35). It would be Nitzsche who would introduce Spector to his cohort of musicians that would embellish nearly all of his greatest work; these would include the vocal trio the Blossoms, from where he would find Darlene Love, along with famous names such as Leon Russell, Earl Palmer, Don Randi, Hal Blaine, and Glen Campbell (Kubernik).

After the success of "He's a Rebel," Nitzsche would become Spector's protégé, his musical alter ego, and his irreplaceable musical arranger. Like Kirshner, Goffin and King, and many others, Nitzsche was fully aware of Spector's strong emotional connection with the youth market, inherently feeling how they felt and focused all his energy into capturing those emotions on record. "Maybe other producers liked their records," said Nitzsche. "Phil loved his records. Phil really was the artist and it wasn't just out of ego. Phil understood the teenage market, he could relate to their feelings and buying impulse" (M. Brown, 124).

Nitzsche, like Spector, had been a shy, withdrawn boy who had found solace away from an unfriendly world in music and as such was as much drawn into the musical world he helped to create, with Spector, as a means by which he himself could escape the harshness of reality; this is possibly why he idolized Spector so much.

"He's a Rebel" had ultimately been inspired by Spector's production of "Uptown," particularly the use of strings, which impressed Pitney to such a degree that he saw it as transforming the simple pop song into a work of art. Spector, however, ignored Pitney's string arrangement and produced it with a much more basic, though equally effective, arrangement, consisting of a simple piano motif over a basic reverberated backbeat. The song's stroke of genius was Darlene Love's driving powerhouse vocal, supported by a full-on gospel choir by her group the Blossoms. Unlike other Spector sessions, often drawn-out affairs with instruments recorded one day, strings another day, and vocals on still another day, all the recording for "He's a Rebel" was completed in one session. While Vikki Carr's version went nowhere, Spector's went to number one on the Billboard charts and number two on the R&B charts.

The song, which broached the theme of the existentialist antihero, was very influential in not only creating the antihero in mainstream pop music but also making way for other songs of the type to appear—particularly a host of Shangri-La songs such as "Leader of the Pack," "Out in the Streets," and "Give Him a Great Big Kiss," as well as Motown's "Wild One." Then there's the whole culture of antihero songs from the Kinks' "I'm Not Like Everybody Else" to David Bowie's "Ziggy Stardust," while post-1960s groups such as the Ramones and Twisted Sister owe much of their image to the rebel heroes of songs like this. For the Shangri-Las' "Leader of the Pack," the song's producer, Shadow Morton, borrowed both the theme and the musical arrangement of Spector's song, while the New York teenage girls captured the sentiment of the song as if they lived the part of the angst-ridden teenagers, unappreciated by society. The main vocal with its high-hook chorus and wailing fadeout became a regular element of the teen vocals of the girl groups, while its "bad girl" association contributed to the assertiveness of the profeminists of the mid-1960s.

Many, particularly the "beatniks," familiar with the authentic philosophy of European philosophers such as Jean-Paul Sartre, may have dismissed this type of music as superficial, insignificant, and mostly "inauthentic," particularly compared to other forms of music of the time, such as folk, jazz, blues, and its more digestible cousin rock 'n' roll. Yet, Spector's recordings of "Uptown," "He's a Rebel," and songs such as Goffin and King's "Tomorrow" could not be considered superficial or inauthentic, despite their strong commercial appeal. In many respects Spector's music and the Brill Building–type songs were, for the most part, as relevant and authentic as any of those other musical forms. The music writer Bob Stanley put the whole issue into perspective when he wrote that Brill Building music was "a blend of different musics and neighborhoods that related to [the] shape-shifting street life much more closely than the venerated, undiluted directness of Pete Seeger's folk or Chris Barber's jazz" (Stanley, 111).

Gerry Goffin, a major Brill Building songwriter often employed by Spector to provide him songs, was very aware of his position as a songwriter and certainly realized the need for authenticity in the lyrics, knowing full well that teenagers wouldn't accept a song as real or meaningful to them if they were not expressing something with genuine feeling (Stanley, 116). Spector was not in himself inauthentic, though he certainly saw pop music as a vehicle for his own commercial success, but knew he needed to get teenagers to write and sing the music that was going to ultimately be for their generation.

JEFF BARRY AND ELLIE GREENWICH

Though the young songwriting couples, Goffin and King, and Mann and Weil (as well as Jack Nitzsche's ingenious arrangements), were essential in providing Spector with the raw material he needed to produce his teenage pop symphonies, it was the third pair of romantically involved writing partners—Jeff Barry and Ellie Greenwich—that would be the indispensable providers of most of Spector's teen-based musical dramas.

Jeff Barry cowrote "Tell Laura I Love Her," with Beverly Ross, for Ray Peterson, but when he married Ellie Greenwich in 1962 they became devoted songwriting partners also. Greenwich and Barry started to write with Spector after getting off to a shaky start when Spector turned up a few hours late to a meeting with Greenwich. Greenwich was annoyed and, not really knowing anything about Spector, berated him for his rude behavior. Spector walked away but returned to her after hearing a song she had cowritten with Tony Powers called "The Boy I'm Going to Marry"; he organized another meeting from which he took that song and "Why Do Lovers Break Each Other's Hearts," both of which would become hits for his artists. The first was a hit for Darlene Wright whose name Spector changed to Darlene Love, recognizing that such a name would have greater teen appeal; the second was by Bob B. Soxx and the Blue Jeans, another name change by Spector that would chime with teen sensibilities.

Spector would regard the partnership he forged with Greenwich and Barry as the most productive of his career and the happiest he had with any of his teams of writers. They connected strongly with the "teenage mind" (Emerson, 151) and wrote songs that accentuated adolescence. "Jeff and Ellie really understood me, really knew what I wanted, and were able to deliver. The others understood, but not as much as Jeff and Ellie did" (M. Brown, 128).

In *Always Magic in the Air*, Ken Emerson wrote of their songwriting approach, saying they had little interest in Broadway musicals or the great American songbook and even less in classical music or jazz. Unburdened by the past and by the ambitions and doubts that the past can inspire, they took themselves and their music less seriously. This freed them to write entirely and unselfconsciously in the present tense of teenage rock 'n' roll, which is why a 2004 *Rolling Stone* publication of the five thousand greatest songs of all time included more by Greenwich and Barry (six, five of which they wrote with Spector) than by any of their songwriting peers.

Greenwich and Barry didn't share their songwriting work between lyrics and music; instead, they "moved easily between each seamlessly. This open-ended creative fluidity made it easier to accommodate a third collaborator in Spector." The three would jam together, each playing their instruments and "singing away like maniacs." Greenwich told writer Rob Finnis that "we'd find some melodic thing, or lyrical thing, that hit all of us at once more or less, because our minds were on the same wavelength" (M. Brown, 129). Written in 1963, "Da Doo Ron Ron" would become the product of their first collaboration and captured all the innocence and charm of their writing process, creating the first of their "silly little things," as Jeff Barry would describe them.

The song was written in two days in Spector's office; the title of the song served "as a punctuation for each stanza as well as the chorus." It was a piece of gobbledygook made up on the spot until a proper lyric could be written, but Spector liked it the way it was, "its infectious, nursery rhyme charm a perfect illustration of Jeff Barry's songwriting dictum of keeping things 'simple, happy and repetitive'" (M. Brown, 129). "Phil was the co-writer on the song," said Jack Nitzsche.

> Phil embellished the song and was the producer. I've talked to Gerry Goffin about that a lot; Phil co-writing songs that he would produce. Phil would always have the writers come over and write in the room with him, and I knew he directed it. They all say the same thing; that without Phil Spector in the room that song wouldn't have been that way. He helped. He knew what he wanted it to be. (Kubernik)

Their follow-up song "Then He Kissed Me" was another exciting tribute to teen romance and fantasy, and as Doc Pomus once observed, Spector had created what would be the first true teen record: "He made the quintessential young record, because it had . . . to do with the wonderful pureness about adolescence. It almost didn't relate to some pimply kid. . . . It transcended. It was this great wall of enormous sound, and somehow through it all there was this lovely . . . romantic, sentimental innocence" (Emerson, 150).

Simplistic themes of love and romance were often used by Spector with his Wall of Sound productions and helped create a kind of "idealistic" world where relationships are romantic, monogamous, heterosexual, and sanctioned by heaven. The doo-wop style, with its simple form, often used by Spector, reenforced this idealism. The "kiss" in "Then He Kissed Me" is not sensual but romantic and spiritual and most importantly a symbol of tradition, signifying the consummation of the relationship. The love is idealized with the kiss, while the song's imagery of the stars "shining bright" presents a highly romanticized view of marriage, a view that is often yearned for by teenage girls. In effect, Spector's production ultimately creates what Mick Brown calls the sonic equivalent of "the dream of satin, tulle and eternal love" (M. Brown, 131–32).

ENTER VERONICA

While Spector would use "La La" Brooks on "Da Doo Ron Ron" and "Then He Kissed Me," as he felt her voice resonated much more with teen desires than the other Crystals singers, it was in the vocal character of Veronica Bennett that he felt his records could best penetrate into the hearts and minds of the youth culture of the early 1960s. Along with Veronica's voice and Spector's highly polished productions, it was the intense romantic relationship that began to develop between them that gave the music much of its honesty and intensity (Betrock).

Veronica Bennett was very much in tune with teenage sensibilities of the time and had just turned twenty the same month (August) that "Be My Baby" was released. She had grown up heavily influenced by the teen music of Frankie Lymon, and it was because she sang like Lymon that Spector was so interested in working with her (Betrock, 130; Emerson, 199, 257).

Despite the overwhelming lushness of Spector's Wall of Sound and Greenwich and Barry's overly romanticized lyrics, it was Veronica Bennett's vocal that ultimately prevented the songs from giving way to complete sentimental mush. Bennett's vocal contrasted with the typically soft, smooth, and more mature-sounding qualities of presixties female singers. Her vocal was raspy and intense, more rock 'n' roll, like a female version of Little Richard or John Lennon. Alan Betrock suggests that her voice is not particularly strong and her range is not great, but she had a unique voice, which was "youthful, sultry and honest." The wobbles and quivers in her voice combined with a roughness and characteristic that accord more to common speech patterns and gives her vocal, as well as rock 'n' roll and certain types of pop music in general, its close identification with teenagers, who seemed to feel in it a genuine sense of personal expression.

Lyrically, Spector's records are based on the young female's attitudes toward idealized love, its wonders, anticipations, expectations, beauty, and heartache—the desire for a husband or boyfriend that will fulfill her needs and provide her with the emotional stability for which she yearns. With songs such as "Da Doo Ron Ron," "Then He Kissed Me," "Be My Baby," "Baby, I Love You," "Walking in the Rain," "So Young," "I Wonder," and "Chapel of Love," Spector vividly caught the imagination of his audience, and with the Ronettes he also captured a

fantasy image of a group, with seductive sex kittens who dared to challenge the conventions of society while simultaneously becoming the
quintessential fantasy girl group of adolescent males of the sixties (Ulti-
mateGuitar.com). The look of the Ronettes, and particularly Veronica,
who is often considered the first archetypal "rock 'n' roll chick," were so
impressive and alluring that modern musical icons such as Amy Winehouse owe a huge debt to their style and image; the most successful
female pop music artist of all time, Madonna, expressed a desire for her
music to "sound like how Ronnie Spector looked" (Harrington).

For many, the Ronettes' song "Be My Baby" best encapsulates and
expresses teenage emotional fantasy, as well as Spector's own personal
connections with teenage emotions at the beginning of the 1960s. The
song is also an excellent example of Spector's knowledge of his audience
and what they would respond favorably to. Although lyrically the song
reverts to the male/female roles of the pre-1960s social order, giving the
man his traditional "godlike" status ("You know I will adore you 'till
eternity"), lyrical depth was compromised in favor of Spector's revolutionary approach to pop music production, primarily because any conflict within the song, either lyrically or musically, would work against
the overall grandiosity of the sound.

Some, such as Albert Goldman, have criticized Spector for creating
"baby food" for an overly emotional audience (*Phil Spector: He's a
Rebel*), as well as seeing Ronnie Spector and her "overly emotional and
whiny" vocal as a result of emotional immaturity. Yet it is a testament to
Spector that he recognized the strength of Ronnie's vocal style and
tonal quality, something that was not necessarily musically brilliant but
had an emotional quality that captured directly teenagers' feelings of
the time, just as Elvis and John Lennon, or in cinematic terms James
Dean, had done. Veronica's voice allows the teenage listeners to identify strongly with their youthful flights of fancy, and even if fans "could
not do it in real life (ask a boy out), the song ("Be My Baby") at least
offered a fantasy where they could approach a boy with confidence and
as an equal" (Keenan, 51). While the lyrics to "Be My Baby" expressed
notions of teen romance, Ronnie's vocal delivery, as well as some of the
song's lyrics (essentially the line "Be My Baby," which passionately and
openly express her innermost desires), was in a sense an unlocking of
emotions, particularly of young teenage girls, that were up until this
point expected to remain hidden.

Ronnie Spector praised Spector's gift in knowing the exact right vocal for his songs when she wrote in her autobiography, "I have to give Phil credit. He loved the way I sang, and he knew exactly what to do with my voice. He knew my range. He knew my pitch. He even knew which words sounded best coming out of my mouth. He knew that 'Be My Baby' was a perfect song for me, so he constructed the whole record around my voice from the ground up" (Spector, 52). From this perspective "Be My Baby" "allowed fans to try on more assertive subject positions," while at the same time "also lets them imagine their assumed future roles" (Keenan, 53).

Ronnie's vocal ideally expressed an anticipation for her future in songs such as "I Wonder." And her vocal delivery in songs such as "So Young" (a cover of the Students' 1958 song that describes a young person's confrontation with parental authority and the lack of independence regarding his own feelings and personal choices, particularly in terms of love and marriage), combined with Spector's production, make the teenager's situation all the more real and convincing. "So Young" was particularly influential on Brian Wilson, inspiring him to cover the song with the Beach Boys, while borrowing the song's lyrical theme for many of his own compositions, most famously "Wouldn't It Be Nice."

THE NEW YOUTH

Overall, these songs became anthems of teenage emotions and fantasy, and with Spector's formidable Wall of Sound reaching the zenith of its expression, it seemed as if teenagers and pop music were becoming a real force to be reckoned with and an independent voice, as well as a very lucrative market, that could no longer be ignored. Such factors finally gave way to the explosion of the youth movement and signified the sheer impact of rock 'n' roll and pop music, which was now, as Jerry Leiber remarked, a multi-billion-dollar industry—of which Phil Spector was a master PR manipulator (*Phil Spector: He's a Rebel*). This industry gave way to the Beatles, the Rolling Stones, Bob Dylan, the Beach Boys, and a whole host of new groups that expressed the political, social, and emotional aspirations and inclinations of the new youth movement that transformed modern culture completely.

In many ways, Spector's productions were essentially idealistic, conforming to the notions of what young teenagers were expected to think
and not necessarily what they did think. Spector created a very particular fantasy world for teenagers, which in many ways created a barrier
between youth and reality; however, by doing so Spector's "pocket symphonies for the kids" separates the older influences of pre-1960s culture, which were dominated by a specifically "adult" perspective, with
that of the new 1960s youth culture, which had been sparked off in
1956 with the success of the Teenagers' "Why Do Fools Fall in Love"
(*Life Could Be a Dream*).

Nearly all of Spector's records touched on the idealism of youth,
where even the titles suggest the notion of ideal romanticism: "Be My
Baby," "Baby, I Love You," "Do I Love You," "Chapel of Love," and
"Walking in the Rain." But his music also encouraged a new spirit of
teenage liberation and female emancipation.

This new social group's emotional confusion and conflict with traditional values became more significantly felt than at any other time previously in history and would become the subject of numerous songs
from Brian Wilson's "Wouldn't It Be Nice" to the Beatle's "She's Leaving Home" and of course the quintessential youth anthem, the Who's
"My Generation." The latter song was to be strongly echoed in the
following decades in many of David Bowie's songs, in the "punk" explosion of the mid-1970s, and succinctly expressed in the "No Future"
anthem of the Sex Pistols' "Anarchy in the UK," while groups such as
the Beastie Boys and Nirvana would continue to express teenage expectations and frustrations with songs like "Fight for Your Right (to Party)"
and "Smells Like Teen Spirit" (MacLeod, 37–38).

5

HE'S A REBEL

Feminism and Civil Rights

FEMINISM

By the time Phil Spector had established his own label and had found the right act with which to create his pop masterpieces, the pop world had become dominated by girl groups, such as the Chantels and the Shirelles, as well as his own girl groups and girl-fronted acts, such as the Paris Sisters and the Teddy Bears. Spector had initially been opposed to women playing in his groups (Thompson, 24), and considering his difficult relationship with both his mother and his sister, it is ironic that he became one of the key figures behind the girl group sound of the early 1960s. While there were others who helped create this remarkable era in pop history, such as Florence Greenberg with the Shirelles and Berry Gordy with the Supremes and the Vandellas, Spector's tremendous success with a number of girl groups and female singers, such as the Crystals, the Ronettes, and Darlene Love, set a template for future girl groups and female pop performers to follow.

Why exactly Spector, particularly during his most commercially successful period in the early sixties, chose to work nearly exclusively with female singers is difficult to determine exactly, but it's most likely that he felt younger women generally had more expressive voices and were able to capture better the moods and feelings of sixties teenagers. The success of the girl group acts of the time most certainly encouraged his decision; incidentally, he had chosen to work with the Crystals as his first Philles act instead of either of the two male doo-wop groups, the Ducanes and the Creations, which he also had had his eye on (M. Brown, 87; Ribowsky, 101; Thompson, 72). Some others, however, held a different view and thought that Spector worked with these young girls because they were much less threatening than male groups. Though there may be some truth in that, considering his forceful handling of Lester Sill, Jerry Leiber, and Mike Stoller, not to mention Bobby Sheen, the Righteous Brothers, and later John Lennon and the Ramones, as well as the myriad of other male singers he had worked with both prior to and after the girl group era. This point of view, however, often brought up as evidence of Spector's manipulative and misogynistic nature (Betrock, 29), is not altogether convincing.

THE "ADORABLE ANGST OF WHITE SUBURBAN GIRLHOOD"

The lyrics of many of Spector's girl group songs can be criticized for disempowering and pacifying young women (dealt with more specifically in chapter 6), as is also the case with many other girl group songs from the early sixties; many lyrics emphasize the "housewifization" and passive love interest of women, whose primary function is "to restore the worker's manhood in the evening and make him fit to return to his drudgery the following day" (Warwick, *Girl Groups*, 130). Also, it was universally considered at the time that "the entire pop industry was controlled by men, for the profit of men, at the expense of young women" (Doggett, *There's a Riot*, 69). Yet it is important to recognize, as does writer Elizabeth K. Keenan, that

> the girl groups were the first—and only—genre of music at the time to focus on the desires and perspectives of teen girls. . . . As a result, the songs showcased girls' experiences in a new way that marked them as separate from both the male rock 'n' roll stars that preceded them and the female pop music stars of the time whose audiences were older. The music, while much more constructed as pop than as the rock 'n' roll of the time, carves out a path for women of later generations, pop and rock and everything in between. (Keenan, 40)

Even more specifically, the music that Spector created with the Paris Sisters and the Teddy Bears' Annette Kleinbard, coming into the new decade of the 1960s and just before his groundbreaking success with his Wall of Sound and girl groups, was significant in bridging the gap between the older sounds of the female singers of the 1950s and the more pop-orientated "girl group" sound that endorsed a new teen perspective. Journalist and music critic Mark Deming puts it well when he states that Spector's work with the Paris Sisters "exists in a middle ground between the pop vocal styles of the 1950s and the girl group sounds Spector would champion a few years later, but it certainly captures the virtues of both genres and chronicles a short-lived but inspired collaboration that worked despite its contradictions" (Deming).

With the success of Spector's white female teen singers and their expression of "adorable angst of white suburban girlhood," the conditions were established for other white-female-angst-ridden teen singers, such as Lesley Gore and Mary Weiss with the Shangri-Las, to make their mark. Gore's songs, while initially covering the same ground of teen melodrama (e.g., from 1963, "It's My Party," "Judy's Turn to Cry," and "Just Let Me Cry") as well as numerous ones dedicated to boys (from 1964, "Boys," "Danny," and "Wonder Boy"), after three successful singles dedicated to white girls' teen angst, she turned tracks and stood her ground with the protofeminist anthem "You Don't Own Me" (December 1963–January 1964). She was seventeen on its release, and it marked a significant about-turn for young girls trammeled by the social conventions of the time.

GIRL GROUPS: THE CRYSTALS AND THE RONETTES

Though feminism was a little-known, or cared about, concept in Britain in the early sixties (Doggett, *There's a Riot*, 68), there was a general move, inspired by the civil rights movement, toward it in America. With Betty Friedan's *Feminine Mystique* (February 1963), as well as her National Organization for Women (NOW), for example, the direction this movement was taking was mainly from a "white middle-class adult perspective" and not from that of the teenage girl (Keenan, 41). The image of girl groups in the public eye, however, suggested to young teen girls that they themselves could also be liberated and independent, mostly from social and parental constraints.

The Crystals, who had been struck by the girl group bug at the beginning of the 1960s, certainly had a finger on the pulse of the times and were particularly savvy to the songs they wanted to sing, as well as how they presented themselves in image and name (Betrock, 29). The success the Crystals had from November 1961 to 1963 provided Spector with his most successful material to date, virtually making him the most exalted producer within the pop music industry of the time. The sheer presence of the Crystals, both their name and image, in the public eye meant that the girl group sound and genre continued to grow and prosper after the popularity of earlier girl groups, such as the Chantels and the Shirelles, began to wane. Essentially, this meant that young girl groups' themes of teenage girls' hopes and desires were not something fleeting but something that had a distinct relevance, particularly as young teen girls (and boys) continued to identify with the songs, and the groups, by buying the music.

The Crystals' triumvirate of "He's a Rebel," "Da Doo Ron Ron," and "Then He Kissed Me" also indicated the direction in which pop music, from a production point of view, could develop, both transcending the simplicity of their rock 'n' roll predecessors and replacing the adult-orientated popular music of previous female harmony groups such as the McGuire Sisters. Keenan observed that up until the beginning of 1960s (though actually from around 1957/1958) "pop music had mostly been associated with white female artists, such as the Chordettes and the McGuire Sisters, who presented a 'young housewife' image and sang sanitized versions of rock 'n' roll songs, while African American female singers found success only on the R&B charts" (Keenan, 42). So not only did these young girl groups have something relevant to say to their intended audience, but also the manner in which they did it, because of the musical brilliance of Spector's productions, meant that what they did have to say, they said with style. An example of one of these girl groups is the Crystals, which was one of the first African American groups to be accepted by white mainstream audiences and one of the first crossover successes even before the rise of the Supremes.

The Crystals made teen girls even more hip and significant than the Shirelles had done a year earlier with "Will You Still Love Me Tomorrow." The fact that their songs were topping the charts meant that the music industry, as a commercial vehicle, couldn't ignore them either. They became, like all successful artists, even more in demand by radio stations, TV producers, concert owners, and promoters, which obviously meant that the winning girl group formula of the Crystals made the girl group a viable commodity in general, encouraging more and more girls to form groups and express themselves in a similar manner.

With the exception of "Uptown," "He Hit Me," and "He's a Rebel," the Crystals had predominantly preoccupied themselves with themes of a more conventional nature of the passive, love-struck girl in modern American society, particularly with their hits "Then He Kissed Me" and "Da Doo Ron Ron." Meanwhile their image and attitude, though a reaction to the sanitized, adult, white, female-oriented music of the presixties, still tended to reflect the more conventional attitudes of the time. Spector's second girl group, the Ronettes, however, more radically challenged these female stereotypes.

Spector recognized the Ronettes as having mass appeal with their sound and image, as well as the bolshie attitude that had been instilled in them by their mother who realized that a more aggressive, go-for-it attitude was necessary to extricate them from the underprivileged social position they held. Ronnie Spector explains in the documentary *Girl Groups: The Story of a Sound* how their mother educated them on how to look older and get into nightclubs when they were underage, all for the advancement of their careers, and they naturally promoted this in their delivery and presentation of themselves and their music. In tandem with the changing attitudes that had come about in post–World War II, the girls became the ultimate example of female empowerment. They impressed on the teenage girls of the time that they could be sexy, beautiful, and feminine while being simultaneously strong, assertive, and successful (both financially and artistically).

Women's liberation and sexual liberation "took some time to coincide" (Doggett, *There's a Riot*, 69). These two aspects of feminist concerns were symbolized by Friedan's *Feminine Mystique* and the more sexually explicit girl group songs of the same period, particularly "Will You Still Love Me Tomorrow," "He Hit Me (and It Felt Like a Kiss)," "Heat Wave," and "Chains." This was coupled with a changing consciousness and the consideration that, as Peter Doggett puts it, "within a morally and mentally constrained capitalist society, sexual liberation represented a goal that was as urgent as any other form of political relief." So feminist concerns inevitably came to the forefront of both British and American society between 1966 and 1967.

The impact made on the culture by the presence of the Crystals and the Ronettes, as well as other Spector groups, such as the Blossoms and Darlene Love, particularly in the early days of television, cannot be overstated. The successful sixties television producer Jack Good, for example, even asserted that the presence of the Blossoms on the popular sixties TV show *Shindig!* was revolutionary in terms of American race politics (Warwick, "And the Colored Girls Sing," 72). The fact that these female singers were presented up front in view of the audience while the backing band, usually male, were either in the background or invisible gave young girls a greater sense of presence in popular culture. In the United States, as well as in Britain, the presenters of TV shows tended to be male (e.g., Dick Clark in *American Bandstand*, Jimmy O'Neill in *Shindig!*, and Sam Riddle in *Hollywood a Go-Go*), and females were seen as simply eye candy. On radio these girl singers could interchange between different personality types, manipulating their vocal abilities to emulate different singing styles and often representing different cultural, racial, and generational identities—black, white, teen, adult, and so forth (*Twenty Feet from Stardom*). On TV, though, they lost their chameleon nature; these girl singers were able to attract the attention away from their male presenters, at least for the two minutes they were on-screen, propelling young females into a role of significant cultural dominance they had never really experienced before.

Spector's success with his girl groups opened the door for an acceptance of other teenage girl performers and girl groups, such as the Cookies and the Chiffons (R. Williams, *Phil Spector: Out of His Head*, 124–25). As well, the door was opened for labels (e.g., Red Bird), which focused primarily on girl group acts, such as the Shangri-Las and the Dixie Cups (who incidentally had been produced by Spector's onetime cowriter Jeff Barry), and even paved the way for megastars like the Supremes, who had started out emulating the look and sound of Spector's girl groups. This meant that the girl group formula of success provided an opportunity for even more teen girls of different social backgrounds to have success in the pop music market, making the female voice (and image) more prominent on radio and TV. This created a stronger sense of power and dominance within the minds of young girls, who within a few years would themselves be leaders of feminist movements and social reforms. In other words the music of the girl groups was an "agency" of "self-determination through romance" (Keenan, 49) or as Susan Douglas put it, the girl groups had "planted the tiniest seed of a social movement" (S. Douglas, *Where the Girls Are*, 98).

BE MY BABY

The massive success of "Be My Baby" was a testament to the potential power acquired by the girls of the 1960s, who had so many more opportunities than their mothers or grandmothers had ever known. No longer did it seem that young girls had to act as passive and submissive "second-class" citizens within the confines of a patriarchal society conditioned to accept the role of the good girl, who was sweet and eager to please. In contrast to this, the Ronettes, and some of the girl groups that followed, behaved in a totally different manner—they were the "bad girls," who knew what they wanted and how to get it.

Though relationships were still the subject of "Be My Baby," it was not in the form of the woman as the submissive partner waiting for the boy to make his move. No, now women could be open about their desires and openly pursue their dreams, even if their dreams were still geared toward a marriage proposal, which ultimately "Be My Baby" yearns for. The sexual undertone to the lyric and the production, however, suggests that the relationship does not need to be endorsed through marriage and that the young girl's yearning is simply the satisfying of emotional, as well as sexual, desire, unconnected with anything outside the individual's own wants.

Girls of the early 1960s did not pursue boys in the same manner that the girl in "Be My Baby" does; therefore, the song introduces, for the first time, an alternative to the conventional social behavior to which teenage girls of the presixties had to comply. Stephanie Coontz, in her book *Marriage, a History: How Love Conquered Marriage*, makes the point that "asking the boy to be her 'baby' runs counter to the gendered expectations of the time, in which women were more likely to be called 'baby' in a relationship (or song)" (quoted in Keenan, 51). Such an attitude expressed by the Ronettes was not confined to just this one song but is a significant impulse running through the themes of many of their other songs. Songs such as "Baby, I Love You" and "You Baby" also "invert gender expectations," while "Walking in the Rain" and its opening line "I want you" expresses the same yearning desire as does "Be My Baby."

By inverting the expectations and behavior of young girls, songs such as these invite the young female listener to throw off the restricted conventions of the time, inverting the traditional roles of pursued and pursuer, and by "singing along, they could imagine themselves as full agents in a relationship, capable of asking a boy out" (Keenan, 51). In this capacity "Be My Baby" and other Ronettes' songs offered young girls the feeling of an "unprecedented surge of freedom" (S. Douglas, *Where the Girls Are*, 87). While the Shirelles had opened the door for more sexually and independently aware young women, the Ronettes, encouraged by Spector's understanding of the power of the group's commercial appeal, established them as a real force and presence and ultimately led to "bad girl" groups, such as the Shangri-Las, as well as more sophisticated girl groups, such as the Vandellas and the Supremes, who would do away with the more naïve aspects of the earlier girl group culture (a reason Jacqueline Warwick gives for not including these two groups in her book *Girl Groups, Girl Culture*; Warwick, *Girl Groups*, 13, 54).

While many songs of the sixties reinforced the gender restrictions on girls of the time, songs such as "Be My Baby," as well as other so-called bad girl songs such as "He's a Rebel," "Leader of the Pack," and "Give Him a Great Big Kiss" (where the singer flirtatiously crosses the bounds of convention by instigating a playful sexual advance in public), "let girls put themselves in the assertive position of the singer" (Keenan, 53). This role reversal saw the boy as a "passive object of the female gaze and her talk," usually the role reserved for the female, and by doing so the young girl "stuck her tongue out at parental and middle-class authority" (S. Douglas, *Where the Girls Are*, 92).

Though lyrically the girl will wait "eternally" for her man, suggesting still the notion of the young girl passively waiting, the girl still expresses her desires freely and openly, making them clearly known. "Be My Baby" presented listeners with a dramatically different kind of girl from the one who agonized over her boyfriend's advances in "Will You Still

Love Me Tomorrow." "Far from worrying about the dangers of sex," wrote Warwick, "the girl in 'Be My Baby' is particularly panting for it, and the parents, who put the brakes on their daughter's reckless romance with 'the Leader of the Pack,' are nowhere to be found" (Warwick, *Girl Groups*, 125). In other words, pushing the boy to make his move is somewhat keeping within the conventions of the time but by actively moving the boy toward making a decision.

Spector's approach to the song, the opening drumbeat and the general arrangement, color the desire in undertones of sexual fervor and delight while waiting not necessarily for the marriage proposal but for an intimate and passionate encounter and union. "Soaring above the music on 'Be My Baby,'" observed Keenan, is "Ronnie's voice, the centerpiece of the song. The singer takes control of the pursuit right away. Even though Ronnie is asking the question 'Be My Baby' [which is] reiterated by the backing singers, her confident, assertive alto indicates that she already knows the answer is 'yes,' making her the inversion of Shirley Owens' hesitant protagonist of 'Tomorrow'" (Keenan, 51).

In this song, relationships for women were expressed no longer as simply the duty of matrimony and childbearing but rather for personal desire and satisfaction, and for this reason Gillian Gaar considers "Be My Baby" as being a "bold statement of desire, anguish and independence" (Gaar, 62). With their expression of yearning desire and their nonconformist, "bad girl" image, which contrasted with the romantic nature of the music, the Ronettes set a precedent in pop, combining "fashion rebellion with in-your-face sexual insurrection" (S. Dóuglas, *Where the Girls Are*, 92). In many ways, they were the beginning of the girl power movement, which would influence the likes of Debbie Harry a decade later, as well as Madonna, the Spice Girls, and Amy Winehouse in the 1980s, 1990s, and 2000s, respectively.

GIRL GROUPS TO GIRL BANDS

The girl bands that first began to form in the late sixties and early seventies mixed the girl group sound and attitude of Spector and Motown with the R&B sounds of the male groups (the Beatles' appearance on *The Ed Sullivan Show* was as much an impression on girls forming bands as it was on the boys). The Luv'd Ones' lead singer and lead guitarist Char Vinnedge, for example, wrote original material alongside covers of girl group songs featured on their album *Truth Gotta Stand*. Los Angeles girl band the Chymes' "He's Not There Anymore," written by the Turtles' lead singer Howard Kaylan, who first discovered them, uses references to the drum pattern on the Ronettes' "Be My Baby." Meanwhile, Californian girl band the Girls covered the Barry Mann/ Cynthia Weil biker song "Chico's Girl," produced by Spector's friend and collaborator the saxophonist Steve Douglas; the song combined aspects of the Ronettes and the Shangri-Las with a "garage" attitude.

These girl group/boy band hybrids, though mostly independent, underground entities, ultimately encouraged the formation of more prominent girl bands such as the Pleasure Seekers, who subverted the more passive role of the girl groups by playing and writing their own music, while expanding the lyrical subject matters for girls to write and sing about. In their song "What a Way to Die," for example, the group sings about untraditional feminine themes, such as drinking beer and enjoying the sight of the male body. Girl bands such as the Runaways, the Go-Go's, and later the Bangles would make a bigger impression and encouraged girls to form their own bands. These all-girl bands wrote their own material and expressed themselves in their own way, challenging their own (and society's) feelings and ideas regarding gender and race, and offered an alternative view as to what it means to be a woman in a male, capitalist system. They were "young girls resisting the world as we know it," as Cynthia Sikes's character, Alicia Meeker, says in the film *Ladies and Gentlemen, the Fabulous Stains* (1982), about three disaffected young girls who form a punk rock band.

Spector's girl groups and solo female performers definitely did not play instruments, at least in view of the public; they were in many ways kept back by individuals such as Spector from becoming "genuine" musicians who could play their own instruments. Yet the very sight of these young girls gave enough impetus to others to challenge the musical expectations of young girls at the time. In fairness to Spector, although he has been criticized for holding many of his artists back, he was also prepared to take risks both musically and commercially by ignoring conventions of public perception, something he clearly did with the Ronettes and other female artists, and was less concerned about offending the sensibilities of the public (Jayanti). "My graduating theme," Spector once told an interviewer, "was 'Daring To Be Different.' The moment I dared to, they called me different. I always thought I knew what the kids wanted to hear. They were frustrated, uptight. I would say [they were] no different from me when I was in school. I had a rebellious attitude. I was for the underdog. I was concerned that they were as misunderstood as I was" (Kubernik).

As such, the visibility of young female performers, particularly alongside young male performers, allowed a new attitude and perception of young girls performing and creating music for themselves; this new attitude has led to a greater visibility of young women within the music industry, and the media in general, today. (Incidentally, Spector's association and promotion of the controversial comedian Lenny Bruce was born largely out of the fact that Spector saw in him a kindred spirit that too "dared to be different" and who also very much appealed to the underdog instinct in him. While Spector's relationship with Bruce is a significant part of his life and very interesting in itself, there is not the space to address it here, and it doesn't directly shine light on Spector's own cultural significance, of which this book aims to do.)

Though it has taken almost fifty years, female musicians are as ubiquitous today as girl groups and female singers were in the early 1960s. Female rock drummers, such as Alicia Warrington and Cindy Blackman, along with other female musicians such as Bibi McGill, the guitarist in Beyoncé's ten-piece all-female band the Suga Mamas; guitarist Wendy Melvoin and keyboard player Lisa Coleman (both of whom played in Prince's band the Revolution); and bass player Gail Ann Dorsey (who has worked with David Bowie and Gwen Stefani); have all firmly established the female musician in their own right. This role was previously seen as unacceptable by the male-dominated, mainstream music industry.

The high-level visibility of these women has become an indication of the changing attitudes of modern society, a sentiment also expressed by Bibi McGill. "I feel like we're making history," she exclaimed. "It's opened up a bigger door to allow the floodgates of women to come through and shine in the music industry" (Rinny). Though Spector's girl groups were not the only ones to encourage a new attitude toward female musicians, they definitely made a significant contribution in that area.

CIVIL RIGHTS

Although it was the white female vocals of Annette Kleinbard that expressed the sentiments of Spector's deep feelings for his father on this first major record, "To Know Him Is to Love Him," signaling the start of his career, the song owed a debt to the Chantels' song "Maybe" (M. Brown, 38), which incorporated doo-wop elements and black gospel sensibilities, as well as its yearning black female vocal. Spector was more drawn to what he felt was the emotional rawness and honesty of black voices, because, as he once explained, there was the sense "of true suffering, natural suffering . . . and I identify with people who suffer" (M. Brown, 89). According to Ronnie Spector, Phil so strongly identified with black people and their culture that on hearing of the assassination of Martin Luther King Jr., he locked himself in his office for three days, a week before their wedding day, and listened repeatedly to the recordings of King's "I Have a Dream" speech (Spector, 134).

Black singers, since the advent of rock 'n' roll, had highlighted the pain of the black communities, while white rock 'n' roll stars such as Elvis and Bill Haley brought mainstream attention to black performers, like Chuck Berry and Little Richard, who were then endorsed by the next generation of pop performers, such as the Beach Boys, the Beatles, and the Rolling Stones. These artists then in turn brought awareness to the blues artists from which rock 'n' roll had mostly originated (Philo, ix). Black activists in the 1960s, such as the poet LeRoi Jones, who saw the pop music of the time as being a symbol of the white man's exploitation of black artists (Doggett, *There's a Riot*, 34–36), condemned white groups for stealing from black culture; but others held the opposite opinion, feeling that they made white society aware of the black people's pain, "injecting Negritude into the whites" (Doggett, *There's a Riot*, 77). Certainly it is true that many whites within the record industry exploited black artists and their music for their own commercial aims; many though, such as Elvis, Mick Jagger and Keith Richards, and John Lennon and Paul McCartney, truly identified with the emotional content of the music and used it as a means through which they could escape the stifling boredom of their own restrictive social conditions.

Spector and his sidekick Jack Nitzsche were equally as reverential toward black music as much as the likes of Richards or Lennon. From its beginning Spector was obsessed with rock 'n' roll and found a strong

connection with the black performers of this music, even if the majority
of his musical collaborators would be white (except for many of the
singers he worked with and whom he apparently treated quite poorly).
Spector was respectful of the origins of the pop sound that blended
black gospel and blues with rock 'n' roll as well as other ethnically
inspired sounds such as Latin Baião rhythms. Mick Brown points out
that

> more than most people, Spector understood that the history of
> American music was largely the story of white imitating or stealing
> from black. Jazz and rhythm and blues were his own favorite music
> forms, and in his year in New York Spector had worked with enough
> black performers to convince him that the emotional rawness and
> honesty of black voices was his favorite instrument. (M. Brown, 89)

Once again Spector's use of black performers with a flavor of basic
black music from doo-wop, gospel, and R&B to other ethnic sensibilities brought a greater awareness of the music into mainstream culture
in both Britain and America. Spector often wrapped these styles and
cultures, similar to how Elvis had packaged his representation of black
music, into something much more digestible for a modern white,
though often youth-orientated, audience. It was essentially a presentation of black music that would eventually establish itself as a basic
currency of modern popular culture, one in which Elvis, the white "king
of rock 'n' roll," would be superseded a few decades later by Michael
Jackson, the black "king of pop."

The young, black female singers had strongly connected with the
new socioeconomic group of postwar teenagers of which Spector's female singers, such as "La La" Brooks, Ronnie Spector, Darlene Love,
and Tina Turner, brought about a greater acceptability of young, black
girl performers. The black female singers that Spector had fronting his
groups, as well as the sexual energy the songs expressed, were more
easily able to find their way into pop culture through the similitude of
white sensibilities and expectations. Black female singers were able to
gradually move into and find acceptance in mainstream white culture.
As the pursuit for civil rights was steadily under way with the emer-
gence of these female artists, young black girls (and boys) found strong
role models in these artists, while young white people were able to

identify with the cause of black people as well as come to accept them as equal.

It was also through these black artists that young white girls were able to throw off their middle-class repression; Susan Douglas wrote that African American culture mocks white culture for being "pathologically repressed" and suggests that one consequence of this is black women have been viewed as

> more sexually active and responsive than their white bread sisters. . . . Because of these stereotypes it was easier, more acceptable, to the music industry and no doubt to white culture at large that black girls, instead of white ones, be the first teens to give voice to girls' changing attitudes towards sex. . . . Under their crinoline skirts and satin cocktail dresses, they were also smuggling into middle-class America a taste of sexual liberation. (S. Douglas, *Where the Girls Are*, 95)

Black girl groups were able to make the crossover more successfully than black males because black women were "less threatening and, in some ways, more comforting to the white public than a black man would be, especially with the intense sexuality and sensuality that the 'new' popular music of rhythm & blues and rock 'n' roll suggested" (Keenan, 45; see also Wald).

As Keenan points out, "African American girl groups had to 'cross over' to white pop audiences through musical style cues (such as close vocal harmonies, string sections, and elaborate production) that signaled middle-class femininity and blurred assumptions about radicalized 'authenticity'" (Keenan, 42). These colored groups Spector produced and transformed into music stars, and their music spoke directly to the emotions and concerns of the youth of the day. These singers were the embodiment, or so it appeared to them, of the teenager's hopes, desires, and aspirations that dominated the U.S., and to some extent the British, charts for most of the early 1960s, particularly from January 1962 with the Crystals' "There's No Other" to December 1964 with the Ronettes' "Walking in the Rain." Spector gave black singers the opportunity to be stars, while his sound and championing of them and their musical heritage paved the way for a whole generation of black artists, who still dominate the popular music industry today.

Spector had these performers holding the top positions on the charts, particularly after the Chantels and the Shirelles had fallen out of favor with their audiences; and since few of them could compete with the overwhelming productions of Spector's songs, his groups maintained the image of black and ethnic groups throughout the early sixties when they became regular features on prime-time TV shows like *American Bandstand*, as well as emerging teen shows such as *Hootenanny* (1963–1964), *Shindig!* (1964–1966), *Hullabaloo* (1964–1971), *Upbeat* (1965–1966), *Where the Action Is* (1965–1967), and *Hollywood a Go-Go* (1965–1966).

When the Blossoms appeared as the house-backing ensemble on the ABC television variety show *Shindig!* (1964–1966), not only did this give them national exposure during the early days of television, but also young black females from all over America were strongly represented. When ABC, however, wanted to hire British wizard producer Jack Good, who had had great success in Britain with the variety show *Oh Boy!* (1958/1959), he insisted on having the Blossoms in spite of the network's initial reluctance to feature nonwhite singers so prominently in a recurring position in prime time. One of the Blossoms' original members, Fanita James, asserts that Good even told ABC executives that he would not do the show without the Blossoms (Warwick, "And the Colored Girls Sing," 69).

Had the Blossoms come to be a representation for the archetypal female backup singers, and did their continued appearance on the show establish such a phenomenon? Warwick claims in her essay "'And the Colored Girls Sing': Backup Singers and the Case of the Blossoms" that "in viewed performances in most popular genres, backing vocalists tend to resemble the Blossoms" (72). But it is a debatable point since the Blossoms didn't appear regularly on TV until *Shindig!* began in September 1964, by which time many other black girl groups were having a huge amount of public exposure, such as the Chantels, the Shirelles, the Crystals, the Ronettes, and the Marvelettes, who had claimed the number one spot with "Please Mr. Postman" late in 1961. What is more certain, however, is that the Blossoms, even though they were established before they met Spector, did owe a significant amount of their actual success to him and that the use of black female backing singers, particularly with Spector's Wall of Sound (and with Motown), made rock and pop artists, both male and female, want to use black female backing singers to capture a more authentic soul sound. The Rolling Stones would famously use Merry Clayton on "Gimme Shelter," as too did Steve Marriott, who used the Ikettes for his soul group Humble Pie, while artists such as David Bowie, Duran Duran, Sting, and Paul Weller would employ female black singers when they wanted to sound more soulful. In order to emanate greater sexual chemistry, Mick Jagger would even borrow his dance moves from black female performers such as Tina Turner. Visually these female-backing vocalists, however, tended to more resemble the Supremes or the Ronettes than they did the Blossoms.

Regardless of which of these girl groups most shaped the black female backing group, young black girls now had a significant number of role models that they readily saw occupying a space in mainstream culture. These new media representatives instilled greater hope within the black communities, particularly among the younger generation, for success and profit in a "white" society, more than did the political figures that fought for civil rights on a political stage that was far removed from people's everyday lives. Spector and his black girl groups thus gave the young black females, and black males too, a greater sense of their own worth.

Motown, although having begun its enterprise almost simultaneously with Spector, looked to the success Spector was having with his black artists within the white mainstream music industry. Although Motown far outdid Spector in terms of the amount of hit singles they produced over time and the number of artists that had achieved success within the Motown company, it was Spector who made opportunities for black artists, such as those at Motown, a more plausible reality. While the mainstream success of Spector's black girl groups may have been seen as a challenge to Motown, they must also have been a source of encouragement to the company that would initially struggle to get his black artists heard on mainstream radio. "Not as enduring or as productive as Motown artists, they [the Ronettes] still had twenty-five Top 40 hits in the early 1960s, a huge presence on the charts at the time when Gordy was trying to figure out the Motown way. Spector was a somewhat forgotten but huge influence on Motown" (R. Williams, *Phil Spector*, 125–26). It is largely because of the success of Motown and Spector's black girl groups that Douglas rightly claims, "White girls . . . owe a cultural debt to these black girls for straddling these contradictions, and helping create a teen girl culture that said, 'Let loose, break free, and don't take no shit'" (S. Douglas, *Where the Girls Are*, 95).

Considering again Warwick's analysis of the Blossoms' *Shindig!* appearances, she accurately outlines the difficulty the group's mixed-race lineup with a white girl, Gracia Nitzsche, wife of Spector's arranger Jack Nitzsche, caused. "Although ABC," she writes "complied with Jack Good's demand to hire the Blossoms, the idea of featuring a mixed-race trio of girls was impossible, unconscionable to audiences in the Southern states . . . so Jean King was used instead of Nitzsche" (Warwick, "And the Colored Girls Sing," 70).

While this was seen as a problem by a big network such as ABC, Spector ignored such prejudice and dismissed any effect a mixed-race group like the Ronettes (who were part African American, Irish American, Cherokee, and Puerto Rican) may have had on the success of his records. As well as encouraging the teen sensibilities of the time, the associated relationship between Spector and Veronica Bennett with "Be My Baby" (and other Ronettes songs), as well as the group's mixed-race heritage and the mixed-race promotional video for the song, embodied "the interracial allure of the era's pop music" (Emerson, 151). And it encouraged mixed-race groups and duos throughout the period, including Sonny and Cher, and Nicky Scott and Diane Ferraz; these groups finally found total acceptance by the end of the century with numerous mixed-race duets by Prince and Sheena Easton, Eric Clapton and Tracy Chapman, George Michael and Aretha Franklin, and Brian Adams and Tina Turner. Today's girl groups are more often than not mixed-race groups, for instance, the Spice Girls, All Saints, and the Pussycat Dolls.

UPTOWN

Spector's songs not only touched an audience on a purely emotional level, allowing them to purge and express their emotional sides, but also drew attention to the social plight and background of all teenagers. Spector gave expression to racial, as well as socioeconomic, concerns, which blacks and other ethnic groups struggled against.

The lyrics of "Uptown" were instrumental in expressing societal concerns alien to much of pop music of the 1940s and 1950s but that filtered through the conscience of the 1960s, a particular time that began to question all these values in such a manner not possible before. For such a reason Alan Betrock thought that the song's lyrics were "the strongest reflection to date of struggling urban youths' desire to climb up the social ladder. It hit home for blacks in ghettos, as well as those actively fighting for their rights down South. Its underlying meaning also capsulated the frustrations of the young and presaged the violence that exploded across America during the street riots of the summer of 1967" (Betrock, 32).

Although "Uptown" indicates Spanish Harlem through its flamenco guitar and castanets, and the lyrics reinforce an idea of a hardworking man of color who, despite facing discrimination every day, persists in struggling to "make it" in America, the song never directly discusses racial injustices but leaves its interpretation open (Keenan, 42). However, the song is unique in that it introduced into pop music the possibility of a social conscience, beginning a trend that became increasingly more common and that would dominate the style of popular song by the midsixties; this was a major reason songs such as the Beatles' "Eleanor Rigby" and Dylan's "Like a Rolling Stone" came to be (or at least influenced their commercial acceptance).

Spector's production highlighted the difference between starkly contrasting worlds, and though it created a romanticized vision of the underprivileged ethnic minorities, it encouraged the listener to contemplate the struggles of these groups, often making the general white, middle-class teen audience identify their own concerns of misunderstood adolescence with those of different ethnic communities, thus seeing themselves as an underprivileged class, as well as finding solidarity with similar downtrodden groups. All of this opened up an awareness of humanity's inhumanity to humankind—a sentiment expressed clearly in the ultimate teen movie *Rebel without a Cause* a few years earlier, while such feelings would ultimately have their fullest expression felt a few years later in the love generation of 1967.

The fact that pop music was able to express these sentiments, while at the same time sugarcoat the message with a sing-along melody, made it unthreatening to the establishment. Yet the emerging youth groups, who would embrace racial integration and look up to the black performers and artists of their time, were angered by the racial abuse they saw in their country.

As Susan Douglas saw the Shirelles as important to the advancement of feminism in the early 1960s, the tremendous success of the Crystals, the Ronettes, and Darlene Love brought young women and black artists further into the public perception, particularly into the young white consciousness, and hence did as much as Little Richard and Ray Charles to bring about a more integrated racial awareness. If it didn't contribute directly to the political concerns of the civil rights movement, it at least offered a cultural background, as well as a mesmerizing soundtrack, to its cause.

6

HE HIT ME

Control and Power

SPECTOR'S MOTHER AND SISTER

Despite all the affection that the young Phil Spector received from the women at home, encouraging both his self-belief and his musical potential, there was a darker side to their attention. They were jealous and controlling, often smothering him more than loving him. In one respect he was the hero, who could do no wrong and from whom the family name and position could aspire to greatness, while at the same time, the sense of responsibility placed on him as the symbolic head of the family was possibly too great a burden for the young Spector to contemplate.

As he got older Spector seems to have felt a great need to break free from his mother and sister, feeling they were always present, keeping a watchful and concerned eye on him. This created a tension between them and forced Phil to grow more distant from them emotionally, if not entirely freeing himself from their interference in his life. There was a stark contradiction though; as Spector tried to move away from his mother and sister, he seemed to become more dependent on their encouragement and support. In fact, his sister Shirley would become his manager, though often getting in his way at the same time, and he would often consult his mother on business, as well as on personal, matters. This love/hate relationship between Spector and his mother and sister would prove to have devastating effects on the other women that came into his life, both romantically and professionally, "establishing a pattern that would characterize his relationships with women for the rest of his life" (M. Brown, 28).

Spector's first girlfriend Donna Kass, who had experienced his mother and sister's jealousy when they accused her of hindering Spector's career because he was spending too much time with her, thought that Phil's own controlling behavior toward her, after the initial honeymoon period was over, was a mirror of Bertha's "suffocating possessiveness" (M. Brown, 28). On many occasions Phil would track Donna down, if she was not where he thought she was supposed to be, and then "spend the night berating her for deserting him" (Thompson, 20). His relationship with Lynn Castle, an aspiring songwriter, whom Phil meet before his big success, was strong, but "his jealousy and possessiveness was becoming intolerable." Castle couldn't take any more of Spector's possessiveness, and she stopped seeing him (M. Brown, 55).

Spector was also insecure about his appearance; he was short and chinless, had thinning hair, and was "an undisguisable high-school nerd" (Marcus, 242), often using charm as well as his musical ability to mask his insecurities. Beverly Ross, a onetime songwriting partner of his, felt he was plagued by "the unhappiness of his childhood and his insecurities over his size and appearance," and would discern that "beneath the veneer of cockiness and wise cracking humor," Spector was actually crippled with self-loathing. "You just had this feeling," said Ross, "that he wanted to get even with everybody for his father dying so young and for him not growing up as every girl's dream" (M. Brown, 62).

Later on, when Spector began to have success, he developed relationships with women more so out of what he could get from them and how they might advance his career, often wounding them when they no longer served a purpose. His abandonment of Annette Kleinbard was one example. Another example was Ross herself, who felt they had formed a strong bond together as writers but that Spector had betrayed her when he reneged on his promise to give Ray Peterson their cowritten song, "That's the Kind of Love I Wish I Had," as the flip side to "Corrina Corrina." Instead, Spector showed his loyalty to his family and gave Peterson a song cowritten by him and his sister (Ribowsky, 74–75). Spector also excluded Ross on the songwriting sessions for "Spanish Harlem" with Jerry Leiber and Mike Stoller, even though he had promised to involve her (Ribowsky, 77). Ross was convinced that Spector was a "user," who had exploited her friendship and then callously pushed her to one side. "It was almost as though he had planned it out. That he was going to eliminate this person and that person and go and get all the credit himself" (M. Brown, 66).

Ross had been so hurt and disturbed by Spector that when she was offered a contract to be a staff writer for Leiber and Stoller, a golden opportunity for any songwriter, she declined the offer, not wanting to be anywhere near Spector (M. Brown, 67). According to Michael Spencer, Beverly Ross "was a compassionate girl, very supportive of Phil. But he dominated her completely. He liked Beverly but he wasn't nice to her. There was always that contradiction in Phil" (M. Brown, 97–98).

His music was in many ways an extension of his ego, as was his relationship to his business colleagues and the women in his life—both romantically and professionally. Spector even as a teenager would be very controlling of his friends and their activities, and later, as Sonny Bono keenly observed, he was the same with his music. "The way he behaved with his friends was exactly the way he behaved with his music," Bono would announce (Thompson, 20). Spector was an egocentric whose need for women's attention was not motivated by sex, as stories by Spencer (M. Brown, 78–79), Artie Ripp (Ribowsky, 72–73), and others (Ribowsky, 82–83) testify, but more so to satisfy his ego. If Phil had the power to charm, as well as the talent to impress and the power to transform people's lives, as in the case of the Crystals and the Ronettes, it is easy to see how women, for example, Ronnie Spector, hungry for fame and success, would be drawn toward him (Ribowsky, 152), but his egomaniacal nature was poison for anyone who came too close, as Ronnie Spector and others, most possibly, Lana Clarkson, would sadly discover.

SPECTOR CONTROLS HIS SINGERS

While Spector felt a need to control his girlfriends, this also extended into his professional relationship with his singers. Though Spector treated his musicians with great respect, often showering them with gifts throughout the sessions, paying them properly, and having everything on contract, he did not have the same respect for his singers. Phil only used them for his own purposes. He wanted not stars but young kids he could control (Ribowsky, 139–41). Spector felt the singers were disposable and that their careers depended on him. He relished the power he had over them, and it was interesting that most of the singers were young girls with whom he could play power games. "We were never allowed any say in what we did at all," claimed Crystals singer Dee Dee Kenniebrew. "We were very young, of course, but we were teenagers making teenage music, and we would have liked, you know, some input. But no way! There was nothing we could do: Phil Spector was our record company, our producer, our everything" (Warwick, *Girl Groups*, 66).

Although Spector could be as manipulative of the male singers he worked with as much as the female ones (something the young Brian Wilson had well observed when he happily took up an invitation to a Spector session), Alan Betrock suggests that Spector preferred to work with young, inexperienced girls because "they offered little resistance on the creative end, and Phil could use their voices merely as one component in the complex and distinctive sound he wanted to create. They were disposable pawns in his gambit for creative freedom and chart domination, and if they would leave, there would be others ready and able to take their places" (Betrock, 29).

After "Then He Kissed Me," "he wanted to rule the roost," said Don Kishner. "He felt he was Numero Uno, which was all he cared about" (Biography Channel). He "could be very demanding in the studio," putting groups such as the Ronettes "through forty-two takes of their first record to get the sound he wanted—some called it crazy; others called it brilliant" (Biography Channel). For others, however, it just showed how "completely unhinged" and insecure he was; he used such occasions in the studio as if "in search of a weaker party to pounce on" (Examiner.com). "La La" Brooks complained that Spector's treatment of her was tantamount to "child abuse." He would sometimes have her in the studio twelve hours straight: "He would put me in the dark and sometimes I couldn't see the lyrics . . . he would say just get into the mood" (Biography Channel).

The Crystals, despite the tremendous success they had had on both a commercial and an artistic level, disbanded within a few years, mainly due to Spector's interference (Ribowsky, 144–45). He replaced singers unexpectedly (the Blossoms sang all the vocals on "He's a Rebel," while the original Crystals were on tour, and on "He's Sure the Boy I Love" [Betrock, 36, 120–21; Gaar, 42–43; *Walk on By*]) and recorded songs distasteful to the group, for instance, "He Hit Me" and "(Lets Dance) The Screw," a song that drew them into the petty squabbles that Spector would have with his business colleagues (Betrock, 32–36, 120–24; Gaar, 43). If others had a moral issue in replacing singers in this way, Phil certainly hadn't. In fact, for many, Phil had no moral dilemma because he considered everyone to be his puppet (Ribowsky, 120). It seems Spector used the Crystals for his own musical experimentations, easily disposing of them once he discovered the Ronettes, who would even replace the Crystals on a number of songs on their own greatest hits album. According to John Clemente, he had "inserted Ronnie's voice on two songs" for the Crystals LP (Clemente, 186), though other sources claim up to four songs were replaced.

Darlene Love, particularly, seemed to have had a difficult relationship with Spector (*Twenty Feet from Stardom*), and when he recorded "He's a Rebel," he "used" Darlene, paying her a once-off sum of $3,000 with no royalty (Thompson, 81). When the record was released it was released as the Crystals, possibly with the intention of cashing in on their success. Love had no profile at the time, singing only as a member of the backing group the Blossoms. She thought this would be her big break, but since she received no royalty she felt she did not really gain commercially from the project, and since she remained anonymous on the record it didn't help her public profile either. When Spector brought her back for another recording, the Barry Mann and Cynthia Weil track "He's Sure the Boy I Love," Love demanded a proper contract as an independent solo artist who would have her records released under her name, but Phil never honored the contract (Warwick, *Girl Groups*, 68–69). After "He's Sure the Boy I Love," Love's trust in Spector quickly diminished; he had reneged on his promise to have her as a solo artist and instead put the song out as the Crystals because he was certain the radio would play a successful group like the Crystals.

Love felt like a caged bird with Phil. He wanted control, and even though Burt Bacharach and Brian Wilson wanted to record her and the Blossoms, Phil would not allow it (Love, 116), keeping Love from the fame many, quite rightly, thought she deserved.

It is to a large degree Spector's treatment of the girls that he worked with and stories such as these told by Darlene Love, "La La" Brooks, and others that many see these young girls of the girl group genre as being deliberately exploited, abused, and then, most often, callously discarded by the producers and managers who took them on (Keenan, 37–38). Indeed, as Warwick points out,

> The story of Darlene Love suggests that when a member of a backup trio tries to assert herself as a soloist, her efforts are vigorously opposed. It is important in our society's thinking to maintain the unity of the backup singing group at all costs, and to avoid seeing these women as whole, self-sufficient, and individual. . . . The symbolic function of the backup trio generally coincides with reductive and controlling stereotypes of black women as selfless sources of emotional and practical sustenance for individuals whose identities are assumed to be more psychologically complex and important. (Warwick, "And the Color Girls Sing," 75).

Though Warwick is mostly referring to solo artists, who employ the services of backing singers to enhance their sound, it most certainly applies to Spector too as a producer, who felt his position as the master craftsman was far more important than the singers who sang the songs and would make the all-important connection with the record-buying public.

The idea that the female singers with girl groups were patronized this way, considered to be lacking in musical ability, separated from the other musicians, and used only as instruments was an attitude of the time. Spector it seems was particularly guilty of this behavior, treating his musicians with reverence and respect, while his singers, both male and female, he gave little consideration. If this was Spector's way of ensuring that they never outshone him, never became stars in themselves, it also helped perpetuate the myth that girls were not "real" musicians, which, considering individuals such as Carole King, Ellie Greenwich, and Carol Kaye (a bass player with the Wrecking Crew), as well as girl group singers such as Shirley Owens and Gladys Horton from the Marvelettes, who wrote their own material, this was definitely not the case.

However, since these girls were never to be seen playing instruments (possibly because it challenged notions of the ideal woman/girl) the resistance toward female musicians and girl bands grew very strong. Some, like Susan Bordo and Jacqueline Warwick, have seen this control over the singers, particularly female singers, extending into the choreography of the black girl groups as "a means of controlling appropriate female behavior on stage" and that their seen presence on TV shows meant "they had to conform to acceptable standards of prettiness and youthfulness in a culture that insisted on an ideal of female beauty based on whiteness" (Warwick, *Girl Groups*, 70).

For some reason, however, it was not just from a business point of view that Spector felt a need to exert control over his female singers, as if they were his personal property and he felt personally violated if they didn't behave the way he wanted them to. According to his friend Michael Spencer, he would treat his girls like "trophies" (M. Brown, 97–98). Spector would show off his wife to his friends when they came over, letting them take pictures of her and then sending her off to bed, while they stayed up playing pool (Spector, 145). It is probably for similar reasons that he sent a telegraph to the Rolling Stones manager, threatening the band to "leave my girls alone," while the Ronettes were touring England with them (Norman, *Mick Jagger*, 129). The possessive adjective "my" here seems to indicate that girls were indeed simply "trophies" that garnered him respect and admiration among his peers and fellow musicians, who more often than not were male. Maybe he was simply paranoid over Ronnie, but this paranoia extended over the whole group, making it very awkward for the other girls to relax while they were on tour. Spector commanded a presence of control, despite his not even being there.

RONNIE AND PHIL

Aspects of Spector's controlling nature were also possibly at the root of his ambivalent relationship with Ronnie Spector, a Galatea to his Pygmalion, a rough diamond that he eagerly transformed into a shining jewel. His great musical skill as well as his "generosity" would be publically displayed by making Ronnie a big star, but as her light began to shine too bright, dangerously close to eclipsing his, he needed to rein her in. "Once I'd made it big," surmised Ronnie, "Phil was too insecure to let me keep growing, because he was terrified that I might one day outdo him" (Spector, 104).

Phil, now "in love" with Ronnie, didn't want to share her, and by 1965 the Ronettes were beginning to deteriorate. Ronnie Spector believes that Spector held her back, intent that she would "stay a dependent little kid from Spanish Harlem." He would keep her in the control room away from other musicians, using the excuse that he needed her with him as his muse, a flattering but obsessive sentiment (Spector, 106–7). He also stopped her from opening for the Beatles on an American tour, jealous she might run away with a Beatle, and pressured her to choose between him and them (Spector, 113).

Phil had begun his affair with Ronnie Spector while he was still married to Annette Merar, though he continued to obsess over his ex-wife, even as he became more deeply involved with Ronnie. Spector, though initially channeling all his emotions into his tentative relationship with Ronnie, later turned his charm into its negative; while Ronnie had, without much doubt, fallen in love with Spector, it was definitely his status as the world's greatest pop producer that drew her to him and ultimately influenced her decision to marry him. Ronnie fantasized about her life as Mrs. Spector: "First off, I'd be a star again. Phil would be so inspired by married life that he'd climb right out of his rut and write half a dozen songs for me, and every one would be an even bigger hit than 'Be My Baby'" (Spector, 133). She was convinced that her marriage to Phil would solve all her problems, that she'd have her own family, her own children to fuss over, and that she would "never feel lonely anymore."

Would she have been so smitten by Spector if the opportunity for him to make her a pop star was not there? Possibly not, and Ronnie ended up paying a very dear price for fame by trading her freedom. Of course it doesn't excuse Spector's behavior toward her, keeping her captive in her home and having her minded and guarded everywhere she went.

The night they married, Phil went to see his mother, who didn't know about the wedding, and sent Ronnie home on her own. He returned that night in a rage, seemingly because his mother had convinced him that Ronnie was only after his money (Spector, 137). Ronnie's wedding night turned into a nightmare, as she had to lock herself in the bathroom to escape Spector's outrage. The marriage became more bizarre with Spector virtually having her fenced in in her own house, letting her out only to drive around in a car with her married initials, VS, painted all over it; Ronnie suspected this was a device Phil used so everyone would know, most particularly Ronnie, that she was his property. He even had her drive around with a dummy version of himself in the passenger seat and started to call her Veronica instead of Ronnie: "He erased Ronnie from his mind. And now in her place, he was trying to create Veronica, a loyal and quiet wife, who would be perfectly happy to waste away with him in the dark corners of his musty old mansion. He may not have been completely aware of it himself but I felt Phil was trying to brainwash me every single day of our marriage" (Spector, 147–48). To Ronnie, Phil was an "expert at mind control."

Spector's need to control every aspect of his life, as well as those close to him, has deep psychological questions surrounding it and was possibly very much related to how the women in his childhood treated and behaved toward him.

Spector's initial desires that he felt for Ronnie resulted in the great pop songs they created together, including "Be My Baby," "Baby, I Love You," "Walking in the Rain," and many more. "He couldn't have made them more personal if he'd sent them as love letters," Ronnie admitted. "He would tell me how much he loved me by writing hit songs, which I would sing back to him. . . . You can trace our relationship through the songs we did together. He courted me while we rehearsed 'Be My Baby,' we fell in love when we recorded 'Baby, I Love You,' and we made love after we listened to 'Do I Love You' for the first time" (Spector, 84–85).

When the attraction and feelings left Spector, nothing much could be done to create any more great pop songs. Possibly Spector questioned his own relationship with Ronnie after many of the songs, though worthy of success, didn't perform on the charts as well as they should and Spector felt the control in his life slipping away. In an effort to cling onto his success, Spector felt he needed to control the very person that had inspired him.

Just as he had done with Darlene Love and the Crystals, Spector abandoned his own muse (and wife) in order to maintain his foot on the ladder of success. Not only once did he replace Ronnie Spector with the Righteous Brothers and then Tina Turner, but also he replaced her a second time when he and George Harrison helped to reignite Ronnie

Spector's career with a collection of songs written by Harrison, including "Try Some Buy Some" and "You." As he had done in their marriage, so too he ignored Ronnie by leaving her outside the record by obscuring her vocal with overproduction. Ronnie described the records as being "like a movie where the star only appears now and then" (M. Brown, 263). Harrison commented on Phil's ineffective behavior and attitude toward the project, saying, "We never got to make a whole album because we only did four or five tracks before Phil fell over" (Harrison, 218). This statement suggests Spector was desperately losing his ability to even stay in control of himself.

SPECTOR AND A CULTURE OF SADOMASOCHISM

Groups such as the Blossoms, the Crystals, and the Ronettes had created a strong image and visual presence for women, who would be seen as escaping from the restraints of domestic boredom. As well, the vibrancy of the music no doubt inspired young girls to form their own groups. Many of the later groups, particularly the punk bands, reacted against the exploitive nature of the music industry and figures such as Phil Spector, who were seen as controlling Svengali types, as well as his treatment of Ronnie Spector, who at first seemed to encapsulate the new woman: strong, independent, successful, and in charge of her own life. Yet she met the total opposite fate, being incarcerated in her own home by the very man who had "rescued" her from the young girl's inevitable life of domestic drudgery.

While Spector's groups did, in many ways, have a significant impact on how young girls and women saw themselves, offering them alternatives to the inevitable occupation of housewife, his groups still displayed a sense of traditional femininity, in which the young girl is primarily groomed for marriage; it is her sexual appeal that is important, even if it is packaged as the "bad girl." Despite the subtle sexual nature of the boy's interest in "Da Doo Ron Ron," for example, "he looked so quiet but my-oh-my," the boy still behaves in a very mild and acceptable manner, that is, "he walks her home." Some commentators have argued that such behavior for the woman was not acceptable for the period, and the girl had to be presented as more vulnerable and passive in order for the song to have commercial appeal (Warwick, *Girl Groups*,

64, 141–53). This may be said too for the follow-up song "Then He Kissed Me," where the boy reverts to an active role and upholds the ideals of the previous generation; the girl, uncertain, "didn't know what to do," what Jacqueline Warwick refers to as "the meek, passive behavior that is necessary to earn a marriage proposal" (Warwick, *Girl Groups*, 64).

This notion of passivity would extend further into emotional and physical abuse as a significant number of girl group songs, such as Gerry Goffin's "Chains" and most notably his Spector-produced "He Hit Me (and It Felt Like a Kiss)," were loaded with seemingly sadomasochistic themes. Most of the girls, though uncomfortable with the material, grudgingly went along with singing them and were seen to be promoting ideas of sexual and social abuse of women, blurring the boundaries between love/passion and violence, and confusing women as to what healthy and positive relationships were about.

Goffin and King's "Chains," for example, deals with a girl who "seems to enjoy being a prisoner of love," as the song moves "from an opening featuring a three-voiced subject, implying that the feelings discussed are shared by many, to the articulation of one individual's experience" (Warwick, *Girl Groups*, 71–72). The song, suggests Warwick, begins "with the premise of community and the implication that the song's message describes common emotions and ordinary behavior" and is, Warwick continues, "hardly the sound of victimhood" (Warwick, *Girl Groups*, 72). The fact that young girls were casually singing the lyrics to these songs, which incidentally motivated their parents to take action and have the songs, particularly "He Hit Me (and It Felt Like a Kiss)," withdrawn from shops, is evidence enough that record-buying young girls were simply unaware of the subliminal and quite disturbing messages that were being promoted.

Warwick observes that the culture "skirts around the song's ["He Hit Me"] message that seems to condone and even celebrate male violence against women in ostensibly loving relations." Warwick points out that no one, apart from parents, had any major concerns with the song's negative influence, as Goffin didn't seem to think the song was "a dangerous courtship model," while Lester Sill simply thought the song was "a terrible fucking song," and Alan Betrock felt the song was a prank played on Sill by Spector (Warwick, *Girl Groups*, 67).

Warwick also suggests that the Crystals were unaware of the song's implications and didn't like it, mostly because it was not very pretty and the recording session was difficult—not because of its "disturbing" subject matter. Warwick is probably right in claiming that the male figures were unaware, if not unconcerned, of the song's negative message, but the Crystals, at least according to Barbara Alston, were certainly concerned about the songs themes: "'He Hit Me' was absolutely, positively the one record that none of us liked. We knew in our hearts that it was going to be a controversial piece and argued on several occasions with Phil about releasing it. Why would five young girls sing something extraordinary like 'He Hit Me (and It Felt Like a Kiss)'?" (M. Brown, 100).

HE HIT ME (AND IT FELT LIKE A KISS)

Spector released the song in July 1962. It is a song that explores notions of "unfaithfulness and an ensuing sadomasochistic relationship, building up to the line 'he hit me and I was glad'" (Betrock, 35). The song it seems was initially quite popular, receiving favorable reviews, while most importantly the kids were happily singing it. Despite its initial warm welcome, some, such as Alan Betrock, believe that Spector didn't release it as a serious chart contender. "It seems impossible to believe," commented Betrock, that "Spector seriously thought this record could be a success." For Betrock it seemed more of an attempt for Spector to antagonize his estranged business partners (Harry Finfer and Co. [Betrock, 35]).

This may be so, but Spector's treatment of the song is very elaborate, and even Barbara Alston claims he labored over the arrangement. She said that "he was so particular about the arrangement and the sound that we had a terrible session" (Betrock, 35), and according to Mick Brown, Spector "attacked the song with manic relish" (100). So, in contradiction to Betrock's remarks above, it seems Spector did very much take it seriously and conceived it as a definite hit single.

It's quite possible that Spector was drawn to the subject matter, just as much as the song's writers, Goffin and King, were and thought it both intriguing and perverse to deal with such a subject. He was excited by the idea that such raw sexual undertones could exist in a pop song, while at the same time allowing pop music to become a means of social commentary, even in taboo areas such as domestic abuse. If "Uptown" had highlighted the plight of ethnic minorities, then surely commenting on the unspoken subject of domestic violence would be a reasonable progression for pop music. The song, though it never actually became a hit, is particularly significant in light of its perceived romanticizing of domestic violence (Betrock, 35; Clemente, 76) as well as its influence on a significant number of female artists since.

The song came about after Goffin and King had heard their babysitter, Little Eva, recounting of how she got a black eye after being hit by her boyfriend. The couple was shocked to hear Eva explain that it was his way of showing that he loved her (Ribowsky, 114), and they both felt it a particularly interesting subject to write about. Though it is difficult to digest after listening to the song only a few times, mainly because it is so unexpected in the girl group genre, the song's lyrics, arrangement, sonic textures, melody, harmonies, and vocal richness are outstanding. It is also brave, if somewhat lacking in foresight for audience acceptance, or more so, societal acceptance, considering it was withdrawn from public release due to parental complaints, a possible indication of society's inability to face up to its problems.

In essence, "He Hit Me" (as does "Uptown") explores the perverted and confused values that lurked beneath the surface of both individuals and society at large; these values distorted the domestic bliss of early postwar America and explain why filmmaker Adam Curtis, in his experimental film *It Felt Like a Kiss* (2009), which examines the decaying American Dream, used it as a title. Curtis's film observes the rise and fall of America through pop culture, and although the title suggests that on the surface things looked wonderful, beneath the cozy veneer there lurked something violent. In this sense the song, along with others such as "Johnny Get Angry," "Please Hurt Me," "Chains," and even "Leader of the Pack" and "Nowhere to Run" highlight the violent undertones that lay beneath the surface of society, the individual, and relationships.

"He Hit Me" has become a subject for the discussion of "the twisted connections between romance, obsession and violence" by Jacqueline Warwick in her essay "He Hit Me, and I Was Glad" (Stras, 104). Here Warwick argues that certain aspects of the song's instrumentation "represent cultural forces that can pressure women to accept dysfunctional relationships as normal" and that "the musical language of the song enacts a virtuosic rationalization of wife or girlfriend battering" (Stras, 104). Though there is something certainly unsettling about the musical language of the song, it is also found in other Goffin and King/Spector collaborations, most significantly, "No One Ever Tells You," which adopts a similar language but focuses more on the first painful experience of lost love and the tragic fact that no one warns you of such experiences.

Warwick observes the song's musical dissonance, which makes it even more unsettling: "Alston's C sharp on the word 'hit' is an uncomfortable triton away from the bass foundation we have accepted, and it creates an ugly dissonance that is every bit as troubling as the words, which are foregrounded in the mix in a production style that is unusual for Phil Spector" (Stras, 103). Warwick also suggests that the Crystals' voices are wooden, unlike their passionate performances on other songs such as "Da Doo Ron Ron" and "Then He Kissed Me," and that the "backing vocals are also in an eerily high tessitura" (Stras, 103). The sound of the strings, long understood as a syrupy soundtrack to fairy-tale romance, she argues, is "complicit in helping the song's protagonist accept physical abuse as a testament of love" and that all of these aspects of the song ultimately result in "a compassionate performance of the unhealthy logic that makes abuse tolerable" (Stras, 103, 104).

It is possible to make the argument that women were mistreated simply because that was the culture of the time and that young producers and managers, as well as the girls themselves, thought this was normal behavior. It is only recently, however, that this culture and attitude, after feminism and women's rights came to the fore, which ironically was given considerable attention through the girl groups that Spector produced, have been challenged. Many commentators such as Alan Betrock, John Clemente, Jacqueline Warwick, Susan Douglas, Elizabeth K. Keenan, Laurie Stras, and Greil Marcus have responded more positively to the success of the girl group era, as well as highlighting the "exploitation" of many of these girls at the same time.

Whether Warwick and others are justified in thinking "He Hit Me" was promoting domestic abuse is entirely another question. The opposite view suggests the song drew attention to its existence and perception in the culture of the time, which saw it as being interconnected to romance; this is certainly how Carole King, the song's cowriter, interpreted the song, as both her husband and she were puzzled about Little Eva's attitude toward her boyfriend's violent behavior.

Whether Spector himself was highlighting domestic abuse or promoting it is not so easy to determine (Goffin claimed that Spector was somewhat masochistic [Ribowsky, 115]). There is probably a number of motives behind his decision to produce it, particularly in the manner in which he chose: partly to highlight the twisted perception between violence and romance in the culture of the time; partly because of perverse elements in his own nature that gave him a sense of dominance and control; and partly because it was a theme that would not only irritate his partners, another perverse characteristic of Spector, but also go against the grain of mainstream pop, something Spector considered himself to be beyond, as well as the possible egocentric challenge of turning such a song into a hit. For Mark Ribowsky, Spector's arrangement seemed to justify "violence against women as a way to true love" (Ribowsky, 114), while David Thompson was more sympathetic to the idea that the song was possibly highlighting the disturbing fact that wife battering was an acceptable cultural norm (Thompson, 78).

Regardless of Spector's reason for recording the song, it is certainly clear that if the culture of the time was reticent to discuss or even acknowledge such social behavior, it was because, as Warwick (and Thompson) rightly points out, the "twisted connections between romance, obsession, and violence were not yet of general psychological interest to the society of the time" (Warwick, *Girl Groups*, 70).

MODERN GIRLS

Over the last few decades, girls have begun to sing and write about their sexual, rather than romantic, experiences, with Blondie's "In the Flesh," Madonna's "Like a Virgin," or Lady Gaga's "Pokerface" being examples. Intertwined with the liberal attitude toward sex in modern pop songs is the notion of violence (toward both women and men), which has become one of the most alluring aspects of today's pop culture and the subject for many videos from female singers such as Rihanna, Lady Gaga, and Beyoncé. Many songs today encourage sadomasochistic relationships, Amy Winehouse's "Do Me Good" or "Sent Me Flying," for example, while other songs, with a similar obsession, reference "He Hit

Me" as if it were a pop cultural signifier of "dysfunctional" relationships. It is interesting to note that cultural critic Lauren Rosewarne, in her book *Part-Time Perverts: Sex, Pop Culture, and Kink Management*, indicates that, in many ways, the "role of pop culture is stimulating and normalizing" such behavior (Rosewarne, 19–23). Considering more recent songs, such as Lana Del Rey's "Ultraviolence," the Cardigans' "And Then You Kissed Me" (which incidentally subverts the titles of two Crystals songs), Florence and the Machine's "Kiss with a Fist," or Courtney Love's insipid MTV performance of "He Hit Me," suggests a culture caught up in the drama of sexual aggression and violence.

While Spector certainly knew how to use the talents and charm of young girls, it seems more likely that he was identifying with a teen emotion and an exploration of their own identity through notions of marriage and their place in society, as well as an expression of the sexual energy that remained locked up inside them. Other girl group music, with their "do lang do lang"–type phrases, as well as their wild uninhibited screams (consider the Tammys' "Egyptian Shumba"), suggests an unleashing of these sexual impulses that found their full expression when groups such as the Beatles and the Rolling Stones came to town.

Though Spector and Goffin may be accused of promoting violence against women, it may also be seen that they were questioning certain underlying concerns within culture, though possibly at the same time making them acceptable and by doing so creating confusion among later generations of teenage pop fans. In her article entitled "Lady Gaga, Miley Cyrus and the Rape Generation," Zoe Williams explains the uncertainty modern culture has regarding its stance on this type of behavior, constantly attempting to steer itself along the thin line between what is considered boundary pushing, taboo challenging, and risqué as opposed to what's "sleazy," "abusive," and "regressive sexist bullshit."

IN DEFENSE OF PHIL SPECTOR

Although many found Spector to be domineering, others saw a different side to him. Gloria Jones, of the Blossoms, sensed a vulnerable side to him, and though ultimately she felt he was "a little punk" (in fact, according to Darlene Love, she felt he was "sneaky" and a "creep"

[Love, 84]), she still respected his talent (M. Brown, 120–21). Fanita James, also of the Blossoms, felt Spector tried to create a happy atmosphere at work, tried to make it a family environment, but possibly Spector, sensing little threat from Fanita, as she wasn't as keen to be in the spotlight, could be more civil to her.

Though Spector treated many of his singers without any conscience, he was not unique in that regard. Motown's treatment of Florence Ballard is a particular case in point, and though there is some truth to Berry Gordy's feeling that he took all the risks and invested all the money, it cannot be helped but thought that these young women were simply commodities in the pop music industry, and very disposable ones at that. The conduct of other managers and mentors was also poor. For example, Leiber and Stoller sold their Red Bird label "for a dollar" and left their acts, mainly young girls, in the lurch (Marcus, 251). Shadow Morton's sudden lack of interest toward his own charges, the Shangri-Las, more or less ended their career. And Florence Greenberg and her final treatment of the Shirelles (Keenan, 42) is another example that reinforces the idea that young girls were, in general, exploited within and by the industry.

It wasn't, incidentally, only girls; boys too were often the subject of managerial or record company exploitation. Groups such as the Beatles, by EMI; the Rolling Stones, by Allen Klein; and the Small Faces, by Immediate Records were all, at some stage in their careers, subject to financial mismanagement, robbed of artistic control, or simply overburdened by work commitments or tied into unfair legal contracts that obliged them to do things they were not comfortable with. Spector's male musicians too felt he pushed them beyond their limits, some even refusing to work with him because of it, and Spector, almost as notorious for his eccentric behavior as for his record making, would reportedly hold his male collaborators at gunpoint in order to intimidate them, making certain they knew precisely who was in control. Spector, legend has it, even pulled a gun on John Lennon, whom he supposedly revered (Biography Channel).

While Spector could certainly be manipulative and controlling in and out of the studio, many cite his treatment of Darlene Love as a major example for this manipulative side of his personality. Without doubt Spector was not interested in making Darlene Love a star, particularly if it meant it would obscure his own name; however, in Spector's defense, he certainly did not simply "use" Love for her vocal talents on "He's a Rebel," as she, like all other musicians on the session, was hired for the record. If some thought Spector had misused her, it must be pointed out that she received $3,000 for a day's recording (Love, 63). For her sessions prior to that she was earning about $200–300 (Love, 60), and even though Love had had a bad experience with Spector, she stayed around for so long because she felt that despite all his "deception" he was a "genius" (Love, 84).

In fact, Spector knew every aspect of his singers' vocal abilities, purposely building the songs around their vocals (Ribowsky, 32). Ronnie Spector readily admitted, "He knew that 'Be My Baby' was a perfect song for me, so he constructed the whole record around my voice from the ground up" (Spector, 52). Spector made many of his singers, including Darlene Love, Annette Kleinbard, Priscilla Paris, Ronnie Spector, Bobby Sheen, the Righteous Brothers, and even Joey Ramone, if not exactly stars, at least well-known and much-loved names within the pop music of the period.

Spector and other companies, such as Motown, have also been criticized for exploiting and manipulating the look and sexuality of young, particularly black, girls by confining them to views of white femininity, particularly in the way they dressed and moved in their performances. Some, however, for example, Elizabeth Keenan, have viewed black girl groups' look and performances from a different angle: "Retraining was also a specific means of projecting an image of 'proper' African American femininity. . . . This restricted femininity reads differently in the face of racist presumptions about African American sexuality that became visible in the rock 'n' roll era and in the fight for civil rights" (Keenan, 46). In a similar manner, Angela McRobbie makes the case for dancing as a means of young girls conforming to stereotypes while at the same time emancipating them; they secretly perform for the male gaze and are not under control. "Dance and music are associated with being temporarily out of control, or out of the reaches of controlling forces," explains McRobbie (quoted in Warwick, *Girl Groups*, 74), while Susan Douglas, as already mentioned, also praises black girl groups for surreptitiously introducing the acceptability of sexuality into white teen culture through dancing and singing.

In terms of the Ronettes, their highly sexualized look was devised not by controlling white male figures such as Spector but by their mothers, while the Supremes gladly styled their own look according to main-stream conventions (M. Wilson, 160). This isn't to say that black sexuality wasn't repressed, but it was a means of these girl groups creating opportunities for themselves, which eventually opened up black culture and sexuality so much so that Madonna deliberately left her image off her debut single in order to be accepted into the black dance charts in the eighties (S. Douglas; Howe; Thompson, 51). Meanwhile, Tina Turner's stage performances, though crossing over into white main-stream culture, did not suppress her black sexuality but in fact celebrated it as much as James Brown did and even influenced a whole culture of white, particularly male performers when her style was adopted by the likes of Mick Jagger at the end of the sixties.

THE VINDICATION OF THE CRYSTALS AND THE RONETTES

While Spector appeared all powerful, some did stand up to him; the Crystals, for one, sued him for unpaid royalties. Though they lost the case, they did manage to secure the rights to their name (Gaar, 43), which Spector had come to own. This case set a precedent and brought about the passing of new legislation to protect artists and the use of their names (Clemente, 77; Warwick, *Girl Groups*, 129).

In 1972, with the help of her mother, Ronnie Spector managed to escape her husband's imprisonment of her, though she had to leave behind all her money and possessions. Since she and the other Ronettes had only ever received one royalty check for $14,000 in 1966 (approximately $4,500 each), which was certainly not enough to live on, Ronnie, in 1985, with the help of music agent Chuck Rubin, eventually took legal action. Rubin was the initiator of the Artists Rights Enforcement Corporation, which aims to restore "royalties and dignity" to aggrieved artists. Finally the courts agreed that the three Ronettes were entitled to 50 percent of all licensing of their material and were awarded an initial settlement of $2.6 million (*Secret History*). After the settlement, Ronnie Spector said she personally felt "vindicated as a woman, a performer and a singer" and felt "vindicated" for finally receiving the due recognition for all the hard work she and the other Ronettes had put into making the records.

Spector wanted complete control over not just the music but also the money and the rights to all the Ronettes' recordings, which according to author and attorney Stan Soocher, were some of the most lucrative recordings being used in TV and film at the time (*Secret History*). Spector thus tried his hardest to undermine the Ronettes, even claiming that Ronnie's sister and their cousin had not even sung on the records and therefore were not entitled to any payments (*Secret History*). Even though the judge had quashed his claims, Spector, unwilling to admit defeat, vindictively wrote a letter to board members of the Music Hall of Fame urging the board to withdraw the Ronettes' name from their list of possible candidates. The members strangely enough conceded to Spector's wishes, and the Ronettes, though major contributors to pop music, will, at least as the situation is at this moment, never be officially considered and honored among their peers (*Secret History*). But Ronnie says she is not too concerned as long as she can sing under her own name and work with those people, among which have been Bruce Springsteen and Joey Ramone, who have continued to admire her musical talents. However, this view of Phil Spector portrays a man with an irregular and unhealthy obsession for control, one that could only, and eventually did, lead to a very unhappy end for him and others.

7

YOU'VE LOST THAT LOVIN' FEELIN'

Collective Consciousness versus Ego Consciousness

SPECTOR'S WINTER OF DISCONTENT

As the winter of 1965 approached, Phil Spector began work on a new song, this time a Barry Mann and Cynthia Weil original. While the initial idea had potential, Spector, by altering the tempo, adding a whole new section, and extending its length way beyond the standards of the pop record, created something that is still considered to be one of pop music's greatest achievements. "The finished song," Mick Brown would write some years later, "was almost twice as long as Mann and Weil's original demo—almost twice as long as any pop song of the time. But Spector refused to change a note. As autumn turned to winter, he prepared to make the biggest record of his life" (M. Brown, 172). The song was "You've Lost That Lovin' Feelin'," while the "winter" that Brown is referring to was not just seasonal but also a metaphorical winter, as Spector struggled with many personal problems, a great many artistic and industry challenges, and significant cultural changes that came in too swiftly for individuals like Spector to be able to deal with.

Though "You've Lost That Lovin' Feelin'" was an epic achievement that would become the most played pop song ever, it suggests something more than just personal loss. The original impetus of joy and enthusiasm that had characterized much of Spector's music, particularly the girl group sound of the early sixties, had given way to a much more aggressive sound and attitude, which had been particularly inspired by many of the British groups that were now becoming popular in America and which had filled an emotional hole left after the assassination of President Kennedy in the winter of 1963. From this perspective the song also suggests the struggles and challenges that the society of the time was beginning to come to terms with.

Along with the British groups, the shadow of Motown was also posing a challenge to Spector's musical empire, as too were his own protégés, particularly the Beach Boys. The group's leader, Brian Wilson, if he had not surpassed Spector's productions, had equaled them. Spector was also facing personal problems, being still emotionally attached to his ex-wife, Annette Merar, while his existing relationship with Ronnie Bennett was becoming more and more turbulent. To compound matters Spector was also beginning to question his own abilities as a producer.

SPECTOR'S LOST CONFIDENCE

A few months prior to "Lovin' Feelin'" and after a number of unsuccessful records with the Ronettes, Spector had teamed up for a third time with the Aldon songwriters Mann and Weil (although it was his fourth time working on a Mann song). The composition that emerged was "Walking in the Rain." Despite everyone's feeling it would be a big hit, the track, however, only reached number twenty-three, and Spector felt the public had lost interest in his music, which to a large degree it had. The naïve sensibilities associated with early pop music were beginning to wane and be replaced by a more grown-up and cynical attitude; love and happiness were being infused with sex and freedom. "It was no longer simple commerce, teen romance or good times but something else: a total immersive experience" (Savage, viii).

Young people, who had grown up with affections toward the Spector sound, and teenagers, who had dreamed of love, marriage, and happiness, as expressed in the songs of the Crystals, the Ronettes, and Darlene Love, had moved past such a state of hopeless idealism. As they began to grow older and experience more of the world, different feelings stirred them, feelings more akin to the raucous sounds of the British bands and the folk rock music that was emerging. But Spector didn't want to face the fact that his music was not moving with the times. Sonny Bono hit the nail on the head when he commented that Spector "duplicated the same sound and the enthusiasm dropped and it was harder to get the records played" (Ribowsky, 169). Meanwhile, Jimmy Iovine, Spector's onetime engineer, would claim that "Phil was a one-trick pony" who had essentially run out of ideas (R. Williams, *Phil Spector*, ix).

In many ways Spector couldn't be blamed for feeling insecure, since much of the music he recorded with the Ronettes was first rate and deserved much more attention than it had received. Nonetheless, Spector should have known that both the industry and the public are fickle when it comes to pop music and that the overpowering force of the British groups, who had for a number of reasons been pushed by the media into public consciousness, made it difficult for many American artists, who were now "beleaguered, uncertain and desperate to find an answer to the sudden and drastic change of status quo" (*The Byrds*), to compete.

As well as these professional and artistic challenges, Spector was becoming increasingly uncertain about his own abilities (M. Brown, 171), and though he had always lacked confidence in certain areas of his life (e.g., his personal appearance and his relationship to his peers), the pressures of success and the expectations he was placing on himself were now becoming increasingly problematic for him. What many saw in Phil as arrogance and egotism was often insecurity and his way of compensating for what he felt were his inadequacies. "Phil's problem," said Nino Tempo, "wasn't that he thought he was too good. It was that he never thought he was good enough" (M. Brown, 135). Spector's neurosis, possibly resulting from the loss of his father, plagued him constantly; he had extreme difficulty flying, even though his profession often demanded him to do so, and it could make the studio environment difficult for anyone, such as producer Terry Melcher (M. Brown, 136), who had to work with him. Sometimes, during sessions, he would spend hours on the phone to his psychiatrist, Dr. Kaplan, looking for reassurance about his abilities (M. Brown, 137).

His first wife, Annette, one of the few people whom Spector could confide in, would often answer the telephone at three or four in the morning to find him on the other end of the line in California, anxiously seeking reassurance that he had not lost his gift (M. Brown, 172). His paranoia could become so pronounced that he would at times watch the tramps in ghettoes just to reassure himself that he was not so badly off or to perversely imagine what his life might have turned out like if things had not gone his way (M. Brown, 135).

Confusion in his love life at this time became another pressure, as his waning passion for Ronnie was doubly complicated by the fact that she was his muse. The loss of his "loving feeling" toward her also meant the loss of his artistic inspiration, which was compounded not only by the musical challenges that he had to face but also by the fact that he was not fully over his ex-wife, Annette. He had never admitted to her his infidelity (with Ronnie) and pleaded with her to get back together with him. He even told Annette he would drop the Ronettes from their contract if she would return to him. She refused (M. Brown, 172). By not loving the woman he was with and not being with the woman he loved (or wanted to repossess), Spector possibly felt in need of a muse. These pressures, all coming at once, were possibly too overwhelming for him.

DIG THE NEW BREED: BRIAN WILSON, MOTOWN, AND THE BRITISH INVASION

Ultimately, the sweet sound of the Spector productions, the lyrical content of idealized love, and the absence of grit and emotional realism mixed with the absence of drug influences and psychedelic attitudes resulted in the youth of the time moving away from his style of music toward more challenging material, which shattered all the illusions about love, life, and the American Dream. Although the so-called British Invasion and the influence of the British bands such as the Beatles, the Rolling Stones, Herman's Hermits, and the Who, to name just a few, was a huge component in the demise of Spector and his American contemporaries, artists such as the Beach Boys, Bob Dylan, the Byrds, the Doors, and Jimi Hendrix also posed a challenge as they too began to explore new musical styles and embrace new ideas.

With the arrival of the Beatles in the United States, life in some ways suddenly seemed more complex. The mayhem surrounding the group, as well as the need for the United States to look beyond itself for fulfillment, was a whole new realization for U.S. culture. In addition, more than before, young girls and boys, with pent-up anxieties, sexual urges, and other subconscious feelings, which seemed to have been lurking beneath the surface for some time, were beginning to find expression. In an interview in 1965, Mick Jagger would express this very idea: "In the last two or three years," he said, "young people, this especially applies to America, instead of just carrying on the way their parents told them . . . they're anti-war, they love everybody and their sexual lives have become freer[;] the kids are looking for something else or some different moral values, because they know they're gonna get all the things that were thought impossible fifty years ago" (*Charlie Is My Darling*).

It was difficult for many musicians and songwriters to compete with the raw energy the Beatles had brought with them, indicating more the change in attitudes than actually inspiring them, but the fact that they looked different, sounded different, and spoke and behaved differently to most popular figures both in the United States and Britain made the youth of the time feel that things were drastically changing and that the age of innocence was well and truly over (*People's History of Pop*). These sudden changing attitudes were so clearly evident to everyone that Spector's devoted arranger Jack Nitzsche would comment that "it just stopped being so much fun. The Beatles were coming" (M. Brown, 171).

If the American music industry had difficulty competing with the Beatles simply on a personality and publicity level, their music was also challenging for the mainstream pop star at the time, mainly because they established a new approach of writing, performing, and recording their own music, a trend that was also being established by many young American musicians, such as Brian Wilson and Bob Dylan, whose raw delivery of his self-composed protest songs in the folk idiom set out new territory to be explored in popular music. The music writer Robert Shelton observed how more poetic, serious-minded individuals, like Bob Dylan, were beginning to become the dominant influence on popular music and culture: "The age of pace is moving us outward; the age of drugs is moving us inward. And the age of new mass arts is moving us upward, inward, outward and forward. In this era of exploration, there are many breeds of navigators, but few more daring than the poet musicians who are leading our pop musicians in new directions" (Savage, viii).

Sam Cooke, when discussing Dylan's impact, put it best when he succinctly said "it no longer matters how prettily you sing but the truth in your voice" (*Rolling Stone*, "100 Greatest Singers"). From this perspective the notion of raw basic "truth" seemed to resonate more effectively with the audiences now than the sugarcoated pop sounds that Spector had spent so much time crafting and developing. The Beatles (and to a lesser extent the other British bands) had managed to merge the influences of sweet, well-crafted pop songs with the rawness of rock 'n' roll and, by singing and playing the songs themselves, were able to deliver a more immediate and authentic sound to their audience.

The Beach Boys similarly had taken the pop sound of Spector and expanded it with more complicated harmonic developments borrowed from jazz, classical music, Eastern music, folk, and music hall. Wilson, like Dylan, the Byrds, and groups such as the Doors, also expanded on the lyrical content of pop music, moving its focus away from the traditional love and relationship theme toward the arena of politics, philosophy, and transcendentalism. Soon the charts became dominated by much more elaborate songs such as "Good Vibrations," "Eight Miles High," "Strawberry Fields Forever," "Paint It Black," and "Break on Through"; Spector's way of competing with these bands was to take his Wall of Sound and simply make it even bigger (Biography Channel).

While Spector was not prepared, it seemed, to move away from his signature sound, his protégés, particularly Nitzsche, were more open. Nitzsche had begun to see a world beyond Phil Spector, and when the Rolling Stones recorded some sessions at the RCA studios in November 1964 (Elliott, 54–55), he was invited to sit in on keyboards, beginning a relationship with the group that would flourish over the next few years.

Working with the Stones was a liberating experience for Nitzsche. Their approach to recording was much different to Spector's. They had a "fuck you" attitude. "There was no guidance at all on those records and very little need for it . . . they changed my whole idea of recording," said Nitzsche (Davis, 105–6). However, while Nitzsche was keen to spread his wings and move out from under Spector's shadow, Spector had his reputation to keep, and moving into new territory was more daunting for him than it was for Nitzsche, who could remain in the background while experimenting with new creative approaches.

If Spector had accepted the fact that his sound needed modernizing rather than stubbornly refusing to change, he may have been able to hold his own in the new musical climate. Instead, he seemed to simply play out a part that the press and the public perceived him to be, that is, the mad reclusive genius, a sentiment later expressed by Ronnie Spector. "What the press wrote about him he became. They said he was a genius, he acted like that. They said he was a mad genius, so he acted like that. They said he was a recluse so he became a recluse. . . . He's afraid now if he fails, the name he has he wants to maintain, he's afraid it will not become a hit and he wants to keep the image of mad genius" (*Phil Spector: He's a Rebel*). Was it easier for Spector to live out the role of the reclusive, mad genius rather than risk failure and possibly reveal to the public what was possibly his worst fear, that his fire had gone out?

Another musical competitor that Spector had to concern himself with was Berry Gordy and his Motown record label, which would harness the energy of many young and very talented black artists, who were beginning to feel a real sense of self-confidence. Gordy set up Motown with the intention of developing a crossover sound like Spector's, who had mixed the songwriting and production styles of white, Western musical cultures from American popular song to the European romanticism of Wagner and Beethoven; this was delivered in a black gospel tradition mostly through the vocal abilities of the black female singers he had employed. Gordy, like Spector, wanted to reap the rewards, which had been denied him with the Jackie Wilson and Barrett Strong numbers he had written but from which only publishers and promoters had profited.

While Spector was one individual almost single-handedly running his label, with some help from Aldon's songwriters and his devoted helpers, such as Nitzsche and Sonny Bono, Gordy had built up and presided over a virtual empire of music industry professionals. The Beatles and the Stones had covered quite a number of Motown tracks, for instance, "Please Mr. Postman" and "Can I Get a Witness," which partially helped to finance the early stages of the Motown takeover of the music industry (Spector's songs were deliberately more elaborate to prevent people copying his sound); this meant that Gordy, who had also sourced the immense talent of the black communities around Detroit and New York, was able to outdo Spector and most other rivals of the crossover sound.

Gordy was also lucky to have gifted individuals in the form of Smokey Robinson, Holland-Dozier-Holland, Marvin Gaye, and Stevie Wonder to contribute in the songwriting, arranging, and production departments, as well as a whole host of highly skilled jazz musicians in the Funk Brothers, Motown's equivalent to Spector's Wrecking Crew; a group of exceptional female vocalists in the form of the Andantes, Motown's equivalent to Spector's Blossoms; and a huge selection of talent from the Marvelettes, who scored Motown's first number one, to Mary Wells, the Temptations, the Four Tops, the Miracles, the Vandellas, and ultimately the Supremes, who were the only real competitors to the ubiquitous Beatles during their heyday in the midsixties.

Not only did Gordy have access to all this talent, but also he had two other things that made his competition in the charts much more effective than Spector's. First, he had a much bigger marketing and quality assurance team, which he put a lot of trust in (Spector took these decisions on himself), and second, Gordy seemed to have the modesty to give up his role as songwriter/producer to focus more on the running of the company. In other words, he didn't seek the personal glory of being the star of the show, as Spector seemed to crave, but worked quietly away in the background.

The Marvelettes, not to mention other girl groups such as the Angels and the Shangri-Las, produced by Spector wannabes Richard Gottehrer and Shadow Morton, were a challenge to Spector's genre of music. But even more so were other Motown girl groups such as the Vandellas and the Supremes, who extended the girl groups' image, sound, and attitude into a more sophisticated form and continued to survive after the girl group genre, as such, began to wane in 1964; thus few other girl groups could really compete with Motown.

"You've Lost That Loving Feeling" was in many ways the apex of Spector's sound—not altogether a new approach but one final encore from his Wall of Sound before the public would "turn their back" on him after the release of, what he felt was, his real masterpiece: "River Deep, Mountain High." Understandably, after such blatant dismissal of his work by both the American public and the music industry, Spector, it would appear, became increasingly nervous about putting out records. Spector simply couldn't compete with these strong musical forces that had begun to emerge, even though their existence was largely due to the tremendous achievements made by Spector in the preceding years. The pressure of it all was ultimately too much for Spector and probably helped drive him into reclusiveness, reemerging only when the Beatles called on him to produce their swan song album, *Let It Be*.

THE TIMES THEY ARE A-CHANGIN'

Though the sixties were still in full swing, something unsettling, though possibly not apparent at the time, was creeping into the consciousness. The late sixties and early seventies was not only a time of great idealism but also a time when a generation had lost its innocence and rebelled (*The Byrds*). During the "Summer of Love," the hippie movement, spurred on by their new attitude of flower power, looked for alternative lifestyles and challenged the white, patriarchal, capitalist consumerism of the post–World War II period, which had glorified the notion of the "American Dream" but had also involved Americans in two devastating world wars. According to the folk singer Arlo Guthrie, people had reached a moment in history when "our traditional thoughts and way of life had brought us to the brink of disaster" (*The Sixties*).

The threat of nuclear war was ever present, and teenagers lived in constant fear that the world they lived in could be obliterated at any moment. "We were young and having a great time," observed Steve Gibbons, the "socially aware" lead singer of the British sixties garage band the Ugly, "but the whole time there was this fear that America and Russia would go to war. Most kids of my age didn't expect to make it through the sixties" (Savage, 19). A new impulse of "thinking for yourself" began to develop, and people, particularly the youth, questioned the establishment. Affluent kids of the postwar boom began to reject the capitalist ideologies and ushered in a new wave of living, which promoted free love, drug experimentation, alternative thinking, and alternative religions (*The Sixties*).

While Lyndon B. Johnson would put forward his policies for "the Great Society," focusing strongly on racial injustice and eradicating poverty, he also escalated U.S. military presence in Vietnam, which essentially dragged the United States and its citizens into the conflict between North and South Vietnam. Americans at first accepted the war in Vietnam as a necessary means of containing the spread of communism (BBC, "Vietnam, 1954–1975"), but as it raged on, many Americans, including high-profile figures such as Martin Luther King Jr. and Muhammad Ali, began to oppose it. The powerful seemed to be irresponsible so the powerless felt they had to do something. Never before had so many Americans protested a war, and by 1967 public opinion had turned completely against it (*The Sixties*), eventually uniting various factions and hoping that a revolution would sweep the "old order and its culture, from power" (Doggett, *There's a Riot*, 14).

Pop and rock musicians were beginning to question society's values, and what it meant to be rich and famous was soured with a tremendous feeling of discontent. For example, when journalist Maureen Cleave met John Lennon at his mock Tudor mansion at Kenwood, she observed that the "spiritual emptiness" in Lennon's life was masked by an "endless consumerism available to the rich . . . objectified in Lennon's life by his cars and television sets" (Doggett, *There's a Riot*, 57).

Lennon's music at this time also gave an indication of society's discontent. For example, he had begun recording "Help!" in April 1965 a few months after Spector's "You've Lost That Lovin' Feelin'" had topped the charts in the UK. The song was a cry that something was very wrong, even though it was covered up by the exhilarating beat and vocal harmonies that turned Lennon's despair into bubbly pop. The flip side, Paul McCartney's "I'm Down," reinforced the notions of discontent felt, and by the second half of that year the Rolling Stones would sum up the culture's sense of dissatisfaction with "Satisfaction (I Can't Get No)," their youth anthem of social rebellion and disaffection. Though Mick Jagger and Keith Richards felt it was only a sketch of the intended song (Elliott, 69), its rawness gave it an immediacy that resonated with the raw emotions and feelings of the time. The song, said writer Jon Savage, "expressed an almost cosmic dissatisfaction with the very consumerism that had thrown the Rolling Stones into prominence"; a year later their single "19th Nervous Breakdown" "hinted at the psychological disturbance that lay beneath the shiny, brightly colored new teen world, at the same time as it sought to push those extremes wherever they might go" (Savage, 40).

Dylan's *Freewheeling* (1963) and the Rolling Stones' *12x5* (1964) demonstrated that antiestablishment thought was becoming a commercially viable art form and that music could be a powerful and extremely necessary force for social renewal (*The Byrds*). Other songs, which also caught the imagination of the culture around 1964 and 1965 but which, whether intentionally or not, expressed a feeling of dissatisfaction and isolation, were "Nowhere to Run," and "Dancing in the Street." The latter song was embraced by young black demonstrators, who adopted it as a civil rights anthem to bring about social change. Dylan's "The Times They Are a-Changin'" became a song of social change. The Kinks, with "You Really Got Me," produced an edginess not heard before in mainstream music and opposed the soft pop sounds of its predecessors, while in September 1964, the Who, influenced by the autodestructive art of Gustav Metzger, began destroying their instruments on stage. In December of that year Sam Cooke was killed under mysterious circumstances, but his song "A Change Is Gonna Come," released posthumously, highlighted the racial inequalities that still existed in America. Meanwhile, seven months later in July 1965, Dylan's revolutionary six-minute, thirteen-second social commentary "Like a Rolling Stone," a song often heralded as signaling the moment when pop (ephemeral, trivial) mutated into rock (enduring, significant), changed the tone of rock and pop music completely (Doggett, *There's a Riot*, 78).

The Beatles, the Stones, Dylan, Hendrix, the Who, the Doors, and many others encouraged, even forced, a new attitude to living and thinking. These bands were, as music journalist Stephen Davis said when describing the impact the Rolling Stones had on the culture of the day, "the embodiment of everything we represent, a psychic evolution . . . the breaking up of old values" (Davis, 124). And by the end of 1965 the music industry would undergo a phenomenal artistic change with the main musical focus shifting away from mono-themed singles to multilayered-themed albums such as *Rubber Soul* (1965), *Aftermath* (1966), *Pet Sounds* (1966), *Blonde on Blonde* (1966), *Revolver* (1966), *Younger than Yesterday* (1967), and *Sgt. Pepper's Lonely Hearts Club Band* (1967).

Barry Melton, guitarist with the sixties alternative rock band Country Joe and the Fish, suggests that the musicians of the midsixties bridged the gap between a consciousness movement and a political movement and that "guitar players were leading the revolution"; school, college, and the steady job were rejected in favor of being a musician, and people were encouraged to march to a slogan of "play your guitar, get a following, start a revolution" (*The Sixties*).

Higher education opened up to everyone in the 1960s, creating a greater awareness of social conditions and ultimately leading, in 1968, to the widespread rejection of authority by students protesting on campuses across the United States and Europe. While middle-class white kids in these colleges were challenging the values of their elders, African Americans were undergoing a revolution of their own, and together they underwent shifts in social, political, and cultural renewal. In 1960 Rosa Parks started the change for racial equality, which led to the passing of the 1964 Civil Rights Act, outlawing segregation. Afro-Americans were connecting and identifying with the homeland, casting off their white-man's chains and chanting slogans such as "I'm black and I'm proud," a position that Spector's black stars had of course encouraged to some degree. Civil rights had exploded with the murder of Malcolm X in February 1965, and revolution was shouted in the streets of Harlem. Jazz musicians, such as Archie Shepp and Charlie Mingus, began to speak out vehemently against white America (Doggett, *There's a Riot*, 45). California in 1966/1967 was a breeding ground for not only hippie counterculture but also black nationalist groups, all with the same conviction that "liberation was impossible in a white-controlled society" (Doggett, *There's a Riot*, 73–74). And this ultimately led to black militant groups such as the Black Panther Party.

When Johnson resigned his nomination to rerun for president, this was seen as a victory of the counterculture and a sense that protests and demonstrations could bring about social change. Jon Savage summed it all up, writing,

> It was a time of enormous ambition and serious engagement. Music was no longer commenting on life but had become indivisible from life. It became the focus not just of youth consumerism but a way of seeing, the prism through which the world was interpreted. . . . It was possible to conceive of an alternative future, to believe that things could be different, that people could be free. (Savage, ix)

COLLECTIVE CONSCIOUSNESS VERSUS EGO CONSCIOUSNESS

It was clear that things could no longer be the way they had been and that the sense of collective happiness that the early sixties had brought, possibly as a result of the collective efforts to defend freedom and democracy in the face of fascism, and that was to a large degree reflected in the pop music of the period, was fading. The culture began to emphasize more the individual, partly promoted by the consumer culture, which was heavily dependent on the notion of personal happiness and identity (Curtis).

The rock music that had emerged by the midsixties was a clear reflection of this change. The Beatles, for example, who had started primarily as a vocal harmony group with a songwriting partnership, had splintered into a group with three distinct songwriters and three primary lead vocalists. The Beatles had moved from the collective "girl group" harmony style of their earlier arrangements, as well as their cowriting approach (which again reflected the girl group songwriting partnerships of that era, such as Mann and Weil, Goffin and King, and Barry and Greenwich), to a more self-oriented approach.

The Beach Boys (and the Byrds) ultimately did the same, and the vocal harmonies of earlier pop groups, particularly girl groups and doo-wop groups, were replaced by groups with little if any vocal harmonies, such as the Rolling Stones, the Doors, and the extremely individualistic voices of Bob Dylan and Leonard Cohen. "Pop and folk were drawing closer. Pop groups wanted depth. Folkies wanted exposure and fame. . . . In many ways, commercial youth culture was beginning to take up the slack of organized politics . . . where their songs mirrored the problems of the world, songs about loneliness, rejection, inhumanity" (Savage, 20–22).

Drug experimentation became an influence of the new music, particularly the use of marijuana and LSD, which was openly talked about within the realms of pop culture. The Who's Pete Townshend, for example, had spoken openly about the use of drugs to aid in experiencing different levels of perception (A Whole Scene Going), while Paul McCartney had publically admitted taking LSD (The Beatles Anthology). The use of these drugs allowed people to have pseudo-spiritual experiences on a deeply personal level, and such personal revelations would be directed "towards powerful social change" (Savage, 109). This would lead to the pop musician's sense of importance in terms of social responsibility, well depicted in a CBS broadcast in 1967, where songwriter Graham Nash expounds his individualistic beliefs in the role of popular music as a political tool (Inside Pop).

Young people were also beginning to understand and express a philosophy of self-awareness, in which "truth" was to be found within oneself and where awareness of the self went hand in hand with an awareness of the world around the self. This philosophy would lead to the conclusion that personal responsibility and social responsibility were indeed different sides to the same coin (*Inside Pop*).

Although the United States had created more opportunities for higher education, the result was that young people could now question the motives of the country (Doggett, *There's a Riot*, 15), while hallucinogenic drugs allowed young people to explore the limits of their own consciousness, thus bringing them to conclude that "consumerism offered poor nourishment for the psyche." Yet, ironically, the consumer culture offered a "web of media" through which they could express and share their own culture, mainly through magazines, films, books, and music (Doggett, *There's a Riot*, 15).

The extreme individualistic attitude of the mod culture, which had emerged in England in the late fifties as a by-product of the war, created an elitist group of self-centered and upwardly mobile individuals and the "first generation to cope consciously with the world that depends more on mass communication than personal relationships" (Savage, 63). A small group at first, the attitude began to spread through the culture, promoting an aggressive, though cosmopolitan, sophistication that rejected the subservient attitude of the postwar era. It was an attitude that was primarily defined by "the slow but steady move from a collective society towards materialistic individualism" (Savage, 63). And this attitude was particularly enhanced through British cultural events, such as the Beatles and James Bond, that found its way into the United States and other Western countries in 1964/1965.

The music that Spector was making was essentially born out of a more collective consciousness, involving the coming together of an assortment of different people with a unique set of skills, from songwriters to arrangers, performers, singers, and session musicians. These people were brought together through the talents of a gifted producer, such as Jerry Leiber and Mike Stoller, Joe Meek, and of course Phil Spector. Many of the new groups did not, however, work in such a collective environment but essentially wrote their own material, expressed their own feelings, and often, at least by the midsixties, took control of the arranging and production of their own music. By the seventies, artists such as David Bowie, Bruce Springsteen, and Todd Rundgren had more or less taken control over every aspect of their music and image.

While the Beatles and the Beach Boys were able to make a transition from collective-conscious artists to ego-conscious artists, many others were unable to do so, and to a large extent, this is why the girl group acts, so integrally connected to a collective consciousness, were unable to survive. Even the ones that did survive had to repackage themselves as individual artists with a backing group, such as Diana Ross and the Supremes or Martha Reeves and the Vandellas. Berry Gordy claimed this was a ploy to charge more money by having essentially two acts perform, a solo artist and a backing group, but it is only an economic consequence of a shift in the consciousness of the period. Teenagers were becoming more aware of their individuality and wanted that represented in their idols.

Spector, though in many ways driven by his own ego, had not the resources to become an individual entity in himself; he could not write and produce the music that fitted into that new mind-set. This mind-set encouraged personal reflection; freedom of thought and action, with songs reflecting personal experiences, feelings, and opinions; and a culture interested in the workings of the inner self and the psyche through exploring ideas of meditation, transcendence, and the fulfillment of personal needs. When John F. Kennedy stated, "Ask not what your country can do for you—ask what you can do for your country," it was relevant in the early sixties when the consciousness was still relatively collective, but by 1965, when such an attitude had disintegrated, Kennedy's phrases were simply scoffed at, particularly since the country had led the people into a pointless war. Instead, the new catchphrases were "Do as you will" and "We want the world and we want it now," reflecting what Jon Savage called "the all-consuming NOW" (Savage, 19).

Spector's was a world of fantasy and romance, not one of political, social, and philosophical speculation. Spector simply couldn't survive in this new artistic environment without a more ego-conscious artist to give his creativity currency; he needed someone like Dylan or Lennon to make him relevant once again.

THE POP SINGLE VERSES THE POP ALBUM

As the culture became more focused on individuality and as the palate of pop music expanded, artists had a greater desire to express all their ideas, both musically and philosophically, and hence a greater need for more space on a record to do so. The Beatles' *Revolver* had been instrumental in bringing about the transition from the single to the album, a point that music journalist Sean O'Hagan made when he commented on the album's importance: "*Revolver* changed everything, shifting the locus of pop from the single to the album, and announcing a period of intense creative momentum that arguably has not been equaled since. . . . It also speaks about another pop culture, that was more idealistic, adventurous and less narcissistic than today's" (O'Hagan).

Meanwhile, the Beach Boys' *Pet Sounds* "reinvented the album as the in-depth illumination of an artist's soul, liberating it to exist as a self-contained art form on a par with literature, theatre, cinema, dance" (Ellen). Savage would express a similar idea, writing that "1966 was the last year when the 45 was the principal pop music form, before the full advent of the album as a creative and a commercial force was heralded by *Sgt. Pepper's Lonely Hearts Club Band* in the summer 1967" (Savage, x). Spector was unwilling, if not unable, to think in terms of albums. He was content to think in terms of linking themes together in a unified whole—one theme, one song.

Also his productions were so big that it took too much energy to focus on that one thing, leaving him behind when the audiences of the midsixties wanted more—more music, more ideas, more detailed cover artwork, and essentially, at least from an economic point of view, more value for money.

Spector again refused to change with the times, whether because he lacked the confidence, because he was too stubborn, or simply because his approach took so long is hard to say, but he saw the single as the real medium for pop music. He greatly expanded its possibilities, not just from a sonic perspective, but also its compositional development; he turned the pop single into a virtual symphony, especially with the revolutionary "You've Lost That Loving Feeling," from which point songs became both longer and technically more proficient. Yet Spector wasn't able to move away from its form and embrace the more popular medium of the midsixties: the album.

YOU'VE LOST THAT LOVIN' FEELIN'

Despite his overwhelming success with Ellie Greenwich and Jeff Barry, Spector had turned once again to Barry Mann and Cynthia Weil for new material. It's possible that he wanted to change songwriting partners to create something different after he had moved his attention away from the Ronettes. He also felt bitterly betrayed by Greenwich and Barry when they topped the charts with the million-selling "Chapel of Love," a song he had dismissed as inferior after recording it with the Ronettes but that Greenwich and Barry, realizing its potential, went on to produce for the Dixie Cups.

Mann and Weil were certainly more socially conscious than the lighthearted approach of Greenwich and Barry, and from a certain perspective it may have seemed more fitting for Spector to have collaborated with a songwriting couple that was probably more in tune with the changing social conscience of the midsixties. Where Greenwich and Barry had displayed a temper and mood that better reflected the innocent, upbeat nature of the early sixties, Mann and Weil certainly would have reflected the more abrasive and unsettling side of the period; consider, for example, the socially aware lyrics of "Uptown," "On Broadway," and "We Gotta Get Out of This Place." From this perspective it could easily be deduced that Spector was keenly perceptive of the changing attitudes within music and the culture of the time, even if society was only on the cusp of change at the end of 1964, when Spector began his work on the song. If nothing else, the song was significantly different in mood and tempo than his previous big hits of "up-tempo avalanches of fulfilled and celebrated love" (Thompson, 121).

"You've Lost That Lovin' Feelin'" was inspired by its composer's admiration for the Four Tops' "Baby I Need Your Loving," a big hit for the Motown group during the summer of 1964. Spector by all accounts loved Mann and Weil's composition the minute he heard it, and once again, demonstrating his talent for turning a good song into a great song, he added his own significant touches. First, he made the song even slower than it was originally intended and then added his masterstroke—a dramatic middle section, measured by a bass riff modeled on "La Bamba," dropping the song to an almost whisper and then building it back up into a crescendo of Wagnerian proportions. This stroke of genius brought the song from a simple love song to something that

transcended anything pop music had ever conceived possible; he ultimately turned the two-minute pop song into a virtual modern pop symphony, while also removing any trace of the song's original Motown
influence. Brown expertly described Spector's genius regarding the
song's production in the following passage from his book:

> Now the fatalistic anguish of loss becomes a desperate plea for rec-
> onciliation and redemption—*"Bring back that lovin' feelin'"*—a plea
> that finally drifts into a far-distant silence, leaving you stunned in its
> wake. A masterpiece of chiaroscuro, of searing emotional light and
> darkness, of pain and catharsis, "You've Lost That Lovin' Feelin'" is
> the very summit of the producer's art. (M. Brown, 174)

Not only did Spector arrange and produce the song, but also he did so
with the very specific voices of Bill Medley and Bobby Hatfield in mind,
a duo that though popular on the live circuit, had yet to have a hit
single. Once again Spector demonstrated his seemingly uncanny ability
to both know the right voice for the right song and production and coax
the perfect performance from the singer.

"You've Lost That Lovin' Feelin'" didn't only expand the musical
dimensions of the pop song but also extended its time frame. In the
midsixties most songs were around two minutes long, but Spector, once
again "daring to be different," challenged the conventions of the music
industry and totally disregarded the radio stations' scheduling, which
liked to have songs come in under three minutes, feeling their audience
would lose interest. Showing his usual disdain for the industry, Spector's song came in at 3:46, which didn't make him very popular, but in
fairness to him, his concerns were more about the art of the song, about
experimentation and emphasizing the popular song as a legitimate art
form that couldn't and shouldn't be constrained by commercial interests.

Many people just didn't get the song, thinking it was too long and
too slow. The influential radio personality Bill Gavin and his "sheet,"
the virtual bible of the radio industry, which was essentially his tips on
what was the best music for DJs to play in order to increase listenership,
actually described the song as "blue-eyed soul has gone too far!" Meanwhile, promotions man Bill Walsh said he had to get the record played
under force and duress but stressed the point that "Phil's music re-

quired undivided attention, and not everybody could understand that" (M. Brown, 175).

Even if there were initial reservations among DJs to play the song, it was essentially "unstoppable." Within five weeks of its release it had entered the top ten, and by Christmas it was number one. Andrew "Loog" Oldham, always one of Spector's biggest fans, considered it "Spector's greatest production, the last word in tomorrow's sound to-day," and took out a full-page ad to promote the song and to challenge British singer Cilla Black's version of it.

Black's version had been produced by Beatles producer George Martin and was initially favored by DJs in Britain, who considered Spector's version to be too "dirge"-like, until Spector sent the Righteous Brothers over to promote it. It is interesting to compare the two versions and by doing so realize how much Spector's production is so much more dramatic and expansive. The "dirge"-like element of the Spector version emphasizes a feeling of lost love as akin to the actual loss of a loved one through death, while Black's version, although well produced and executed, simply doesn't delve so deep into the human emotions of loss and pain and comes over simply as a standard song of unrequited love.

The midsection of Spector's production, in which Bill Medley and Bobby Hatfield interchange vocals, particularly Hatfield's high-pitch yelps, which far outshine Black's, and that propel the song toward its massive climax, is often considered one of pop's greatest moments. The dynamics of Spector's song spread almost entirely across the range of the pop music of the day, whereas Black's fits neatly into something that was more or less standard for the time and suited the palate of DJs and music lovers, who didn't feel the need to challenge already-existing and established tastes. Spector, on the other hand, pushed his listeners to reach that bit higher and feel that bit deeper than they were used to. For this reason, Righteous Brother Bill Medley claimed it to be "one of the first grownup, sensitive-male songs of the era—marking the end of the teen-idol years" (Myers).

The sheer size and scope of the song, as well as the lack of initial interest among the music industry, really exposed "the overall mediocrity" of the business, and many years later Spector would reflect that "Lovin' Feelin'" was "the summit of his achievements with Philles" (M.

Brown, 176). "I would guess," explained Spector, "'You've Lost That Lovin' Feelin'" really captured something for me":

> It said the most to me as far as a production was concerned at the time. It was made as an honest shocker and was made as an experiment. It was really not made to necessarily become number one. That was not its goal. You see the main force that I have that drives me is probably the same force of why Wagner wrote music. To make a forceful message, to have a forceful approach, to present his dynamic feelings through his music. This is the way I see a record. (Kubernik)

"Lovin' Feelin'" made a huge impression on the pop musicians and songwriters of the time. It expanded the pop format; its musical palate and undoubtedly the duration of the pop song allowed the evolving pop musicians of the day to give more depth to their records. Brian Wilson's music, especially *Pet Sounds*, is hugely indebted to the song, as was the Beatles' *Sgt. Pepper's Lonely Hearts Club Band* (Myers) and the grand and expansive rock-opera style of bands such as the Who and later Queen. In many respects, one might say "Lovin' Feelin'" was the sixties precursor to "Bohemian Rhapsody."

8

HE'S SURE THE BOY I LOVE

Mentor and Protégés

BRIAN WILSON AND THE BEACH BOYS

Phil Spector's collaborators, such as Nino Tempo, Sonny Bono, and Jack Nitzsche, as well as songwriting partners like Gerry Goffin, all worshiped Spector and took many of his ideas into their own projects. While Goffin would collaborate with Spector as a songwriter, Nitzsche found a true role model in Spector, and working with him endowed Nitzsche with a sense of purpose and importance (M. Brown, 122–24). Nitzsche admired Spector's ambitions to create an orchestral pop sound, often daring him to enhance his Wall of Sound. If Spector was the visionary, then many felt Nitzsche was undoubtedly the architect. After a successful career with Spector, Nitzsche took many of the skills he had honed and applied them to the sound of his next music collaborators, the Rolling Stones. Nitzsche joined the band in the midsixties as their indispensable arranger, playing on and helping produce almost all the records they would make at the RCA studios in California, including *Aftermath* and *Between the Buttons* (Davis, 243). Sonny Bono, a promotions man for small local labels, worked for Spector as a general dogsbody, simply wishing for Spector's genius to rub off on him. His determination paid dividends after writing "Needles and Pins" with Nitzsche and having a big hit with "I Got You Babe" with Cher. Of all the American artists inspired by Spector, however, it was probably

Beach Boy Brian Wilson who was to have the greatest impact on the sixties.

Wilson began to idolize Spector after hearing Darlene Love singing "He's Sure the Boy I Love." Wilson said the record "opened up a door of creativity for me you wouldn't believe. . . . Phil Spector opened it up for me." And when Wilson heard Spector's "Be My Baby" on his car radio, while driving down Sunset Boulevard one afternoon, he had to pull the car over and absorb every bit of this new sound. It was, he said, "the best song he had ever heard" (Hartman, 58; B. Wilson, 82).

Brian was so affected by "Be My Baby" that he once locked himself in the recording booth of his studio and listened to the track on a loop for five hours in the dark. He memorized every note and sound and wrote "Don't Worry Baby" for the Ronettes in honor of his idol (B. Wilson, 82). On recording the song for the Beach Boys, Brian had tried to capture the Ronettes' sound opening with Hal Blaine's iconic drumbeat for "Be My Baby." "I was unable to think as a producer until the time I really got familiar with Phil Spector's work," Wilson once explained. "That was when I started to design the experience to be a record rather than just a song." Brian was so impressed with Spector, with both his songs and the productions, that he had the Beach Boys cover a number of them, including "There's No Other (Like My Baby)," "Then I Kissed Her," "I Can Hear Music," and "So Young." "The man is my hero," Brian Wilson said in an interview in 1977. "He gave rock 'n' roll just what it needed at the time and obviously influenced us a lot" (Kubernik).

Brian even began to use the same studios as Spector, such as Western Recorders, Gold Star, and Columbia (Pinnock). Brian would also sit in on many of Spector's sessions, watching carefully how his idol worked: how he set up the microphones, how he set the levels on the desk, and how he would overdub layers of each instrument to give them all greater and greater depth. He would observe how Spector created a unique voicing by layering a single melody with multiple timbres. Brian even poached Spector's musicians, the Wrecking Crew, for his own recordings (Ames Carlin, 43–47).

Though Larry Levine claimed that "Brian was one of the few people in the music business Phil respected" (Levine), other accounts suggest that Spector was little impressed by Wilson and all his praise. He rejected Brian's "Don't Worry Baby" as a song for the Ronettes (seemly because he couldn't get a writing credit on it; Clemente, 185), as well as "Don't Hurt My Little Sister," and seemed to go out of his way to insult the young Brain, rewriting the latter tune and then using it as a jingle called "Things Are Changing (for the Better)." He also invited Brian to play piano for him on a session but then dismissed his playing as substandard (B. Wilson, 85).

By the Beach Boys' third album, *Surfer Girl* (1963), Brian had taken over full control of shaping the sonic textures of the album and, following in the footsteps of Spector, stopped performing live and began to focus solely on writing and producing songs. He wrote songs not just for the Beach Boys but also for a variety of different artists that included such groups as Jan and Dean, who would directly copy Spector on songs such as "You Really Know How to Hurt a Guy"; Rachel and the Revolvers; and a Ronettes-inspired group called the Honeys. Though Brian was hugely influenced by Spector as a producer, he didn't simply copy his idol; instead, he created sounds that resonated with his own spirit, as the following passage from Domenic Priore's book suggests:

> The Ronettes had sung a dynamic version of The Students 1961 hit "I'm So Young" and Wilson went right for it, but took the Wall of Sound in a different direction. Where Phil would go for total effect by bringing the music to the edge of cacophony—and therefore rocking to the tenth power—Brian seemed to prefer audio clarity. His production method was to spread out the sound and arrangement, giving the music a more lush, comfortable feel. (Priore, 29)

As a response to the Beatles' *Rubber Soul* (1965), Brian created his pop masterpiece *Pet Sounds* (1966), an epic achievement in which Brian used a "bewildering array of resources, more than Spector and the equally iconoclastic Burt Bacharach combined" (de Forest). Wilson brought the notion of the Beatles album of complete polished songs to its next level with the influence of Spector's production standards, creating a complete studio album with great songs, performances, and production, and making the album the true focus of the pop and rock artist. In *Pet Sounds*, Brian fully realized Spector's vision of the "pop symphony" (Pinnock). "Wilson considers *Pet Sounds* to be a concept album centered around interpretations of Phil Spector's recording methods and by doing so he captured the essence of modern culture" (Moorefield, 16). Rolling Stones manager and Spector admirer Andrew

"Loog" Oldham even took out a full-page ad in *Melody Maker*, encouraging everyone to buy it and calling it the "greatest album ever."

With his next project *Smile* (1967), he attempted to create what he called "a teenage symphony to God" and continued to emulate Spector's use of large ensembles; he also expanded his use of exotic instruments, or traditional instruments played or recorded in unlikely ways (Ames Carlin, 81). Though Brian did not realize his vision completely with *Smile*, the tracks he completed for the album, such as "Good Vibrations," "Heroes and Villains," "Surf's Up," and "Our Prayer," give a good indication of just what Brian was trying for. "Good Vibrations" was probably the pinnacle of his achievements. Peter Ames Carlin described "Good Vibrations" as a psychedelic about the nonverbal communication between people. The song transcends Spector in moving into a more spiritual dimension both musically and lyrically (Ames Carlin, 84–106).

The spark of inspiration taken from Spector's records gave Wilson the creative impulse to push the boundaries of the pop genre, inspiring songwriters and musicians from the Beatles to Leonard Bernstein (*Inside Pop*). The Byrds' Roger McGuinn describes to Mark Dillon the effect Brian's Spector-inspired music had on his own group:

> Just as Brian would play "Be My Baby" every day, McGuinn was similarly taken with The Beach Boys. "I remember listening to 'Don't Worry Baby' and 'God Only Knows' just about every morning." . . . "It was really inspirational. It was almost like going to church." . . . McGuinn recalls [Terry] Melcher telling drummer [Hal] Blaine to "get the feel like 'Don't Worry Baby'" [for "Mr. Tambourine Man"]. . . . The jerky guitar chord that appears in the instrumental break in "Don't Worry Baby" runs throughout "Mr. Tambourine Man." (Dillon, 31)

THE BEATLES

Though hugely influenced by many of the male rock 'n' rollers of the 1950s, the pop music of Spector and the girl groups of the early sixties also had a big impact on the Beatles' sound; the group was often praised for being so adept at "adapting songs by US girl groups" (Clayson, 99, 105). In total the Beatles included five girl group covers on studio albums, which was the most covers they included by any particular group of artists, and they covered at least seven girl group songs for their live set. Although Spector's girl groups were not directly represented in this set, his earlier Teddy Bears track "To Know Him Is to Love Him" was covered by them in their Hamburg days and was recorded for their Decca audition in January 1962 but wasn't released until 1994 with their *Live at the BBC* sessions. The group was also a big fan of the Brill Building songwriters who provided Spector with most of his songs. "Not only did they base their harmony sound on that of black girl groups like the Shirelles," wrote Stephen Barnard in his *Illustrated History*, but also "they modeled their earliest songwriting efforts on the work of Gerry Goffin and Carole King, master suppliers of girl group material. Their lyrics followed the conversational mode by Goffin in songs like 'Don't Say Nothing Bad About My Baby'" (Barnard, 62).

While the Shirelles had altered lead vocals on some of their earlier songs, Spector would alter the lead vocals on nearly all the Crystals' recordings; the first few singles were being sung by Barbara Alston, the next few by Darlene Love, and then finally a third singer, "La La" Brooks. The fact that the tonal character of the voice changed for the same group; that the girls formed themselves as a unit as opposed to a lead singer and a backing band; and that the girls all wore the same outfit helped to fashion this concept of a uniform male group with different vocalists for different songs, which is what made the Beatles unique.

While some of John Lennon's earlier ballads were inspired by Spector's work with the Paris Sisters, other songs attempted to capture Spector's raucous Wall of Sound, particularly those of the Ronettes. Lennon's composition "Tell Me Why" echoes the Ronettes' "The Best Part of Breaking Up" and was Lennon's attempt at "a black New York girl group song" (Spitz, 489). Lennon also covered "Be My Baby" on his *Rock & Roll* album in 1975 as well as recording a cover of "To Know Him Is to Love Him'" (retitled "To Know Her Is to Love Her") but with a Wall of Sound approach, which Spector had not yet developed for the original Teddy Bears' version. At the same sessions, though, it wasn't released until the compilation *Menlove Ave.* album in 1986. The opening track to this album, "Here We Go Again," was incidentally cowritten and produced by Spector.

Lennon's "All You Need Is Love" directly borrows its opening line from Spector's recording of Arlene Smith's "Love Love Love" (though the Vandellas' "Love Makes Me Do Foolish Things" is also a strong influence). And his "Merry Xmas (War Is Over)" is virtually Spector's Wall of Sound infused with the melody to "I Love How You Love Me" (Du Noyer, *John Lennon*, 536). McCartney, always keen to mimic his idols, also borrowed Spector's heavy, reverberated sound for his track "That Means a Lot," which unfortunately didn't see the light of day until the *Beatles Anthology* was released some thirty years after the song was first recorded.

Spector's involvement and effect on the Beatles is much broader than this and is covered in a separate chapter (chapter 9), but it is significant to point out that from a cultural point of view, the Beatles had absorbed the sensibilities of the girl group sound and look and mixed it effectively with the rock 'n' roll roughness of Elvis and Chuck Berry, creating an androgyny that would allow women a more active involvement in modern culture as well as allowing young boys a means in which to explore the feminine elements of their psyche. Susan Douglas claims,

> That drawing from the rock 'n' roll of Berry and Little Richard as well as from the "soft" call-and-response layered harmony styles of the girl groups, the Beatles pushed the conventional musical codes of masculinity and femininity up against each other in a way that evoked making love with your clothes on. . . . John's gravelly voice led in to falsetto cries suggesting that male sexuality wasn't so threatening, female sexuality was perfectly normal, and the two could exist together harmoniously. (S. Douglas, *Where the Girls Are*, 117)

THE ROLLING STONES

The Rolling Stones, though not traditionally associated with the pop music of Spector, owe a great debt to him for their early success, particularly since their initial manager and producer Andrew Oldham was totally in awe of Phil Spector, seeing him as the physical embodiment of his childhood idols: the fictional hustlers Sidney Falco in Alexander MacKendrick's *Sweet Smell of Success* (1957) and Wolf Mankowitz's

Johnny Jackson in *Expresso Bongo* (1959). "It was Falco's unapologetic zest for the Hustle that I loved," wrote Oldham in his book *Stone Free*.

Oldham was "Britain's answer to Spector," and as Spector represented the new breed of music producer in America, Oldham, adapting Spector's combined "auras of recording genius and a gangster," was a totally new kind of manager in Britain:

> Before Oldham, managers . . . had been older men with no interest in the music beyond what it might earn them, and no empathy with their young charges or with teenagers generally. . . . Oldham was the first manager to be the same age as his charges, to speak their language, share their outlook, mirror their rampant heterosexuality, and seem motivated by their collective ideals as much as by financial gain. While engineering managerial coups that, at the outset, seemed little short of magical, he was naturally and undisputedly one of the band. (Norman, *Mick Jagger*, 92)

Like Spector, Oldham craved stardom. "To be sure in his egotism, arrogance, grandiosity, self-indulgence and lack of self-control he was far more like a modern rock star than any of them, especially Mick" (Norman, *Mick Jagger*, 179). It was an attitude that would influence other hustlers of the music industry, particularly Sex Pistols manager Malcolm McLaren.

Oldham was not only impressed by Spector's business acumen when dealing with the music industry executives but he was also a huge fan of Spector's music. "He had this little machine in his car that played singles. He kept playing me the Crystals and the Ronettes, day after day," remembered his friend Dave Berry (Oldham, *Stoned*, 267–69). Oldham also tried, though unsuccessfully, to emulate Spector's production style on the Rolling Stones records, and before applying the Wall of Sound to the Stones, he made a few precautionary experiments with other artists. He recorded a version of "To Know Him Is to Love Him" with Cleo Sylvestre and versions of "Then He Kissed Me" and "Da Doo Ron Ron" with the Andrew "Loog" Oldham Orchestra, with the latter including Mick Jagger on vocals. As much as Oldham tried to reproduce Spector's Wall of Sound (Norman, *Mick Jagger*, 131) with the Stones' more R&B influence, he instead created what Bill Wyman later called his "wall of noise," referring to Oldham's incompetent job of recording and producing the group's early work. Stones expert Martin Elliott pointed out that

Oldham "seemed to be determined to construct a British mirror image of the Phil Spector success story" (Elliott, 50).

Following the success of their Lennon and McCartney–penned "I Wanna Be Your Man," the Stones were struggling to do anything creative in the studio, so Oldham called on the help of Spector and songwriter Gene Pitney, who had written Spector's hit "He's a Rebel" (Davis, 77). Spector more or less wrote "Little by Little," the B-side to "Not Fade Away," while effectively producing the two tracks. The Stones and Spector also recorded two other songs: "And Mr. Spector and Mr. Pitney Came Too" and "Andrew's Blues," a "pornographic monologue by Spector dedicated to his British disciple in chief" (Norman, *Mick Jagger*, 131). While "Tell Me" was clearly inspired by the commercial success of the Beatles songs, the production was another attempt at reproducing the Spector sound, the heavy reverb on Jagger's vocal being a good example. Spector would also later play bass on "Play with Fire," while his sidekick Jack Nitzsche played keyboards, harpsichord, and piano, with only Jagger and Keith Richards contributing anything from the Stones (Davis, 116). Spector also suggested that the Stones capture an authentic blues sound by recording in Chicago, the home of their blues heroes (Davis, 90).

With help and advice from Spector, Andrew Oldham set up his own independent record label, Immediate Records, to which he signed the McCoys, Fleetwood Mac, Rod Stewart, the Nice, and the Small Faces; the label's slogan, "happy to be part of the industry of human happiness," was inspired by Spector's records label slogan, which boasted "Tomorrow's Sound Today."

Spector's girl group sound along with the upbeat soul sound of Motown would come to play a key role in providing the soundtrack for the elitist mod culture that would emerge in the early sixties. Spector's thrilling Wall of Sound productions fitted into this lifestyle, and so groups such as the Crystals and the Ronettes became a large part of the soundtrack of the mods lifestyle. The Rolling Stones would come to be seen as representatives of this new breed in the UK, and individuals such as Oldham came to represent the quintessential mod with his excessive lifestyle and go-getter hustler attitude, an attitude epitomized in Oldham's eyes by Phil Spector.

THE WHO

The British mod band the Who had a sound that was not too similar to that of any girl groups, unlike mod revivalists the Jam that, a decade later, unashamedly borrowed much from the girl group genre. The group did, however, include the Vandellas' track "Heat Wave" into their live set as well as the classic "Dancing in the Street" in the late seventies, where the opening drumbeat of their version references "Be My Baby."

As the Who became more successful, they began to explore the possibilities of new musical forms and recording techniques outside of their R&B roots. The group's principal songwriter and musical director Pete Townshend pushed the boundaries of the single and the album to its limits, incorporating ideas from his art college days, and their stage act became an expression of New Wave art ideas, particularly the Futurists, who attempted to dismantle the conventions of art. In terms of their songwriting and production approach, the group followed on from the psychedelic ideas that had begun to emerge during the mid-1960s, particularly the ideas of Wilson's *Pet Sounds* and the Beatles' *Sgt. Pepper's Lonely Hearts Club Band* to create what became known as rock opera.

However, without the impact of Spector's Wagnerian-style production on pop music of the 1960s, Townshend most likely wouldn't have been able to conceive of his rock operas, which often employ the same bombastic elements as in Spector's productions (think of the dramatic timpani over the weighty piano chords and sound effects of rain pouring down at the opening of "Love Reign over Me"). There's also the use of leitmotifs in *Quadrophenia* (1973) and the dramatic buildup toward the near Wall of Sound at the end of the album. Spector's influence can be felt as well in Townshend's writing, as the riff to "Then He Kissed Me" is referenced on the track "Smash the Mirror" in their rock opera *Tommy* (1969). And he uses Spector-type arrangements in sections of "A Quick One while He's Away" and Wilson/Spectoresque *Pet Sounds* influence on both *Tommy* and *The Who Sell Out* (1967). The use of falsetto throughout *The Who Sell Out*, particularly in songs such as "Our Love Was" and "Sunrise," blend elements of masculine and feminine, in other words a blend of girl group pop with the raucous sound of rock 'n' roll. The band would also acknowledge Spector's influence when they included "Be My Baby" and "Da Doo Ron Ron" in their mod-inspired film *Quadrophenia* (1979).

The Action was another mod-influenced band of the mid 1960s whose lead singer, Reg King, was considered by some to be one of the few great white soul singers of the time. The group, though produced by Beatles producer George Martin, achieved little success but did become inspirational to a number of bands in the 1970s, bands that wanted to merge the soul sound of the 1960s with the raw sound of punk. King's band covered a number of girl group songs including the Ronettes' "Do I Love You" and "You Baby" ("The Action").

The American pop trio the Walker Brothers also adopted Spector's Wall of Sound with great success, most significantly with their Frankie Valli cover "The Sun Ain't Gonna Shine Anymore," as well as employing it on "Make It Easy on Yourself" and their cover of the Ronettes' "Walking in the Rain."

MOTOWN

Motown founder Berry Gordy knew that if black music could be popularized he could have a very successful operation with his Motown record label. After Spector's success with his black artists with mainstream white audiences, Gordy purposely moved away from the traditional black sounds of R&B and adopted the white sound and style of the Brill Building in order to "cut across barriers" (Stanley, 187).

Before Motown really found its feet, most of its material borrowed from the Brill Building formula, while early songs by the company's most prized songwriting team, Holland-Dozier-Holland, experimented with Spector's signature sound with songs such as the Marvelettes' (aka the Darnells for these records) "Too Hurt to Cry, Too Much in Love to Say Goodbye." Though the Wall of Sound was abandoned by the HDH team, their compositions, particularly for the Supremes, were definitely influenced by the pop formula of Spector, particularly the use of strings to sweeten and uplift the songs.

Apart from the musical influence, Gordy adopted a similar business approach to Spector for making the label the brand rather than promoting particular artists, although the individual acts would capture more of the spotlight at certain times, and the Supremes would attract more

attention than nearly all the other acts put together. During the midsixties, it was the overall formula sound of Motown that was the focus and
that sold. Acts were groomed to be Motown artists, and like Spector the
same musicians (the Funk Brothers and backing singers, the Andantes,
who were often used to sweeten, if not cover up, flaws in the main
vocal) were utilized for the purpose of continuity and conformity.

SPECTOR THROUGH THE SEVENTIES: BRUCE SPRINGSTEEN

Bruce Springsteen began his musical career in the vein of Bob Dylan
and Van Morrison. The social realism of Dylan and the harsh, gritty
vocal delivery of Morrison characterized his early records, but Springsteen also had ambitions that lay beyond emulating just two of his idols.
He was intent on merging all the elements of rock 'n' roll that were
defined by the music he had grown up with.

Springsteen was ambitious enough to attempt to roll all his musical
influences into one landmark album, which would compress the whole
culture of rock 'n' roll since its inception with Elvis Presley through to
American soul and British-based R&B, as played by the Beatles and the
Rolling Stones. He centered this musical landscape around a Dyla-
nesque lyrical style that depicted the struggle of the American working
class but colored by the epic grandeur of Spector's Wall of Sound.
"Springsteen was set on making the great American album—the soaring
vocals of Orbison, the poetry of Dylan, the guitar of Duane Eddy and
the sonic textures of Spector" (Kirkpatrick, 40).

The single "Born to Run" was to be the main commercial vehicle for
the album, and Springsteen's producer Mike Appel purposely sought
out Jeff Barry to discover some of Spector's production tricks, with the
hope that they could create for the song an atmosphere as thrilling and
exciting as Spector had done for "Be My Baby" and "Da Doo Ron Ron"
over a decade earlier. Spector's onetime engineer Jimmy Iovine was
also brought in, and together Springsteen, Appel, and Iovine created a
Wall of Sound that included layered guitar tracks, sustained pianos,
"heavy echo and reverb," and even a "Spectorish glockenspiel" (Kirkpatrick, 41). Ultimately, the trio managed to produce something that
would get as close to Spector as anyone else had attempted, and Spring-

steen, for all his earlier attempts to capture America's imagination, had produced a virtual rock classic. "Born to Run" became Springsteen's magnum opus—an effectively innovative reworking of Spector's approach that chimed perfectly with its time and that Spector biographer Richard Williams colorfully described as being "like a hot rod running on melted-down Crystals records" (R. Williams, *Phil Spector*, 18).

PUNK, NEW WAVE, AND GLAM ROCK

When rock 'n' roll made it possible for even those with little musical talent to make it big, the New York Dolls set out to claim their place in the sun. They blended the showmanship of the Stones with an androgynous image and sound of the New York girl groups. The Dolls looked to the studio techniques of Spector to capture for them a commercial record that would be as outlandish and bombastic as their look and attitude. Unfortunately, the Spector collaboration never worked out, and the band finally settled for two Spector-influenced producers— Todd Rundgren and Shadow Morton.

It was, however, the Morton-produced second album *Too Much Too Soon* (1974) that more closely resembles the sound of the girl groups than does their Rundgren-produced debut. Morton had styled his productions of New York girl group the Shangri-Las on Spector's record-making approach and even borrowed themes already made popular by Spector in his songs, particularly the theme of the lone, misunderstood biker in "Leader of the Pack." Morton worked with Spector's songwriting partners Ellie Greenwich and Jeff Barry, and together they picked up where they and Spector had left off. Morton then styled the Dolls around the same formula.

Too Much Too Soon borrows heavily from the girl group sound with its layered doo-wop-style backing vocals and rich female voices that harmonize on many of the tracks. Nina Antonia describes, in her biography of the group, how the "'oohs' and 'woawoahs' recalled sixties girl groups," while guitarist Sylvain Sylvain's "teen angel background vocals" and singer David Johansen's "imaginative flaky lyrics evoke Dolly locations and emotions" (Antonia, 81).

The approach of the Dolls to capture the immediacy of the girl group sound and early rock 'n' roll as a counterattack to the pretentiousness of the current music styles was something that the next generation of teenagers and new musical hopefuls instinctively felt was the way forward. The Dolls had little success commercially but ultimately awoke the next generation of kids up to the fact that they didn't need to be musical virtuosos to play rock 'n' roll.

New York groups such as the Ramones, Blondie, and many of the CBGB bands formed out of the encouragement they garnered from the New York Dolls, and both the Ramones and Blondie took a similar approach to the Dolls in attempting to capture something of what had been lost in the early days of rock 'n' roll. Both groups used much of Spector's girl group pop sensibilities in their overall sound, and in some ways both groups were an extension of the girl group formulae.

Blondie's first incarnation was a girl group called the Stilettos, "a combination of the aggressive Shangri-Las rock and the round, solid vocals of the R&B girl groups" (Porter and Needs, 47). Being from New York, the New York girl groups informed them with a style and attitude, and much of the language of, Debbie Harry's earlier compositions, as well as her overall look, adapted from girl group language. As well, they used the language of pop culture of the 1950s and early 1960s, which made the early Blondie work sound slightly kitsch and more self-conscious than the previous generations' use of it. Writer Everett True suggests as much, saying, "If songs like 'Heart of Glass,' 'Call Me' and 'Atomic' hadn't achieved success, Blondie's first three albums would be held up today as prime examples of post-60s girl group garage pop" (True, 35). And DJ Rodney Bingenheimer termed Blondie "the punk Ronettes" (Che, 49).

Spector's larger-than-life productions of pure pop sensibility appealed strongly to Harry's idea of fun, while she saw herself and her boyfriend, Chris Stein, as forming a similar type of songwriting partnership to Spector's married songwriting teams Greenwich and Barry, and Goffin and King. Harry and Stein's successful partnership as songwriters and performers signified how the music of the time had changed over a decade. Harry and Stein had come into the era of self-contained songwriter and performer, via the careers of Brian Wilson, Bob Dylan, and the Beatles. Blondie had taken the girl group sound, attitude, and female vocal into the era of punk rock.

Spector had offered to produce Blondie, obviously seeing something in Harry that reminded him of his success with his own girl groups, particularly the Ronettes, as Harry's punk attitude reflected a similar attitude that the Ronettes had expressed a decade earlier. Harry and her group, however, turned Spector down and instead formed a musical alliance with the girl group producer Richard Gottehrer, who had scored a big hit with the group the Angels and their song "My Boyfriend's Back," which incidentally had kept Spector's first release for his new group the Ronettes off the top spot. The Angels, however, had a slightly edgier and less romantic attitude than Spector's girl groups, who were "less threatening to the male ego," as Jay Warner had suggested in *American Singing Groups: A History from 1940s to Today* (Warner, 79). Harry had intentionally set out to be more threatening than many of the previous generations' girl performers. She declined Spector's offer to record her group, possibly because she was aware of the control he might try to impose on her; she was a forward-looking feminist who wanted control over her own life and artistic creations, or possibly she simply recognized that Spector had passed his peak.

The Ramones were another rock 'n' roll group that had been greatly inspired by the pop music of Spector, as well as the earlier rock 'n' roll that had influenced the New York Dolls and Blondie. They were determined to reawaken the simplistic approach of early 1960s pop records, such as those made by Phil Spector.

Spector had been introduced to the Ramones in the midseventies by Barney Kessel's sons, who saw them as the new Beatles. And at the turn of the eighties, as they struggled over the next few years to make any considerable impact on the record-buying public, they approached Spector with the intention of him producing an album that would give them the commercial success they hoped for and that they felt was well overdue. The Ramones' involvement with Spector is covered in more detail in chapter 10.

ROY WOOD, TODD RUNDGREN, AND JIM STEINMAN

George Harrison, Brian Wilson, and Bruce Springsteen were all very taken by Ronnie Spector and wrote and recorded songs for her. Springsteen would rewrite "You Mean So Much to Me" for her, while Wilson had written "Don't Worry Baby," and Harrison had penned a number of tracks including "Try Some Buy Some," which Spector had produced as an attempted comeback for her. The record did not achieve for her a second chance at success but did make a dramatic impact on one David Bowie, who admitted, "I love this song so much; it made me fall in love with the singer . . . my heart went out to her" (Pegg, 238). Bowie had initially caught the attention of pop music lovers with his unique brand of glam rock—a sound that allowed the charts to be recolonized by a teenage consumer culture for the first time in a decade—and a genre of pop music in which Bowie first made a profound impact, infused with a generous dose of gender bending. He had originally planned to include the song "Try Some Buy Some," which he had made part of his live set, on his aborted *Pin Ups 2* album of covers, though he eventually featured it on his 2002 album *Reality* (Buskin). Earlier songs such as "Teenage Wild Life" featured engineer Chris Porter, Tony Visconti, and Lynn Maitland to provide what Visconti described as "the Ronettes-type backing vocals" (Pegg, 229). While Bowie undoubtedly had drawn inspiration for his musical ideas from everywhere, including Spector, the original "grandfather" of glam rock, Roy Wood had deliberately set out to recapture the essence of Spector's sound.

Roy Wood began his music career as the guitarist, vocalist, songwriter, and the musical driving force behind British group the Move, delving into a variety of different pop and rock genres that were typically British in style and nature. When Wood changed his musical direction to incorporate elements of classical music, he was impelled to form a new group, ELO, with Jeff Lynne. Wood and Lynne wanted to expand pop's musical palate in the manner in which the Beatles had done, and by layering overdubs of numerous cello parts on their first recording, "10538 Overture," Wood had essentially adopted Spector's Wall of Sound.

Unfortunately, due to disagreements with the direction ELO should take, Wood left to form what would become the start of a new form of popular rock, bringing with it an immediacy that paralleled the exuberance of the early 1960s. Wood's new group, Wizzard, was Spectorscopic, employing two drummers, two sax players, and two cellists: "He was about to become the Grandfather of Glam . . . a Brummie fusion of Rock 'n' Roll and Phil Spector's Wall of Sound. The seventies started when Wizzard released their first single 'Ball Park Incident' . . . an epiphany akin to Jesus walking on the water and turning it into wine. Here was the past and the future all rolled into one" (Gallagher).

With songs such as "Ball Park Incident," "See My Baby Jive," and "Angel Fingers," Wood moved toward a style that was typically American. The songs referenced American girl groups, and Wood employed Spector's technique of layered instruments and percussion. The music also expressed the same warmth that Spector had expertly captured at the height of his creativity; however, since Wood had essentially gone back in time with his Wizzard project, the songs essentially became nothing more than novelties and more a vehicle for Wood to display his expertise at imitation, covering an array of different pop styles and genres, rather than creating something unique (McGee).

Though still content to imitate (expertly though, it must be said) rather than create something unique, in 1973, Wood went further than anyone since Spector in capturing the spirit of Christmas on record with the Christmas classic "I Wish It Could Be Christmas Everyday": "I'd been thinking how it had been ages since anyone had done a decent rock 'n' roll Christmas record. Phil Spector . . . was probably the last. Initially I considered doing something stripped down and folky for a solo album, but then I thought if it was good enough for Spector it was good enough for Wizzard" (Staunton).

Coming from a similar background to Wood were two other prodigious musicians/producers who were essentially weaned on the music of Spector: Jim Steinman and Todd Rundgren. Steinman was only eight years Spector's junior and grew up a teenager in 1960s New York. He was the typical target audience for Spector's teen-oriented music, and so it is no wonder that Steinman would go on to write music with a similar bombastic, Wagnerian feel to it. This music would both ideally suit the big dramatic/operatic voice of his most celebrated collaborator, Michael Lee Aday, better known as Meat Loaf, and fit perfectly into an era in which rock opera would come to dominate the musical landscape.

Steinman's most famous work, *Bat Out of Hell* (1977), can certainly be compared to Springsteen's Wall of Sound–inspired production *Born to Run* (*Classic Albums*). The album's title track certainly draws similarities with Springsteen, the feel and themes of which echo Springsteen's work. Although more possibly the album is an antithesis to Spector's idealism, the big sound of Spector is heard throughout the album. The motorbike sounds that are heard toward the end of the album's title track, and that indicate the imminent crash of the song's hero, are drawn from the inspiration of another Spector admirer and imitator:

Shadow Morton. As well as Spector, Steinman was highly influenced by
the tragic country songs of Hank Williams and the "death disc" shock-
ers, such as Ray Peterson's "Tell Laura I Love Her," the Shangri-Las'
"Leader of the Pack," and the "rural suburban teenage angst" of Bruce
Springsteen. Steinman wanted to write the "most extreme crash song of
all time." "There is something so thrilling to me," he once said, "about
that operatic narrative that involves a cataclysmic event, especially one
so perfectly in tune with a teenager's world, and rock 'n' roll, as a car or
motorcycle crash" (*Classic Albums*).

"Bat out of Hell," suggests writer Tom Quirk, in his curiously titled
book *Endlessly Horny for Wonder and Magic: How Jim Steinman's
"Bat out of Hell" Perfectly Captured the Pre-Pubescent American Id
(and Nearly Ruined Me for Life)*, sounds like "Phil Spector producing
Bruce Springsteen covering the Who, only a lot more bombastic"
(Quirk, 4). Just like Spector, Steinman claims to be as equally influenced by Wagner and rock 'n' roll and tried desperately, as did many of
his generation, to recapture the magic of the sixties. Considering again
Steinman's music, Quirk suggests, "Its roots were the same as punk
rock though in many ways it was the antithesis of it" (Quirk, 4).

As with Springsteen's "Born to Run," Steinman brought in Spector's
onetime engineer Jimmy Iovine for his *Dead Ringer* (1981) album,
most probably, as with Springsteen, to try to source some of the Spector
magic. Later in his career Steinman would replace Spector on the Celine Dion album *Falling into You* (1996) after Spector became disinter-
ested in the project. Steinman attempted a version of Spector's "River
Deep, Mountain High," but the end result is synthetic and crass, lacking the innovation of the Spector original. Spector was far from flattering of Steinman's efforts, however, calling Steinman a "bad clone of
yours truly," but Steinman famously responded to the slight by saying,
"I'm thrilled to be insulted by Phil Spector. He's my God, my idol. To
be insulted by Phil Spector is a big honor. If he spits on me I consider
myself purified" (Steinman). This is an obvious indication of just how in
awe of Spector Steinman was.

Todd Rundgren, an exceptionally gifted multi-instrumentalist, like
Wood was eager to display his skills at mimicry in terms of both composition and production. Rundgren was hired as a substitute to Roy Wood
to provide a Spectoresque production to the New York Dolls' debut
album, which fused Brill Building–type songs, rock 'n' roll, and girl

group "teen alienation" (Antonia, 81). Sometime later, possibly for the same reason, he became Steinman's producer on the *Bat out of Hell* album and applied a particularly effective Wall of Sound approach to it, even referencing the iconic drumbeat from "Be My Baby" on the album's second track, "You Took the Words Right out of My Mouth," while the handclaps at the end of the track are a nod to the girl group productions of the early sixties.

FROM THE 1980S TO TODAY

While the 1980s experienced a revival of girl groups, many of which borrowed from their sixties counterparts, a number of male bands also found their sound or at least part of their sound in the sixties girls groups. The Scottish band the Jesus and Mary Chain's debut album *Psychocandy* (1982) opens with a reference to Hal Blaine's opening drum pattern for "Be My Baby." Such an action emulates both seminal British and U.S. punk bands the Damned and the New York Dolls, who also referenced girl groups at the start of their records. Groups such as the Cocteau Twins and Teenage Fanclub, and current noise pop outfits like the Raveonettes (even the name suggests Spector's girl groups from the sixties), all claim Spector's influence on their music (Hochman).

One of the most successful and influential bands of the 1980s, the Smiths, also owes a debt to Spector and his girl group sound. After seeing a *South Bank Show* (a British TV show) special on the songwriting team of Jerry Leiber and Mike Stoller, the band's guitarist Johnny Marr decided he wanted to become one member of a top-class songwriting partnership (Fletcher, *Light That Never*, 3). Although influenced by many singers and groups, including Patti Smith and Neil Young, Marr's main influences were drawn from the songwriting teams of Phil Spector's Brill Building songwriters (Fletcher, *Light That Never*, 191).

If Marr had been drawn to the girl group sound and those songwriters who had chosen to write for them, it was primarily from a purely musical perspective. Marr was fascinated with the structures of songwriting, the harmonic structures over which moving melodies could be constructed. He was also interested in sound, and so the sonic elements of the arrangements as well as the production quality of the records, particularly with the Spector records, also drew him toward this style. "Holding Phil Spector as one of his main influences," Marr has expressed that "I wanted my guitar to sound like a whole record" (Devereux, Dillane, and Power, 45). So many of the string arrangements and the multilayering of guitars owe their gratitude to Spector's Wall of Sound (Morrissey).

While Marr had been seduced by the musical and production values of the girl groups, and their songwriters and producers, the Smiths' enigmatic front man Morrissey had interests in these groups and songwriting themes that were more to do with the overall aesthetics of the period as well as the social and fashion aspects from which the girl groups drew their inspirations. Morrissey felt an affinity with the tragedy of the themes expressed by many of the girl groups.

According to Len Brown, in *Meetings with Morrissey*, female singers appealed to Morrissey more than the male singers of the sixties: "Female singers seemed to be risking and that's what made them so dramatic and interesting to me. It seemed better to open your heart and throw it away" (L. Brown, 202).

Morrissey intrinsically understood how the female singers were plucked, mostly by opportunistic figures such as Phil Spector, from various social strata at a time when the swinging sixties hit factories had no shortage of eager young girls waiting for their big break. They thus "approached the material they were given with a singular passion, throwing themselves into every song with the full knowledge that their careers depended on it" (Fletcher, *Light That Never*, 59).

Over the last twenty years, girl groups have once again dominated the pop charts. While the late eighties and early nineties saw the British charts being taken over by Spector-like producers Mike Stock, Matt Aitken, and Pete Waterman, more recent girl groups and girl bands today have carried over some of Spector's influence. Groups such as the Spice Girls, Girls Aloud, Destiny's Child, and the Pussycat Dolls, as well as the alternative groups like the Pipettes, Vivian Girls, and the Dum Dum Girls, derive a sound from the sixties girl groups and particularly Spector's Wall of Sound. One of these modern female singers who particularly stands out as a true inspiration from the Spector girl group era is Amy Winehouse.

It was when she discovered the Shangri-Las and their heartrending paeans that Winehouse began to feel a strong association with the girl group sounds of the sixties. Her newfound love affair with Blake Fielder Civil developed around her newfound love of sixties music, and both inspired her second album *Back to Black* (2006). Nick Johnstone suggest the songs from the album, such as "Rehab," display touches of the Vandellas' "Nowhere to Run," the Angels' "My Boyfriend's Back," the Ronettes' "Recipe for Love," and the Shirelles (Johnstone, 82), while most reviews compared the album to Motown and sixties girl groups. "Amy comes across like Dinah Washington crossed with 1960s girl group the Ronettes," wrote Jamie Hackim (Newkey-Burden, 81). The brass, rhythms, and overall sound of tracks such as "Rehab," "Back to Black," and "Tears Dry on Their Own," as Johnstone suggests, are Motown blended with a "Spector chemistry," while coproducer Mark Ronson, who used sixties-styled vocal group the Dap-Kings, as well as authentic sixties studio equipment and recording techniques, re-created a classic sixties girl group sound for Winehouse.

Amy adapted the familiar and very popular look of the beehive, stilettos, and miniskirt, modernizing it with tattoos and piercings. She became a twenty-first-century Ronnie Spector; even Ronnie herself thought it was her when she first saw a picture of Winehouse. By a mixture of natural evolution and specific tailoring to suit a certain image that she wanted to portray to the press, Amy brought a Spector-influenced girl group sound and image back to public awareness; it rekindled Ronnie Spector's career and early girl group songs. "To Know Him Is to Love Him" and "Be My Baby" became favorites again.

SPECTOR IN THE MOVIES

Though sound was predominately Spector's arena, and it was mainly musicians and other music producers that were mostly inspired by Spector, filmmakers such as Martin Scorsese found that Spector's music could also be used as an effective enhancement of their visual medium.

In Scorsese's film *Goodfellas* (1990), he uses three Spector productions, "Christmas (Baby, Please Come Home)," "He's Sure the Boy I Love," and "Then He Kissed Me," to heighten the atmosphere of particular scenes. In his first major motion picture, *Mean Streets* (1973), Scorsese opens the film with the Ronettes' "Be My Baby," in an effort to capture the essence of a New York Italian American neighborhood, while simultaneously creating the necessary impact to engage the audience from the beginning. Whether, as Spector claims he made Scorsese's, Robert De Niro's, and Harvey Keitel's careers because he allowed them to release the film, even though they had not sought permission to use the music, is questionable, though certainly a serious point of contention (Jayanti). However, as with *Goodfellas*, Scorsese certainly recognized the importance of the right music to enhance the visual images, and Spector's recordings lent themselves wonderfully to these movies, greatly enhancing their visual aspects in a similar way that the classical and avant-garde pieces in Stanley Kubrick's *2001: A Space Odyssey* (1968), for example, also did.

Chris Columbus's *Adventures in Babysitting* (1987) opens with Spector's classic "Then He Kissed Me," once again setting the mood for a teenage romantic comedy, similar to the feelings and moods felt by those teenagers during Spector's reign in the sixties. Other "brat pack"–type movies of the eighties also used Spector's teenage pop symphonies to create a believable emotional reality of teenagers for teenagers. Films such as *The Big Wednesday* (1978), *Quadrophenia* (1979), *Stripes* (1981), *Sixteen Candles* (1984), *Little Shop of Horrors* (1986), and *The Pick-Up Artist* (1987) all use Spector's music with some kind of enhancement. But it is Tony Scott's use of Spector's much-admired "You've Lost That Lovin' Feelin'" in *Top Gun* (1986) that not only created one of the film's most memorable scenes, in which Tom Cruise's character makes an horrendous attempt to serenade Kelly McGillis, but also helped in making Tom Cruise a household name. The 1987 teen movie *Dirty Dancing* would also feature Spector's "Be My Baby" as its focal point, making a huge hit of the movie and transforming Patrick Swayze from a capable actor into a movie star with a tremendous box office draw.

While many directors employed a soundtrack of Spector's songs to enhance the emotional impact of their films, others took Spector's infamous personality, at least as it had been portrayed in the media, as a point of inspiration for their distorted fictional characters. Russ Meyer's bizarre, gun-wielding Ronnie "Z-Man" Barzell in *Beyond the Valley of the Dolls* (1970; the film uncannily includes a scene in which "Z-Man" puts a gun in a girl's mouth and shoots her brains out) and Brian De Palma's unscrupulous character Swan in *Phantom of Paradise* (1974) are good examples. More recently, the animated TV series *Metaloca-lypse* (2006–2013) also featured a character, Dick "Magic Ears" Knub-bler, that resembled Spector's public persona.

Other films have felt the need to show the significance and influence of Spector in the biographies of individuals such as Brian Wilson in the movie *Love and Mercy* (2014; the role of Spector was played by Jona-than Slavin, but his one scene in the movie never made the final cut); Sonny and Cher in the TV movie *And the Beat Goes On: The Sonny and Cher Story* (1999); the biopic of Tina Turner in *Tina: What's Love Got to Do with It* (1993); John Lennon's history with Yoko Ono in *John and Yoko: A Love Story* (1985); and the fictional account of the Brill Build-ing enterprise in *Grace of My Heart* (1996), in which John Turturro plays a character very much resembling Spector. Spector would also make an actual appearance in Dennis Hopper's cult classic *Easy Rider* (1969), playing a silent drug dealer. Spector had also agreed to finance an earlier project of Hopper's called *The Last Movie* (1971) but backed out at the last minute, leaving Hopper in the lurch. With the success of *Easy Rider*, Hopper had little trouble finding a backer for the film a few years later.

Most recently, Spector's court case has attracted the attention of filmmakers and writers such as Vikram Jayanti and David Mamet. Both Jayanti's production, *The Agony and the Ecstasy of Phil Spector* (2009), and Mamet's *Phil Spector*, with Al Pacino in the lead, take a very sym-pathetic view of Spector and the circumstance surrounding Lana Clark-son's death. Mamet's tagline for his film "the truth is in the mix," while paying homage to Spector's studio skills, also suggests there is a lot more to the case than what came out in court, or at least the facts as they were presented or interpreted. Mamet and Jayanti are not, howev-er, the only intellectuals to show admiration for Spector's talent. British playwright Tom Stoppard had a 1982 play called *The Real Thing*. Stop-pard's character Henry, a Stoppard stand-in, declares that, while he was producing his dramas, he "was spending the whole time listening to the Crystals singing 'Da Doo Ron Ron' and believing that the Righteous Brothers' recording of 'You've Lost That Lovin' Feelin'" on the London label was possibly the most haunting, the most deeply moving, noise ever produced by the human spirit" (Corliss, "Phil Spector's Greatest Hit").

Along with the films that owe a debt to Spector in one way or another, there are also numerous books based on the character of Spector,
such as in James Robert Baker's 1986 fictional novel *Fuel-Injected
Dreams*. As well, there are articles and biographies on Spector, most
notably Tom Wolfe's "The First Tycoon of Teen"; Mick Brown's *Tearing Down the Wall of Sound*; and the less well known but uniquely
titled *I Was the First Woman Phil Spector Killed*, a collection of essays
by songwriter and Spector's onetime cocollaborator, Beverly Ross.

9

GET BACK

Master and Servant

SPECTOR AND THE BEATLES

After the death of the Beatles' original manager Brian Epstein in August 1967, Allen Klein managed to seduce three of the four Beatles to sign a managerial contract with him. Klein was a hard-nosed businessman who had spent time in prison for tax evasion and had over a short space of time managed to attain control over many of rock 'n' roll's most successful artists, for example Sam Cooke, the Rolling Stones, and Phil Spector. While John Lennon, George Harrison, and Ringo Starr were impressed with Klein's track record, Paul McCartney was distrustful of Klein and instead chose his father-in-law, the American lawyer Lee Eastman, to represent him.

On January 27, 1970, Allen Klein, now in essence the new Beatles manager, offered the major job of editing the Beatles' chaotic "Get Back" material to Phil Spector; this project would later become the album *Let It Be* (Miles, *Beatles*, 367). How Spector came to be involved in the Beatles' project seems to be a rather convoluted affair. According to Beatles guitarist George Harrison, Spector was in England to discuss Harrison's solo album, and Harrison invited him to the studio where Lennon was recording his single "Instant Karma" (*George Harrison*); that ultimately led to him editing the Beatles album. Others claim Spector had requested an opportunity to produce the Beatles, since they

now shared the same manager, Klein, and was actually in London spe-
cifically to discuss involvement in the *Get Back/Let It Be* tapes (Du
Noyer, *John Lennon*, 26) and that it was Lennon who had invited Spec-
tor to "produce" his "Instant Karma" single (M. Brown, 252), which
Beatles expert and friend Barry Miles claims was really an audition for
Spector to do the *Let It Be* album.

Another angle to the story is that Klein, trying to impress Lennon,
said he could get the "great Phil Spector" to mix the "Get Back" material to an acceptable standard (M. Brown, 250). Klein's reasons for ap-
pointing Spector are not clear; maybe he thought Spector was the best
producer to do the job, or possibly he wanted to create a greater rift
between those who had once had an influence over the group, such as
producer George Martin, and get them out of the way, to exert a greater control over the group. But certainly Klein wanted to profit from any
available Beatles material, such as the unfinished "Get Back" album, as
well as the film of the recording.

If Klein, as it appears, was determined to control the Beatles, he was
sadly mistaken, as the Beatles, arguably the most successful entertainers
of the twentieth century, would eventually use the rift over management simply as another excuse to extricate themselves from both their
contractual agreements and what had now become the heavy burden of
being a Beatle.

By whatever means Spector ended up at the "Instant Karma" session, the result, according to Lennon's bass player Klaus Voormann, was
incredible: "He turned up the volume all the way, and we heard the
count in . . . even that sounded incredible. And what followed just blew
us away" (M. Brown, 252). Lennon, continued Voormann, was ecstatic:
"In a few minutes Spector had concocted a fervid, almost claustropho-
bic sound beyond anything the Beatles could have achieved," and he
told Allen Klein he wanted Spector to produce his solo album and
possibly the *Let It Be* record as well (Doggett, *You Never Give*, 115;
Miles, *Beatles*, 367).

Spector, who was now a virtual recluse after the failure of "River
Deep, Mountain High," was ecstatic with the prospect of working with
the "biggest" band in the world. The opportunity was the antidote to his
fading self-belief and the very thing he needed to coax him out of
retirement. For Harrison and Lennon, Spector was a kindred spirit; he
had, like them, "grown up with his ears full of Eddie Cochran and the

Del-Vikings" (R. Williams, "Other Side"), and his early sixties records were a huge inspiration. Working with the "great" Phil Spector was as equally as thrilling a prospect.

LET IT BE

According to Barry Miles, Spector began remixing the *Let It Be* tapes, on March 23, 1970, at both Lennon's and Allen Klein's request, though McCartney was not informed of it (Miles, *Beatles*, 372). Glyn Johns, the engineer for the sessions, had attempted a mix and had a completed album ready for the group's approval on January 5, but none of the Beatles were happy with it. He tried another mix, but still no one was satisfied (Miles, *Beatles*, 374–75; Shapiro, 90).

When Spector came in to mix the sessions, all the recordings were in an abysmal mess, nothing had been cataloged or marked, and Spector was essentially working in the dark as he made his way through hundreds and hundreds of takes and overdubs. It was primarily for reasons such as this that John Lennon claimed, "Phil Spector came in and listened to every take. . . . He listened to about one thousand million miles of tape, which is why the Beatles couldn't face the album. . . . Phil Spector has redone the whole thing and it's beautiful. . . . He was given the shittiest load of badly recorded shit with a lousy feeling to it ever, and he made something out of it" (Miles, *Beatles*, 374–75).

Lennon, even though he thought the recordings were "shitty," was before Spector's involvement fiercely intent on having the unsatisfactory Johns version released, as it would finally burst the bubble of the Beatles myth (Riley, 487–89), something Lennon had become particularly hateful of. The "Get Back" album was to be McCartney's idea of a "honest" album, which he also hoped would appease Lennon's annoyance of the overproduction of their earlier albums (M. Brown, 250).

By the end of the whole saga, however, Spector had turned what was intended to be the rawest of Beatles albums into the "most orchestrated album they ever made," presenting them simply as they were as a band, without studio embellishments and trickery (Shapiro, 92). Despite Spector's efforts, the album was generally considered a disaster, though mostly only by the Beatles' cohorts and music critics.

Unfortunately Spector, who had always entertained a desire to produce the Beatles, was to find himself in the middle of a very awkward situation, not only with the group, in terms of their musical direction, but also with four individuals who felt imprisoned in the corporate entity that was called "the Beatles." Their personal bickering, exacerbated by the Beatles circus; their disagreements with George Martin (Sandford, *McCartney*, 159); their contractual obligations; and the legal battles with external parties that wanted to profit from them, made the whole affair even more complicated for Spector. To add to all this confusion, Spector found himself in the middle of the group's long-standing love affair with the British public, an affair that was becoming more and more strained due to the band's internal problems.

As Glyn Johns had suggested, "It was an unfortunate period in their lives—as a band," and unfortunately Spector became a kind of a "patsy" for their ultimate breakup (Glyn Johns, Rock and Roll Hall of Fame interview, November 19, 2012). The obvious demise of what was Britain's great love affair with the Beatles could not be due, at least in the eyes of their public, to the group, which was by now a British institution considered second only to Shakespeare (Riley, xii). There had to be someone else to blame, somebody at whom the British public could point the finger, namely, Yoko Ono, Allen Klein, or Phil Spector— essentially all non-British figures (Jayanti). According to Spector, it wouldn't really have mattered which American producer had touched the album; the British press would have taken umbrage at the fact that anyone non-British should interfere with their great artists (M. Brown, 254; Ribowsky, 253).

From a strictly musical point of view, a number of criticisms were made against Spector's production. He was criticized mostly for interfering in the Beatles sound, for taking liberties with the recordings, and for applying his Wall of Sound to their raw rock 'n' roll approach, although they had used the studio as much as Spector had done in terms of sonic enhancements. The song that caused the most reaction was McCartney's "Long and Winding Road," where this simple piano ballad "became a production extravaganza with fifty musicians and vocalists overdubbed onto the basic track." McCartney hated the results, complaining that Spector had swamped his work in a Mantovani-style arrangement in which the simplicity of the song's message was lost. Spector's defenders said that he had simply responded to the natural romanticism of the song. McCartney also moaned about the presence of female vocalists on the track, although he had already and would continue to use female vocalists on his records (Miles, *Beatles*, 378; Womack, 275). McCartney would later cite this interference with his work as a key element in his forthcoming lawsuit to formally disband the group (Miles, *Beatles*, 378).

Glyn Johns felt the end result was "disgusting," and George Martin also seemed to have issues with the recordings, but Martin had somehow got his nose out of joint during the previous album's recordings, and relations between the group and him were not so good at this point. George Martin also felt that Spector had overproduced the album (*Nation's Favourite Beatles*) by applying his signature sound to it.

> It would be honest, no overdubbing, no editing, truly live . . . almost amateurish. When John brought in Phil Spector he contradicted what he had said before. When I heard the final sounds I was shaken. They were so uncharacteristic of the clean sounds the Beatles had always used. I was astonished because I knew Paul would never have agreed to it. In fact I contacted him and he said nobody was more surprised than he was. (Miles, *Beatles*, 374)

In addition to the internal squabbling of the group and their imminent breakup, Spector won himself few friends in the manner in which he approached the overdubbing of the album, though possibly if the Beatles, with the exception of Ringo, had turned up to the sessions, Spector may have been easier to work with. Apparently he caused so much confusion and frustration trying to apply his Wall of Sound to the project that Ringo, by all accounts, had to order Spector to calm down (Miles, *Beatles*, 373).

On the more positive side, some of Spector's work was generally acknowledged as improving the original recordings. The live-in-the-studio recording of "Two of Us," for example, was, according to Barry Miles, "brilliantly enhanced by Spector's postproduction, which gave the acoustic instruments a richness missing from any previous Beatles' recording" (Miles, *Beatles*, 376). Miles also praises the work done on "Across the Universe," on which Spector added an orchestra and a choir; the result was "one of the highlights of the Beatles' career," justification in itself for Spector's involvement in the creative process, particularly since the song had been abandoned at a previous session

(Miles, *Beatles*, 376). Mick Brown claims that it was "a pretty song that had sounded feeble in its original version" (M. Brown, 254). Spector had done a major job of sweetening up very rough and unusable material, and using strings to cover up mistakes and sweeten the sound, of which "Across the Universe" was a prime example.

Glyn Johns blames what he called Lennon's "mental breakdown" for souring the whole affair. Lennon seemed to enjoy the controversy and disruption around the group at this stage, having grown so disillusioned with being a "Beatle" (M. Brown, 255). According to Beatle expert Ian MacDonald, Lennon played all the wrong notes on the bass for "The Long and Winding Road" and generally wanted to sabotage anything the Beatles did, which understandably angered McCartney (MacDonald, 339–40).

All of the bickering among the group, the press intrusion, and the public's biased reaction makes it very difficult to determine the real objective feeling toward Spector in terms of the project's final sound. Martin is correct in suggesting that the clean sounds often associated with the Beatles were not there in the final result, but if the sound was to be "almost amateurish" then surely the sounds wouldn't be as clean as usual. This seems like a feeble excuse to cast the blame on Spector since he didn't record much of the album, which had been done by Glyn Johns. Spector obviously felt his job was to produce a record that would have commercial appeal, and since much of the recordings didn't have that, Spector was left to improvise how he could. In his favor Spector managed to piece together what was, by everyone's thinking, an atrocious mess of unfinished work, and to do that in itself was an achievement.

Most of the controversy over the album seems to have come from McCartney; unhappy with Klein's involvement with the group and suspicious of the group being exploited, he seemed to use the orchestration of some of his songs as a means to legally oust Klein from the position of Beatles manager, thus reassuming control over his own group and their destiny. McCartney particularly cited the interference of Klein in employing Spector to remix the sessions; that he was not consulted on any artistic decisions seems to be untrue. On hearing the final versions all Beatles gave their approval, even McCartney, despite what others, such as Martin, had later indicated (Miles, *Beatles*, 373). McCartney would later tell Paul Du Noyer that Spector was simply caught in what was fundamentally a feud between McCartney and Klein (Du Noyer, *Conversations with McCartney*, 76–77). If truth be told *Let It Be* suffered mainly from the fractures within the group, and the idea that the band could actually revert to a small rock 'n' roll band akin to their early days in Hamburg or at Liverpool's Cavern Club was naïve to say the least.

Despite Spector's difficult task and the criticism directed at him, the album still captured the imagination of the public, selling 1.2 million copies. When commentating on the "Let It Be" single, Brown rightly observes that "while it may not have pleased the critics, the mood of plangent sentimentality that Spector invested in the song captured the imagination of the public as the perfect epitaph to the Beatles' career" (M. Brown, 255). This is probably a more accurate understanding of Spector's attitude toward the whole project since the Beatles' personal assistant, Peter Brown, even asserts that Spector was a real fan of the Beatles and was more intent on helping the group than purposely sabotaging them (M. Brown, 251).

The album also scored a Grammy Award, which McCartney, ironically, happily collected, though forty years later he would undo all of Spector's work, rereleasing the album as *Let It Be, Naked* (2003). However, the publicity around the group's split, coinciding with the album's release and the launching of all four Beatles' solo careers, was more than enough to dramatically increase the records sales alone, regardless of its musical greatness, or lack of it.

Despite the clashing egos and heavy demands laid on everyone involved, even the public themselves, *Let It Be* accurately captured the prevailing attitudes of the time as the culture gave up on the sixties' promise of a utopian dream and began to come to terms with the difficult challenges of revolution, war, and economic decline. Spector's involvement with the *Let It Be* record meant that he was intrinsically connected to the entire cultural ethos of the sixties. He was there at the dawning of a new youth-led exuberance both as a producer in his own right and in connection to the Beatles when "he cast himself as a symbolic protector, shepherding them into his own promised land, as if he were engineering the vast changes beginning to pour in from Britain" (Riley, 235). And finally he was there at the end of the decade side by side with the Beatles, not only leading them to the stage for their final curtain call, but also declaring with them that the "dream is over."

The Beatles more than any other group reflected the ideals and aspirations of the sixties, while their breakup symbolized the fading of people's dreams and hopes of peace, love, unity, and happiness. Spector as he had shepherded the group in their early years was now given the task of guiding its members, at least two of them—John Lennon and George Harrison—onto their individual paths of self-discovery.

PHIL AND JOHN

Phil Spector was the pop music titan Lennon always wanted to work with (Riley, 480), while Spector found a definite kindred spirit in Lennon and admitted he "was like the brother I'd never had" (M. Brown, 261). The two men had a great deal in common with each other as they both loved early rock 'n' roll and would each use it as a coping mechanism after losing their fathers at the age of nine. As a result of their loss they both became angry at the world, each feeling a terrible sense of pain, abandonment, and insecurity, and influencing their view that pain is a prerequisite to being a real artist (M. Brown, 261). When Lennon sang the lines on the opening track, "Mother," of the *Plastic Ono Band* album, "Father you left me, but I never left you," it must have resonated strongly with Spector, who would his whole life mourn the loss of his own father.

Instant Karma

With his two previous singles, "Cold Turkey" and "Give Peace a Chance," Lennon was determined to use his music as an honest expression of art and not just commercial entertainment. Lennon's impulsive personality had made him disillusioned with the slow process of the Beatles, and he now wanted to break free of them in order to give his art a real immediacy. His first two singles had definitely achieved this, and he wanted even more to capture it with his third release, "Instant Karma." Lennon had become familiar with the concept of Karma during a Beatles sojourn with Maharishi Mahesh Yogi's ashram in 1968, and his Libran sense of justice attracted him to the notion of a universal law that would rebalance the injustices of the world. Influenced by his impulsive personality and the modern need to have everything instantaneously, Lennon preferred to view Karma as something that should be immediate instead of something that took effect across lifetimes. Lennon's Karma was to be as instant as coffee was to the consumer society of the time (Riley, 485). In accordance with his notion of immediacy, Lennon wanted to write, record, and release the song as fast as possible, like bread delivered fresh to the consumer, and so began recording the song the same morning it was written (Miles, *Beatles*, 367).

Though, at least according to many sources, Spector's involvement on the record was purely random (or serendipitous), Lennon was so impressed by Spector's results that he wanted him to produce all his future solo work, finally collaborating with him on four albums. Paul Du Noyer praises Spector for making "Instant Karma" reflect Lennon's message so effortlessly and so brilliantly.

> Instant Karma . . . is a sonic triumph. Contracting Spector was the final coup in the song's production and was the start of an historic two-year partnership between Lennon. Even though Spector's involvement seems accidental it, nonetheless, managed to capture the definitive sound Lennon was searching for; "the definitive sound of post Beatles Lennon" (Du Noyer, *John Lennon*, 26).

John Lennon/Plastic Ono Band

The *John Lennon/Plastic Ono Band* album (1970) was to be even more immediate than the three previous singles, becoming a vehicle for Lennon's recently discovered Primal Scream therapy, in which psychotherapist Arthur Janov encouraged Lennon to let go of his emotional and artistic crutches and to allow his true feelings to guide his art.

This approach, to be open and honest, would make it difficult for the album to have any real chance of commercial success. Though viewing his own records as artistic ventures, Spector had always considered the commercial aspects of his records too. In this case, however, he deferred to Lennon's wish to overlook commerce for art. With Lennon's *Plastic Ono* album, Spector abandoned his Wall of Sound approach and produced Lennon in all his raw emotion. Klaus Voormann said, "Phil knew what was the best approach for this particular album. . . . He didn't have to do his big sound; he could do something very fine, delicate and sensitive, whatever was appropriate for the song and the moment" (M. Brown, 260–61).

Spector, while being notoriously disrespectful to others in the music business, was diplomatic and cautious and put himself aside for Lennon. Was this because he felt Lennon was a greater artist than himself, or was it because it was the only way for him to be accepted into the top levels of the rock and pop aristocracy, a place occupied by only the Beatles, Elvis, and possibly Dylan? Regardless of the reason, Spector managed to aid in capturing what would be for many the quintessential Lennon album. "The Beatles were an act," Lennon said before recording the album; "now I get to be John Lennon" (Riley, 518). Lennon was at his most open and honest; this was difficult for some Beatle fans, who were more accustomed to the pop artistry of Lennon's Beatle period. Yet *Plastic Ono* is for many others the greatest insight into, not only Lennon as a musician and artist, but also an honest account of the crippling effects that success and fame can have on an artist. "Even to this day the album makes for acid listening and scopes out a definitely primitive sound that would make fiercest punk sound thin. . . . It remains one of the great self-deflating gestures in the history of pop culture. Its emotional glare defies everybody's fondest illusions about Lennon" (Riley, 500–501).

Though Lennon complained that Spector had really little to do with the album, an accusation also made by Harrison on his records, it seems peculiar that if he did little that they would continue to collaborate with him on their next few solo records, records that were generally regarded as the best of their respective solo careers. Even if Spector had little to do with the production of the album, as Lennon claims, his piano playing alone on the song "Love" is worthy of some recognition, creating a sound and mood that foreshadowed the feel of Lennon's most lauded album both commercially and artistically: *Imagine* (1971).

Imagine

Throughout the three-week session at Lennon's home studio in Tittenhurst Park recording Lennon's best-known and possibly most-loved solo work, *Imagine*, Spector once again generously humbled himself to Lennon's artistic pursuits, allowing Lennon's artistic designs to fashion and shape the album. Instead of insisting on his usual larger-than-life treatment of songs, Spector allowed the "nuances" of Lennon's songs to express themselves in simple, honest, and intimate arrangements, as Lennon had desired. He infused each of Lennon's songs "with a rare warmth and intimacy" and encouraged Lennon "to sing more movingly than at any time in his career" (M. Brown, 263).

To "sweeten" the songs and make them more radio and consumer friendly, at least more than the *Plastic Ono* record had been, Spector added strings. According to commentators such as Mick Brown, however, Spector did much more than just add strings simply to make the album ready for popular consumption. Rather, he crafted a series of perfect settings and caught a mood that would make *Imagine* the most perfectly realized and the most commercially successful album that Lennon would ever record, and in the title track he provided a song that would endure as a globally acknowledged anthem for peace. If the work is to be measured by its enduring impact, the hearts it touches, and the hope it inspires, then in a sense *Imagine* was Spector's finest accomplishment as a producer—even if his name was only in small type (M. Brown, 264).

Imagine, Lennon would later quip, was a commercial version of *Plastic Ono* with "chocolate on top for public consumption" (M. Brown, 264). At any rate Spector had ultimately helped Lennon shape both his most widely acclaimed and his commercially successful album, as well as capturing or at least helping to capture what was Lennon's most personally direct record.

Imagine's title track has become a universally acknowledged peace anthem, and while the lyrics owe a significant debt to Yoko Ono, the music, with Spector's assistance, delicately captures the utopian dream of a true idealist. Although "Imagine" is a particularly standout track that has gained iconic status over the years, other tracks on the album also owe a gratitude to Spector's innovation and inspiration. Paul Du Noyer notes that Spector's strings on "It's So Hard," "hovering in the light Hollywood-oriental style," "magically" uplift the song (Du Noyer, *John Lennon*, 44), while his production, "echoing to the heavens," on "I Don't Want to Be a Soldier" "pulls out all the stops, including King Curtis' saxophone as well as the fusillade of rock guitar" (Du Noyer, *John Lennon*, 46).

On the follow-up single to "Instant Karma," "Power to the People," Du Noyer notes that Spector's studio skills made a real difference to the song.

> To the swirling sax of ace sessioner Bobby Keyes, Spector added a full-blown gospel choir for righteous conviction. Next he multi-tracked the sound of the musicians tramping feet. But then he whipped the whole number up into something that was far lighter on its feet, much more supple and funky, than the basic composition implied. It was the first-ever call to mass proletarian action that you could dance to. (Du Noyer, *John Lennon*, 39)

Lennon, however, would later go on to dismiss the recording, if not the song, as a piece of "shit" (Du Noyer, *John Lennon*, 39).

"Jealous Guy" was a tune that Lennon had originally composed in India under the title "Child of Nature." In its original form, Lennon, inspired by his sojourn in India, attempted to reconnect both with nature and with his lost "inner child." In truth, Lennon had never really been a "Child of Nature," finding himself more at home in cities, such as Liverpool, London, and New York; and, although refusing to abandon the melody, he changed the lyrics to reflect something more sincere in his personality, namely, his self-absorbed and jealous side.

Jealousy and possessiveness was a subject that Lennon had tried to address a number of times in his earlier Beatles compositions, but none had quite captured this unsettling side of his personality (Blaney, 84) as well as "Jealous Guy" had. The stark, thin drum sound and hollow, sparse piano created the same abrasiveness that he and Spector had captured on the *Plastic Ono* album, although this time softened by a tasteful arrangement of "soothing and creamy" strings (R. Williams, *Phil Spector*, 164).

Spector and Lennon's production of the song has made it one of Lennon's most beloved solo pieces and was eventually brought to number one by Roxy Music, which had covered it as a tribute to Lennon six months after his murder in December 1980. While the Lennon/Spector production on the track "Imagine" best captures the idealistic nature of Lennon's personality, "Jealous Guy" expertly captures his darker, more possessive nature.

Like "Imagine," Lennon's Christmas song "Happy Xmas (War Is Over)," now a popular classic featuring on every Christmas album release and filling up the airwaves for the entire month of December, is essentially another peace anthem and heavily indebted to Spector's *Christmas Gift for You* album. It is also indebted to his Ronnie Spector comeback record, the George Harrison–penned "Try Some Buy Some," which he had asked Spector to replicate the backing of (Blaney, 59). And another influence, though probably subconsciously on Lennon's part, is the melody from "I Love How You Love Me" (Blaney, 536).

Riley observes that Lennon's later Beatles songs and his earlier solo work such as "All You Need Is Love," "Give Peace a Chance," "Imagine," "Power to the People," and "Happy Xmas" very expertly and unconsciously attempted to "define its audiences rituals" (Riley, 537). He also rightly observes that Spector was instrumental in bringing Lennon's vision to realization on three of these records. Thus Spector would define for, at least the second time, the thoughts and feelings of a generation.

The Rock 'n' Roll Album

Though Lennon had achieved mainstream success with *Imagine*, his follow-up *Somewhere in New York City* (1972), which he mainly produced himself, was considered a disaster (Du Noyer, *John Lennon*, 57). Though considered "egotistical," "witless," and "embarrassingly puerile" on its release, Peter Doggett claimed it as one of the most important political statements of its time (Doggett, *There's a Riot*, 1). While his personal life and financial situation were in extreme disarray, Lennon had also found himself facing a plagiarism suit from Chuck Berry's publisher, who claimed that his song "Come Together" had borrowed heavily from Berry's 1957 "You Can't Catch Me." Lennon had flown to Los Angeles to escape his unhappy personal life in New York, and all this hit him while he was there. Lennon cut a deal to record a new album, which would ensure him an advance from his record label (Capitol) until his Beatles legal battles had resolved themselves while at the same time compensating Berry. His plan was to cover old rock 'n' roll songs, effectively making an album "of the songs that I love" (M. Brown, 282).

Essentially, Lennon would return to his Quarrymen days as a teenager, when everything was less complicated. He decided he didn't want to be responsible for the album in any capacity but would simply sing the songs, release the album, and make the returns on his financial and legal responsibilities. In this capacity he turned to Spector as the producer, offering him full control and full production credits (on the previous albums Spector had only been coproducer). Finally Spector had gotten what he had always wished for: to produce the highest caliber of rock 'n' roll musicians and be fully in control of the process. But Lennon had not anticipated what the album would become and the mayhem that the sessions would bring. Spector had previously worked with Lennon in England; however, this time it was different. Spector was now on comfortable ground in his own comfortable surroundings.

While Lennon was content and expecting to record an old-style rock 'n' roll album with a small-beat combo of a few musicians, Spector had put the call out for his usual monstrous group of musicians that he had used for his gigantic Wall of Sound productions. Spector soon wore out Lennon's patience, a personality that found it difficult to sit still at the best of times, but also considering his emotional state, Lennon most probably wanted to mask his personal unhappiness and express his frustrations by simply playing old rock 'n' roll songs. Instead, Spector, either not aware of Lennon's situation or simply letting his ego take control, began to apply his usual Wall of Sound tactics of arriving to the studio late and then spending hours setting up mics, testing sound levels, and endlessly rehearsing the musicians' parts. Lennon even had to tell the security at the A&M studios that he was working with Phil Spector before he was allowed in (Riley, 572). Spector's personal concerns, particularly his divorce from Ronnie, also became an increasing issue with the production of the album.

Exasperated, Lennon started drinking, and fights soon broke out between Spector and Lennon, Spector receiving a black eye on one occasion (M. Brown, 283–85). May Pang, Lennon's girlfriend at the time (while he was estranged from Yoko Ono) who had accompanied him to Los Angeles, says, "Phil wanted control. That's basically what it came down to. And he kept holding John at bay—like it's my show and not yours. It was an ego trip" (M. Brown, 286). Others, such as Tony King, a promotions man for Apple, thought Spector was "suffering from having been big, and no longer being as big as he was, but still wanting everybody to think he was. So there was all this grandiose posturing going on. . . . Very Phil-insecure—a lot of challenging remarks, putdowns" (M. Brown, 285).

To make matters worse, Spector, realizing the potential of these recordings, paid for the studio time himself, making it difficult for Capitol, Lennon's record company, to get them back, and in the end negotiating with them to the tune of $94,000 (Riley, 581). Apparently a U.S. Marshal was called in to retrieve the tapes from Spector (M. Brown, 289).

Rock 'n' Roll had been recorded with Spector over the months October to December 1973, before Lennon parted company from Spector, reconvening the album a year later with himself as producer. On the final release, only five tracks from Spector were included: "You Can't Catch Me," "Sweet Little Sixteen," "Bony Moronie," and "Just Because."

On sober reflection Lennon said of his gifted, erratic collaborator, "I'm fond of his work a lot. His personality I'm not crazy about." But Spector never lost a sense of his own importance. Speaking in 1976 he announced, "I only went into the studio to do one thing, and you can tell this to John Lennon. They were making records but I was making Art" (Du Noyer, *John Lennon*, 95). If anything truly worthwhile came from Spector's involvement with the record, it was that his unstable behavior was a definite "warning sign to Lennon that he needed to get his act together" or he would soon become as dysfunctional as Spector (Riley, 574–75).

PHIL AND GEORGE

Harrison had essentially moved away from the two-minute pop songs of the Beatles' intent, just like Lennon, to focusing on a more personal and artistic expression. From this point of view it may have seemed odd, for Harrison, though a big fan of Spector's music, to have chosen him as his producer. Danni Harrison, the interviewer of the documentary *George Harrison: Living in the Material World* (2011), had questioned Harrison on this point. "Yeah I suppose it was," was George's whimsical reply, "but he needed a job at the time and I needed someone to help me " (*George Harrison*). It's also possible that Harrison was impressed by the sound that Spector had created both on *Let It Be* (Shapiro, 103) and on Lennon's "Instant Karma," which was a definite departure from the Beatles' style.

Regardless of the reason, Spector encouraged Harrison to make an album with all the unrecorded material he had from his Beatles period. Spector recognized the wealth of emotion in these songs, which the other Beatles had ignored, and if he had achieved nothing else in his collaboration with Harrison, he was instrumental in allowing Harrison to make the transition from being a "second-rate" Beatle into a world-class solo artist—offering him guidance and a sense of security in the wake of the Beatles. To help Harrison realize these songs in the studio, Spector assembled a virtual "Wrecking Crew" of musicians, a lineup that included Ringo Starr and Alan White on drums, Billy Preston on keyboards, and Eric Clapton and George Harrison on guitars, for what was to become Harrison's acclaimed *All Things Must Pass* (1970).

Despite his enthusiasm for Spector, Harrison seemed to be initially unhappy with the direction Spector chose to take the album but, trusting Spector's abilities, went along with it anyway (*George Harrison*). Years later Harrison reissued the album, taking off much of what Spector had originally done. The sleeve notes for the reissue claimed that the songs needed liberating from a production that "seemed appropriate at the time but now seems a bit over the top."

Whether Spector had "overproduced" *All Things Must Pass* or not, he certainly offered invaluable advice to Harrison on what would be a more commercially viable record and encouraged Harrison to release "My Sweet Lord" as the album's first single, despite its religious connection. Spector wasn't afraid to push whatever it was that was commercial, even if it might challenge the audience's perceptions. Whether Spector was aware of anything other than commercialism when it came to releasing records is an interesting point. And was he as aware, as Harrison certainly was in this case, of the anger people might feel in receiving something of a spiritual nature, particularly the references to foreign religious themes, in pop music? "I thought a lot about whether to do 'My Sweet Lord' or not, because I would be committing myself publicly (to my beliefs), and I anticipated that a lot of people might get weird about it. Many people fear the words 'Lord' and 'God.' [It] makes them angry for some reason" (KSHE 95).

Regardless of Spector's attitude toward Harrison's dilemma with the release of the song, his insight (and possibly his courage in disregarding the public's responses to his "art") sent "My Sweet Lord" to number one. It was the first number one for an ex-Beatle and certainly helped

All Things Must Pass into the top of the charts when it was released at the end of 1970.

Harrison was not always open to Spector's ideas in this matter, however. For example, when he urged Harrison to change the lyrics of his song "The Ballad of Frankie Crisp," which he felt would ensure him quite a few cover versions, Harrison said "those words were written because that's what it was" (Harrison, 208). Harrison's concern was self-expression; for Spector, it seems it was the song's commercial potential.

Though "My Sweet Lord" was a huge success, selling over five million copies (Shapiro, 107), for Harrison it was also his downfall after he was accused of plagiarizing the melody from an early sixties tune, "He's So Fine," recorded by a girl group called the Chiffons. This was ironic since it was largely due to Spector that the girl group sound became such a success. Though others, including Lennon, had recognized the song's similarity, if only slight, to the Chiffons (Shapiro, 108), Harrison claims it was mostly influenced by the Edwin Hawkins Singers' "Oh Happy Day." Possibly Spector should have been more aware of the similarities encouraged Harrison to make slight changes to the melody in order to steer it away from any likely lawsuits.

Harrison's "notorious tendency to perfectionism" (R. Williams, *Phil Spector*, 152), and his need to control everything, most likely stemming from the fact that he had little control in the Beatles, meant redoing parts over and over until they were right (he apparently redid the slide on "My Sweet Lord" over ninety times [Thompson, 170]), which ironically exacerbated Spector. Overall Spector seemed to feel a complete lack of control, not just over Harrison's perfectionism, but also over his environment (the English weather and food, as well as the continuous presence of the Hare Krishnas, there at Harrison's request, seemed to distress him). Lack of control over his environment was something that had always made Spector extremely nervous and as a result caused him to regularly absent himself from the studio. Harrison, however, interpreted it as Spector simply not being there when he needed his help (Shapiro, 104).

Spector began to drink to deal with the situation, which soon became a problem for everyone (M. Brown, 258). However, it seems that Harrison's perfectionism and the Hare Krishnas, and so forth, were not the sole cause of the drinking. It is more likely that because of the lack of control over the project he began to doubt if the album was going to sound good. Brown makes the point that "as much as anything else, Spector was drinking to ease his nerves. More than anyone, he respected the Beatles' place at the pinnacle of the musical hierarchy, revered them. . . . At the same time he was terrified of the possibility of failure and rejection" (M. Brown, 258). The backlash from the *Let It Be* album was undoubtedly still fresh in his mind.

As a result, Spector left the *All Things Must Pass* sessions before it was finished, leaving instructions on what, in his opinion, needed to be done to bring the album up to its best. Though Harrison felt Spector had paid insufficient attention to the project, Spector justified his departure by saying he had given the album all the attention it needed and that a consummate professional such as Harrison would surely be able to add the finishing touches to the record himself. Spector was by all accounts getting homesick, and he knew it was not a good environment to be in with his drinking becoming a problem, so he probably made the right decision.

Spector tolerated a lot on the recording of *All Things Must Pass*; however, many musicians were relieved when Spector left (Thompson, 170), and Harrison, a devotee of Hinduism, would famously say that with Spector he came to realize the true value of the Hare Krishna mantra (*George Harrison*).

It would be unfair to think that Spector contributed little to the sessions, and certainly he not only brought much of his skill to the production but also, more importantly, gave Harrison a sense of worth about his songwriting talent and did a lot to encourage him in the studio. Spector's letter to Harrison after he temporarily returned to the United States indicates a genuine concern for the record, Harrison's songs, and Harrison himself as an artist, performer, and vocalist, which was obviously the key instrument in expressing the album's spiritual message.

> I'm sure the album will be able to be remixed excellently. I also feel that therein lies much of the album because many of the tracks are really quite good and will reproduce on record very well. Therefore, I think you should spend whatever time you are going to on performances so that they are the very best you can do and that will make the remixing of the album that much easier. I really feel that your voice has got to be heard throughout the album so that the greatness of the songs can really come through. (Beatles Bible)

Due to the religious themes in many of the songs, a few, such as critic Ben Gerson, have seen the album as having "an air of sanctimoniousness and moral superiority which is offensive" (Gerson). Riley sees the album as "overproduced," while many see the third disc of the album as simply unplayable (R. Williams, *Phil Spector*, 156). Despite these comments, others have viewed the album, on both its first release and still today, as Harrison's best album and as a great achievement in rock music, dubbing it "the *War and Peace* of rock and roll," and forging the "seventies new rock idiom" (Ribowsky, 256). The online music guide AllMusic called it "crafted material that managed the rare feat of conveying spiritual mysticism. . . . Enhanced by Phil Spector's lush orchestral production and Harrison's own superb slide guitar, nearly every song is excellent." The website Ultimate Classic Rock called it Harrison's "declaration of independence"; *Rolling Stone* magazine said, "The production is of classic Spectorian proportions, Wagnerian, Brucknerian, the music of mountain tops and vast horizon" (Gerson); and Nicholas Schaffner, in his book *The Beatles Forever*, called the record "the crowning achievement of both their (Harrison, and Spector) careers" (Bergstrom). Its influence on music through the last four and a half decades cannot be overstated as the following review expresses: "How many guitar-driven, echo-drenched bands have come around since, mixing powerful rave-ups with moody, reflective down-tempo numbers and a spiritual bent? . . . One listen to 'Let It Down' and you'll understand a big part of how 'Dream Pop' came to be" (Bergstrom).

However the success of *All Things Must Pass* again rests on the fact that it was a Beatles solo record, as well as being a triple album, the novelty aspect of which may have attracted more attention than usual. Another consideration is that Harrison had produced an impressive body of work, which had seriously raised the public's estimation of him. He was no longer considered a second-rate songwriter in the shadow of Lennon and McCartney but instead seen as a songwriter of the highest caliber who had been overlooked for too long. This newfound status undoubtedly attracted a concentrated amount of attention that brought favorable critical appraisal, which inevitably increased sales.

The plagiarism connected to the album's flagship song, the dominance of glam and punk during the seventies, Lennon's death in 1980, and Harrison's virtual reclusiveness in terms of the music world have all contributed to pushing the album into relative obscurity. As a result, it is much less popular today than Lennon's *Imagine* or McCartney's *Band on the Run* (1973), even though for its time it was the most commercially successful of all the ex-Beatles albums.

The fact that the album has been the most successful of all the solo Beatles projects seemed to justify Spector's involvement while also reaffirming at least to Spector that he was still the great genius producer. Meanwhile, the Grammy Award–winning album *The Concert for Bangladesh* (1972), at Madison Square Garden, took six months to mix (Richard Williams claims the album only took a week to mix, but Harrison spent months over the artwork for the album [R. Williams, *Phil Spector*, 163]); however, it only took four hours to record (*George Harrison*). The album was a tremendous achievement, producing a reasonable sound (though others have called it atrocious [Thompson, 181]) to what must have been a difficult task, considering the number of musicians, the noise from the crowd, and the environment in which it was recorded. Chip Madinger and Mark Easter in their book *Eight Arms to Hold You*, however, question the extent to which Spector was actually involved in the whole *Concert for Bangladesh* project (Madinger and Easter, 436), while Harrison seemed to give more credit of the sound recording to sound engineer Gary Kellgren. The album is, however, a milestone in that it started the whole charity concert idea, which came to its pinnacle with Bob Geldof's Live Aid in 1985, as well as capturing Bob Dylan's only live performance since his motorbike accident in 1966. In whatever capacity, Spector was part of it all and must again have been a source of reassurance for Harrison, replacing the once steady hand of Beatles producer George Martin in guiding his ideas through the whole recording process. Even if he had done little in terms of the actual recording, the reassurance of his presence is certainly a testament to how lauded Spector was as a record producer among Harrison and his friends.

10

END OF THE CENTURY

Decline and Fall

RIVER DEEP, MOUNTAIN HIGH

By 1966, Phil Spector's perfectionism was having drastic effects on nearly every artist on his label, simply because he wasn't releasing any of their records. "Every time he made a record," said Ronnie Spector, "he'd find some flaw that nobody else in the whole world could hear, and refused to put it out" (Spector, 108–9). Every time a record didn't do well, it would send Spector into a prolonged depression, and one such unsuccessful record, Ike and Tina Turner's "River Deep, Mountain High," may even have driven him into retirement.

Even though, for many, Spector had reached the peak of his musical brilliance with "You've Lost That Lovin' Feelin'," he felt, on some level, that he had outdone it with his production of "River Deep, Mountain High." He was certain that it would have been, and certainly he felt it deserved to be, a massive hit, outdoing all his other records combined. Not only did it not become a hit, but also it was completely ignored, disappearing from the charts within a matter of weeks. In America, no one played the record, and nobody bought it either. Spector, naturally, felt rejected by both the music industry and his public. He felt the industry, despite all the great music he had given them, had simply abandoned him. He also felt that both the public and the industry just couldn't understand his music, certainly since his music, as already mentioned, was becoming more and more elaborate, demanding more from the listener. In many ways Spector's latest material was created not as commercial disposability but for artistic longevity.

In Britain, the record had hit number one, but the British musicians, who in many ways were a lot more innovative and original than in the Unites States, always had more respect for Spector's work, and Spector always had more respect for British tastes (even if he never felt quite at home in that country [Jayanti]). As a result of all this, Spector retaliated by taking out an ad in *DownBeat* music magazine entitled "Benedict Arnold Was Right," comparing himself, and his treatment by the music industry, to Benedict Arnold, the U.S. general infamous for betraying his country by supplying the British with information. Once again Spector would make himself very unpopular within the U.S. music industry.

To many, Spector simply came across as a spoilt child that just couldn't get the attention he craved. "When Phil Spector released a song," according to one commentator, "he expected the world to listen. Yet by the middle of the decade, the public was not listening as intently as the producer would have liked" (Examiner.com). However, others, such as Ike Turner, claim that Spector had become bored with pop music and that he had confided to him that "River Deep, Mountain High" was to be his final curtain call before retiring from the profession (Thompson, 145). Spector, it seems, was not concerned about success; he was more interested in creating something "good" (Thompson, 145) and would later play down the drama of the whole affair, when he told filmmaker Vikram Jayanti that he simply spoke his mind, killed the record, and retired (Jayanti). He was only twenty-six.

If Spector was behaving like a spoiled child, there was some justification to his disappointment; whether it justified the trade paper ads is another question, but Spector, or at least the record, deserved a much better reception than it got, and it is interesting that Jack Nitzsche thought the song was dismissed because people don't like you when you get too big. "He had thirteen hits in a row without a miss. Around 'River Deep, Mountain High,' people started to want him to fail," exclaimed Nitzsche (Examiner.com). Spector's onetime friend and musical companion Marshall Leib suggested a similar reason for the song's lack of success (Ribowsky, 224), while others speculated that the rivalry between radio stations meant it didn't get played, which inevitably hurt the record sales (Thompson, 145).

Spector himself felt it was for largely political reasons that his music was being ignored, while Ike Turner was firmly convinced that it was solely because of racial politics that the song was dismissed:

> If Phil had released that record and put anybody else's name on it, it would have been a huge hit. But because Tina Turner's name was on it, the white stations classified it as an RB record and wouldn't play it. The white stations say it was too black, and the black stations say it was too white, so that record didn't have a home. That's what happened to "River Deep, Mountain High." (Examiner.com)

Spector would echo Ike Turner's feelings during a memorial speech he gave at Ike's funeral, saying, "When we did 'River Deep, Mountain High,' people said you can't put Ike and Tina Turner's name on that record. It won't sell because they are rhythm and blues and it's a pop record." During the same speech Spector would once again claim to defy the music industry's narrow-mindedness, saying, "I signed Ike and Tina Turner, it won't even say featuring Tina Turner; it's Ike and Tina Turner" (Friedman).

Perhaps "River Deep, Mountain High," with its black vocal and white pop music, was out of time with the black movement, which encouraged black singers to take pride in their own music. Although there had been successful mixed-race records, by the time "River Deep, Mountain High" came out in the midsixties "changes were underway. Black politics was radicalized. With black pride, there was an increasing feeling that African Americans should support and protect their own culture. Music had to be explicitly black to appeal to black audiences" (Billig, 110).

The personal and professional links with the Jewish tradition of Tin Pan Alley were also loosening. Phil's collaborator and admirers were now beginning to offer more variety than just Spector's brand of pop, not to mention the British bands, all of which made Spector's pop lose its luster; simply making the Wall of Sound bigger wasn't really the answer. By all accounts even those involved in the project were not so interested in it. The song's cowriter Ellie Greenwich was not impressed with the final result, apparently ripping it from the turntable and hurling it across the room when she first heard it (Love, 119). In contrast to Greenwich's reaction, her writing partner on the song, Jeff Barry, is quoted as saying that he couldn't understand why it never became a hit

(BBC Radio 2), even though he too seemed to dislike the song initially, feeling it had become an ego trip for Spector (Thompson, 144).

In truth, Spector was just going out of fashion; people had heard enough of the Wall of Sound, and to a large degree Spector was aware of that and decided it would be best to retire, blame his musical demise on the ignorance of the American music industry and the record-buying public, and crawl off to lick his wounds.

Spector should have known better than to respond quite the way he did, being intelligent enough to know that the public can be fickle and that the consumer culture by its very nature survives on the novelty of new and different things. Spector, by being on the scene for nearly a decade at this stage, was no longer novel and different; if anything he had become almost an institution.

Considering everything, Spector's ego did get badly bruised by the fact that he had set out to make the greatest pop record of all time, even paying Ike Turner $20,000 just to keep out of the way, as well as another $25,000 to record it using a massive assortment of musicians, including Mick Jagger and Brian Wilson. The amount apparently overwhelmed Tina Turner so much that she found it difficult to perform in the studio, only for it to become a complete failure, on both a critical as well as a commercial level. Psychologically, "its initial failure had floored the unstable elements of his personality, accelerating his unraveling until one of music's biggest personalities was all but silent" (Examiner.com). Today, however, "River Deep, Mountain High" has come to be seen in a totally different light and is duly regarded as the classic it was envisioned to be. The near veneration the record receives today makes the initial treatment of Spector, as well as the song and Ike and Tina Turner, even more reprehensible.

Along with the enthusiasm the song has attracted as a production, it has also come to be considered one of Tina Turner's greatest vocal performances, a performance that Spector pushed her hard to create. Spector had planned to record five tracks with Tina, including the Motown classic "A Love Like Yours (Don't Come Knockin' Everyday)"; these other tracks were recorded, vocals and all, quickly and effortlessly, but "River Deep, Mountain High" was singled out to be different. Spector's attitude in this regard indicates again just how little Spector considered the idea of the album, with all tracks equally significant and effective. For Spector the single was still the focal point of pop music, and this particular single Spector was determined to transform into the most significant piece of art that the pop world would ever experience.

According to Tina, Spector made her sing the opening line "when I was a little girl" "500,000 times"; they had spent two weeks together rehearsing the vocal before even stepping foot inside a studio. Spector's engineer, Larry Levine, recalls that Tina's vocal performance was outstanding and almost the highlight of the session: "She grabbed that microphone and gave a performance that . . . I mean, your hair was standing on end. It was like the whole room exploded" (Thompson, 143). As a result, Tina's vocal on the record has set a challenge for many other highly regarded female vocalists to cover, including Celine Dion, Dolly Parton, Sisaundra Lewis, and Annie Lennox.

POP TO ROCK TO PUNK ROCK: SPRINGSTEEN, NEW WAVE, AND THE RAMONES

Spector's music had captured the newfound enthusiasm of the postwar baby boomers, becoming the soundtrack to the first generation of a new consumer society of U.S. and British teenagers at the turn of the 1960s. Meanwhile, the new consumerism had promised them the world, but by the end of the 1960s, such promises had given way to disappointment and frustration. The beatnik Neale Pharaoh, in his autobiography *Just Me and Nobody Else*, put it aptly when he wrote, "Young people are suffering from an enforced schizophrenia[:] the glossy package of the pop world and the hard realities beneath conflict" (quoted in Savage, 51). And this disappointment was to be deeply felt by the next generation of teenagers.

The use of the Wall of Sound in Bruce Springsteen's "Born to Run," for example, was in some ways an ironic statement of how life for many Americans had turned out and that the promise of the American Dream, which Spector's music would often reflect, had been left unfulfilled. Though the American Dream may still be a vague hope for some, the actual reality for many leaves "tramps like us" with a slim chance for anything better than a "suicide rap." The slowed-down and depressing quality of Springsteen's "Racing in the Street," which echoed "Then He Kissed Me," also suggests as much, particularly when the lyrical theme of the song looks back achingly to a period of fun, excitement, and the vigor of youth. Springsteen creates a semipastiche, as if to document the last dying embers of an era, contrasting it with the stark reality of the present. In "Racing in the Street," writes Richard Williams, "Springsteen set his lament for an obsolete culture against the riff from 'Then He Kissed Me,' slowed down and stripped of all its original exhilaration and given an entirely new potency" (R. Williams, *Phil Spector*, 18).

The Spector Wall of Sound, which filled the airwaves with joy, is now the expression of frustration, anxiety, and a need to break free from the unfulfilled idealism of Spector's generation. While Spector's music created an idealism that perfectly reflected the early sixties, Springsteen's more realistic characters were, as the sixties dream faded into oblivion, much "less youthful in their view of the world around them" (Kirkpatrick, 65).

The same sense of anger and frustration and the deliberate searching for something more than life can offer was expressed a few years earlier in the New York groups of the early seventies, when five boys of immigrant families formed a group that would offer them a way out of their dead end lives. The New York Dolls had grown up, like Springsteen, with the notion that in America anything was possible and that life was exciting and they were eager to live it. Rock 'n' roll assured them of that fact, but as the era drew to a close the originality and freshness of the decade seemed to dry up, and they continued, in the fashion of bands such as the Rolling Stones, with cross-dressing and shock tactics, to challenge the conventions of the time.

Other groups such as Blondie and the Ramones also searched for the excitement of Spector's music of the early sixties, but as the attitudes of the times had drastically changed, the pop music of Spector had to be infused with a more aggressive attitude. Both groups had initially turned down Spector's offers to produce them, probably because they were aware that his time was over; though the Ramones would eventually make use of his production skills, they finally accepted what they already intuitively knew, that "there's a new sound but he doesn't have it" (*Phil Spector: He's a Rebel*).

The attitudes of these New York bands would ultimately ignite a whole new culture in Britain, one that was intent on starting pop from a point of year zero, and although drawing on the immediacy of the pop music of the early sixties, it set out to do away with the artifice of studio production, as well as the notion of pop stardom. Groups such as the Sex Pistols and the Clash balked at the past, but unfortunately the record, which had become the main marketing tool since Phil Spector's grandiose productions, still needed studio trickery to create an impressive sound that could compete with the rawness of live performance. Even though Spector and his contemporaries no longer found acceptance among the British punks, groups such as the Sex Pistols still employed much of his studio artifice, and the layered guitars on *Never Mind the Bollocks* was essentially Spector's Wall of Sound: "The multi-tracked wall-of-sound guitars sound as exciting as rock 'n' roll gets—this is Phil Spector taken to an illogical and molten conclusion. The Sex Pistols may have come to destroy rock 'n' roll or maybe the media gave them that role, but the so-called sexy young assassins ended up reinventing it" (Robb).

By the midseventies, Spector had begun to reemerge from his self-imposed exile. He signed a number of deals with record companies, including Warner Brothers, on which he produced a number of records with Cher and Polydor. With Polydor he produced Dion's *Born to Be with You* (1975), drawing on their shared love of 1950s doo-wop; but Dion disowned the album, while the critics "panned it" and record buyers "shunned it" (Little). In retrospect, *Born to Be with You* has come to be seen as one of the greatest and most influential records ever made and was hailed as such by the likes of Andrew "Loog" Oldham, Pete Townshend, and Primal Scream's Bobby Gillespie (in the AllMusic review and in the *Telegraph*).

Spector's behavior around this time, however, was becoming more and more erratic, which was possibly compounded by an almost fatal car accident he had had in 1974. Following the Dion album, Spector teamed up with the legendary Leonard Cohen to record *Death of a Ladies' Man* (1977), but this was not the record it was expected to be, essentially because Spector's Wall of Sound didn't particularly marry well with Cohen's more intimate acoustic style. Three years later Spector's work with seminal punk group the Ramones brought Spector significantly more success and made him relevant again, if only briefly.

THE RAMONES

The Ramones, like the New York Dolls, based their musical style on the simple, up-tempo, two-minute pop songs akin to early sixties bands, extending their pop influence to include the Bay City Rollers (Melnick and Meyer, 56) and the girl groups of the sixties. They even took their name from no greater a pop icon than Paul McCartney, who before his Beatles fame used the pseudonym Paul Ramon (Melnick and Meyer, 32; Ramone, 42); the name would chime with the family and evoked names of sixties girl groups such as the Crystals and the Ronettes (Warwick, *Girl Groups*, 212).

Since the group is often seen as the herald of the new punk movement of 1976, and as such did a lot to establish and influence the seemingly aggressive and overtly political punk movement that developed in Britain that year with the Sex Pistols and the Damned, it's hard to imagine the Ramones as having evolved from such a strong pop sensibility. Yet from another perspective the Ramones embody much of what pop was about, particularly recapturing the feeling of Phil Spector's early records:

> The Ramones' roots lay in the baroque pop of the Spector-produced Sixties girl groups like the Ronettes and The Crystals—albeit with a minimalist interpretation that stripped away the lush harmonies and 20-piece orchestras, the introductions and codas. Just because Johnny played loud with relentless down strokes that initially cut his fingers to ribbons didn't mean the Ramones' spiritual brethren were MC5 or the Stooges or the angry late Seventies British punk bands. (True, 136)

THE RAMONES AND THE GIRL GROUP SOUND

The Ramones were simple yet radical and strongly identified with the outcast teen rebel of the fifties (True, 149), an image evoked in girl group songs such as "He's a Rebel" and "Leader of the Pack." It was an image that brought them back to their displaced adolescence, back to a time when music was simply about having fun: "whatever happened to the radio," Joey Ramone would inquire in their song "7-11"; "where did all the fun songs go?"

The Ramones were rumored to sound-check with songs by the Beat-les, as well as Phil Spector, the Beach Boys, and Herman's Hermits; "there was no conscious MC5 or the Stooges" (True, 54). Their desire was to re-create the simple pop songs of the sixties with catchy melodies and lyrics, which could express the feelings of the kids of the postsixties generation in the same way those sixties songs affected them growing up. "Rock bands utilize the teen ideal in their lyrical imagery," wrote Ramones biographer Everett True (True, 5) and suggests that Joey Ramone was deeply in tune with sixties girl group sensibilities:

> Joey details in time-honored girl group fashion the beauty of young love that takes place amongst the most mundane, humdrum of sur-roundings—convenience stores, Space Invaders machines, record swaps—before the entire story goes horribly wrong, again in classic girl group fashion. The oncoming car goes out of control—"it crushed my baby and it crushed my soul." If ever a man was born out of his era, it was Joey Ramone. This man was female teen angst personified. (True, 166)

Right up till late in their career, Joey drew from the Spector girl group impulse, particularly songs such as "She Belongs to Me" from 1986's *Animal Boy* (True, 206) or "Merry Christmas (I Don't Want to Fight Tonight)," from 1989's *Brain Drain*, which echoes the Ronettes' "The Best Part of Breaking Up" (True, 226). A song such as "I Want to Be Your Boyfriend" is not too different to the sensibilities of many of the girl group songs; the theme of yearning love and the language of "sweet little girls" and "boyfriends" mixed with the desire to be romanti-cally involved is absolutely the vocabulary of the girl groups, while the melodic and harmonic structures, often very basic in form with the Ramones, is close to the musical form of Spector's girl groups.

The chant forms of "Hey Ho," for example, in "Blitzkrieg Bop," hold a common currency with much of the girl group vocalizing of "Da Doo Ron Ron," "Shoop Shoop," "Doo Lang," or "Na Na Ha Ha"; these nonword vocalizations are often the hook line of the song. Other songs such as "Judy Is a Punk," "I Remember You," "Oh I Love Her So," "My My Kind of Girl," and "Sheena Is a Punk Rocker" are unapologetically girl group in their lyrical and musical style. And "What's Your Game," though full of Beatles references, also sees Joey's voice going into, what True described as, a "Ronnie Spector trembling overload for almost the first time: sweet backing vocals and an acoustic guitar help tell the story of one more outsider, one more girl shunned by the pack" (True, 83).

The Wall of Noise

The Ramones took the same bombastic attitude toward their records as Phil Spector had done toward his, though their attitude was less precious and they spent only a fraction of the time recording them. It was also Spector's production techniques that influenced their studio sound, as their drummer/producer Tommy Ramone tried to capture a "punk" version of Spector's sound on their records, virtually creating a Wall of Noise (*End of the Century*). Their debut album, recorded and mixed in only five days, provided a "direct link" between girl groups such as the Ronettes and seventies punk and nineties grunge bands such as Nirvana (True, 54).

Regardless of their pop credentials, by the time the Ramones had started out, radio had become "corporate" and "homogenized" (True, 66), which meant there was little room for quirky groups such as the Ramones. New Wave record producer Andy Paley says the Ramones didn't stand a chance with the radios of the day, which weren't into classic pop, and the Ramones wanted to play fun music (True, 66). However, DJs such as Rodney Bingenheimer, a Spector enthusiast, became a fan of the Spector girl group–inspired acts, such as the Ramones and Blondie, and as a result the Ramones were his first guests on his ROQ New Wave and sixties show on KROQ-FM (True, 66). Meanwhile Sire Records general manager Howie Klein set up one of the United States' first punk rock radio shows after seeing the Ramones play (True, 66).

In 1978, for their *Road to Ruin* album, the Ramones recorded Jack Nitzsche's/Sonny Bono's "Needles and Pins," which followed "Don't Come Close," and people worried that they'd softened their sound for commercial success. While some Ramones fans appreciated the versatility of Joey's voice and figured the Ramones' forte lay in releasing great pop-punk singles in the tradition of Spector and other sixties groups, others such as Johnny Ramone felt the Ramones had a unique sound and "should stick with it" (True, 119). But as Tommy Ramone argued, *"Road to Ruin* reflected not just the Ramones' enduring love for sixties pop, but a nagging desire to expand beyond the confines of

120 seconds in search of a new vocabulary of harmonic hooks, albeit linked to the guitar-crunching sonics established on their first three albums" (Heylin, 315–16). With such an approach being adopted, it made sense that the band would call up the production skills of a sixties icon such as Spector.

The Kessel brothers invited Spector to a Ramones gig at the Whisky a Go Go in 1977, but he was more attracted to the girl fronting the band Blondie, the group sharing the bill (M. Brown, 322). According to David Kessel, Spector loved the Ramones. Spector "got" the Ramones straightaway, their "irreverence," their vitality, and the way they connected to an earlier, less self-conscious era of rock 'n' roll. He understood that it was back to Buddy Holly. He thought they were the best rock 'n' roll band in the United States (M. Brown, 323).

Roy Carr was a journalist from *New Musical Express* (*NME*) who was with Spector during the Ramones period and was writing a screenplay based on his life. According to Carr, in February 1977, Spector first offered the Ramones $200,000 to sign with him, but they turned him down (True, 137, 138). Eighteen months and two albums later, with the Ramones still not having the commercial success they desired, Seymour Stein, the head of their record company, Sire, negotiated a deal with Spector on the group's behalf. Spector remixed for the Ramones two tracks for *Rock 'n' Roll High School*, the opening title track and the song "I Want You Around" (True, 128), before working on a full album.

End of the Century

Despite their mutual respect for each other and even though their biggest hit came not only with a Spector production but also with a Spector song, "Baby, I Love You," the resulting album *End of the Century* (1980) did not bring the band to where they had hoped.

Recording for the album began at Gold Star on May 1, 1979. Spector took control of the group, virtually replacing the band with his own musicians and making it clear he was only really interested in Joey. According to Carr, Spector looked upon Joey as a male Ronnie Spector. Joey knew a lot of rock 'n' roll history—the doo-wop "street corner New York stuff," which impressed Spector (M. Brown, 323).

With Spector already being a hero to the band and particularly to Joey, the group sought him out, knowing he was keen to work with them; the problem, which they failed to recognize, though, was his controlling personality. There must have, however, been some realization as to his eccentric nature and a gut feeling that Spector was not necessarily the right person for the job since they had already turned down an offer from him eighteen months before, but now, desperate to have a hit and make some money, they were relying on him. Their pop singles were perfect for Spector; in fact, the Ramones were so focused on writing and making good pop records that no one, least of all their record company, could understand why they were not having hit after hit.

The group didn't realize just how eccentric and overpowering Spector could be; he virtually dominated the group, the album, and the recording, as if they were one of his girl groups from the sixties. According to Ed Stasium, nominally musical director of the project, Spector's behavior was insane: "The volume was incredible. He would make the band do take after take after take. I have it written down. He listened to 'This Ain't Havana' over 300 times. No one knew why. He was jumping up and down and swearing" (True, 139).

Phil wanted to make the biggest album ever, not the biggest Ramones album ever or Spector album ever, just the biggest album ever (True, 140), and because of that he drove the band to distraction. Popular legend has it that he made Johnny Ramone play the opening chord to "Rock 'n' Roll High School" for eight hours straight (*Phil Spector: He's a Rebel*). According to Stasium, Phil was "searching the cosmos for a sound and with that antiquated equipment he couldn't find it. At the end of the day Johnny was, 'I'm outta here.' The rest of the boys were up in arms" (True, 140). Carr says Spector wasn't really aware that they were a tight-knit group such as the Beatles or the Stones, where each aspect was essential to the overall band, but instead saw them as Joey Ramone and his backing group.

Baby, I Love You

The final insult to the band was Spector recording the Ronettes' "Baby, I Love You" with his own musicians, pushing the band out of the way and adding strings to the Ramones' usually less sophisticated and for many "unadulterated" sound—definitely not understanding and producing their sound. According to Johnny, who had spent most of the album in his motel room "twiddling his thumbs" (M. Brown, 328–29), "Baby, I Love You" was the worst thing they had ever done in their career, even though it seemed to be his suggestion in the first place to cover Spector (although his original suggestion was to cover "The Best Part of Breaking Up" [Ramone, 90]). If some of the group hated the song, causing internal problems and resentment toward Spector, it was Joey who, obviously taken with Johnny's original idea, had encouraged Spector to record the song under the impression that the producer was "going to make me Ronnie Spector" (M. Brown, 325). According to Thompson, Spector definitely saw something in Joey that made him think he could in fact turn Joey into some male "punk" version of the former Ronettes' lead singer.

Even in its original release for the Ronettes, "Baby, I Love You" should have fared better in the United States, where it hadn't even broken the top twenty; and though not as immediate as "Be My Baby," it was certainly as good, particularly for a follow-up, keeping the same upbeat and romantic lushness that its predecessor had. The two songs were similar to the Supremes' sister songs "Where Did Our Love Go" and "Baby Love," which had both become major hits for the Supremes, the first being almost an advertisement for the second.

Why the Ronettes' second single didn't do as well is a little puzzling, but so is the fact that not too many of the Ronettes songs did as well as they should have, despite their actual pop brilliance. It is understand-able that the singles that followed "Baby, I Love You," such as "The Best Part of Breaking Up," "Do I Love You," "We Were Born to Be Together," and "Is This What I Get for Loving You," all classics in themselves, failed to do anything in the charts because of the over-whelming interest in the Beatles' arrival in February 1964, and the flood of British acts that followed them. But this was not the reason for the lack of interest in "Baby, I Love You," which had no real competi-tion on its initial release, particularly since the Beatles wouldn't arrive for another three months and the only other competition Spector had was his own other artists, the Beach Boys, and Dominique's "Singing Nun."

According to True, Spector didn't want to do the Ronettes' song because it was too close to Ronnie Spector, whom he had recently divorced, as well as being in a protracted lawsuit over the ownership of the songs for years, but Stein and Joey convinced Spector to record it

(True, 146). Dave Thompson's account seems to contradict this story, claiming that Spector insisted the Ramones record either "Baby, I Love You" or strangely enough a Bob B. Soxx song, "Not Too Young to Get Married." Even though the Ramones were essentially a pop act with a certain edge and quirkiness that allowed them to fit neatly into the punk sensibilities that were emerging, particularly in the UK, Spector's covers seemed to be just a bit too much of a departure for the group.

Despite the controversy over the song choice, Spector managed to create not just one great track in the original version by the Ronettes, but also an equally unique and compelling production almost twenty years later, even if it didn't entirely suit the group or the time for which it was recorded. However, this seems to be a matter of opinion, even among Ramones fans, many of whom seem to find something attractive about the song, which gave them their biggest hit while also giving the actual song itself a chart position that it had always deserved. True believes the production of "Baby, I Love You" was as great, if not greater than, the original, claiming that "the soaring strings, the double tracked vocal harmonies, and the thunderous wall of drums was pure heartbreak and denial, all wrapped up in 3.49 minutes of pop perfection. One of the greatest singles ever—not Ramones singles but singles ever" (True, 147).

The song brought the group lots of new attention, particularly from young girls, who would crowd the gigs not to see the Ramones but to hear "Baby, I Love You" (True, 147). For many it was certainly a testament that the Ramones could be so versatile. Punk often parodied early musical periods; the Dolls and the Damned had done so. While Sid Vicious would become notorious not just for his iconoclastic image but also for his parodies of Frank Sinatra, it would be difficult to see the Sex Pistols, for example, doing something in the same pop style. Unfortunately, it didn't help the band's credibility when the song was used on an ad for the Yellow Pages.

Success or Failure?

Apparently Spector labored over six months mixing the *End of the Century* album, which took $200,000 to make. Even though *End of the Century* had been their biggest success to date and they had originally signed a two-album deal with Spector, they couldn't face the prospect of recording with him again.

Fans who were not enamored with *End of the Century* blamed the replacing of Tommy Ramone, who had defined their sound on the first four albums and created much of what fans loved about their records, for its failure. Shunting Tommy Ramone aside may not have been deliberate, suggests True; however, the evidence points to the contrary, with Tommy being replaced as producer, while the Ramones were chasing that elusive hit on albums such as *End of the Century*, *Pleasant Dreams* (1981), and *Subterranean Jungle* (1983; True, 111). Since Tommy had left the touring band, in the same vein that Spector and Brian Wilson had done, to concentrate on the studio recordings, the others felt he was not integral to the band and so was replaceable, yet it was essentially Tommy that had guided the group musically and had virtually created their defining sound on their early albums.

For some fans, and Joey almost certainly, *End of the Century* was the zenith of their career—the Wall of Noise meets the Wall of Sound. Joey was in virtual seventh heaven; he "loved every minute. He didn't want to leave. He loved Phil. Phil loved Joey. Joey had a little bit of Ronnie in his voice" (True, 141). For others, however, and definitely Johnny, it was the beginning of the end (True, 136–50). Johnny hated it because Spector was disrespectful to the Ramones' original blueprint by soloing out Joey. Dee Dee Ramone seems to have grown fonder of the album over time and thought Joey and Phil were a great combination as Spector brought the romanticism out in Joey: "I never thought that could have been an appeal of the Ramones, but he (Joey) meets girls everywhere in the Ramones songs—the Cat Club, the Burger King, 7-11, every time he turned around, he spotted someone else. He was a romantic guy" (True, 144). Like Johnny, however, Dee Dee was frustrated with Spector's approach: "I like beauty to be instant not to be labored over," he would comment (*Phil Spector: He's a Rebel*). This is not surprising, coming from a person with a notoriously hyperactive and addictive personality.

Despite Dee Dee's inclination to get bored easily, finding relief mainly through rock 'n' roll and drugs, he was a perceptive individual and a creative songwriter who was aware of his surroundings and the people in them. Dee Dee would have been as respectful as Joey when it came to Spector, as he too was a big sixties pop fan, but he was insight-

ful enough to see the difficulties Spector brought to the Ramones project too, and it is telling that he saw Spector as being like a little boy in
the studio who didn't know what to do (*Phil Spector: He's a Rebel*).

Dee Dee's impression would suggest Spector's naïvety in recording
within the postsixties aesthetic, particularly in punk rock whose high-
octane energy was often the result of spontaneity, though certainly
some studio trickery was required. And there was the labor-intensive
approach Spector was more used to applying, not to mention his possible lack of confidence in the studio since his heyday in the sixties. It
also suggests the brattish nature of Spector's personality, the need to be
in control and to be at the center of everything. The Ramones album
wasn't about the Ramones but about Spector (and to some extent his
newfound star Joey Ramone).

Regardless of whether the band had taken the right approach in
using Spector is mostly a matter of taste and opinion, even if it seems
most likely that he overstepped the mark with regard to the principal
task of a producer, which is to bring out the essence of the artist in the
production. Spector was never one to focus on the artist as a star but
more how the artists could be used as instruments in his productions,
something that could be applied to singers who could be interchanged
between vocal parts, such as the Paris Sisters or the Crystals. But this
seems pointless for an established band such as the Ramones, and True
put it well when he makes the point that "Phil had never worked with a
band before, his artists were more of his conception" (True, 142).

Spector's presence on the album helped it to become the band's
biggest seller, apart from *The Anthology*, reaching number forty-four in
United States and fourteen in Britain; however, it caused confusion and
certainly created a greater rift among band members (True, 149). While
Tommy Ramone saw Spector's involvement as "a complex event" (True,
150), Joey, with the benefit of hindsight, articulated his feelings to the
U.S. journalist Jaan Uhelszki: "Phil liked to dominate and manipulate,
so it was a little strange. But it felt like I was performing for the master.
He's a passionate, high-drama person. I still admire him—but during
his episodes nobody was enjoying any of it. We were pissed off with his
drinking, his antics, high drama, and the insanity" (True, 142). To make
the whole Spector episode even more complex, Seymour Stein was
eventually forced to sue Spector to get the Ramones' master tapes back
for release as Stein had sold Sire to Warner Brothers, Spector's label.

After *End of the Century*

While the Ramones were hungry for commercial success and ultimately stardom, they sought out Spector because they believed he could turn their music into hit records. "Phil is a legend and we wanted to work with a legend," said Johnny Ramone. If the process did not turn out to be what they thought it would be, the follow-up album *Pleasant Dreams* certainly brought the Spector album into focus, and this collaboration seemed to work better; at least there wasn't all the drama there had been with the Spector album. One British paper suggested that the 10cc songwriter Graham Gouldman, who was brought in to produce the album, "has succeeded where Spector failed, coercing the brothers into the eighties on a wave of sympathetic, harmonic skill" (True, 167–68). Joey, however, was not convinced that Gouldman was the right producer for the Ramones, and he definitely didn't take to him in the way he had taken to Spector (True, 163–64).

Joey's feeling that Spector was a musical genius, however, is equally as clouded as that of, say, Jerry Leiber and Mike Stoller's dismissal of him, as Joey was simply a starstruck fan, overwhelmed by the idea that he could become a star through Spector. The other Ramones, particularly Johnny, were aggrieved at Spector's dismissal of the rest of the band, ultimately leaving the group, bar Joey, out in the cold, and for turning a Ramones record into a Spector record. If Johnny felt Spector's approach didn't suit their music and that listening to the opening chord of "Rock 'n' Roll High School" for hours was not what punk rock was about, it seems the Ramones had not done their homework on whom they were getting involved with in the first place.

It seems their initial reaction to Spector a few years before, when they turned down his offer to produce them, was more intuitive of the punk sensibility and probably a more accurate understanding that Spector was no longer the great producer he once was and that he had lost touch with reality in many ways, if not also out of touch with rock 'n' roll. The Ramones, eager to break the charts, ignored their intuition and instead went for what they thought would be their commercial breakthrough; in other words, they acted out of desperation, and their disappointment was the result.

The Ramones album was one of the last significant things Spector was directly involved in, though he had attempted on a number of occasions to produce current artists in the 1990s and 2000s. Celine Dion was one, though difficulties with Spector and Ms. Dion's company resulted in the project being abandoned. Another was indie rock group Starsailor, for which Spector was hired for their 2003 album *Silence Is Easy*, though he and the group would part company after just two songs.

While Spector's professional life was becoming increasingly more erratic, to say the least, difficulties in his personal life, particularly after the death of his son Phil Jr. from lymphatic leukemia, were forcing him to become more and more reclusive and paranoid. His onetime admirer Andrew "Loog" Oldham would describe Spector's decline in the following paragraph in his book *Stone Free*:

> After the early successes with Lennon and Harrison, many of his projects began with so much promise only to die crib deaths . . . the Ramones, Dion, Leonard Cohen and Celine Dion. . . . It wasn't so much Back to Mono as back to darkness as guns, wigs, gates and guard dogs not so much keeping the world out as they kept the tycoon of teen in a prison of his own devise. The lights went out on Casa Phil. (Oldham, *Stone Free*)

The disappointments and difficulties (with the obvious exception of his son's death) Spector may have been dealing with during this period, however, were nothing compared to the traumatic personal difficulties he would encounter over the next few years, when he would be charged and later convicted of the murder of the actress Lana Clarkson.

COURT CASE AND IMPRISONMENT

On February 3, 2003, Lana Clarkson was found dead in Spector's Pyrenees castle in Alhambra, California. She died instantly when a snubbed-nose .38 Colt Cobra revolver was discharged in her mouth.

Clarkson had small parts in the movies *Scarface* (1983) and *Fast Times at Richmond High* (1982), along with many TV appearances. She also took the lead in Roger Corman's *Barbarian Queen* (1985) but never quite made the big time. She had worked as a hostess at the "House of Blues," the establishment where she first met Phil Spector on the same night she was murdered. Clarkson's death was officially ruled a homicide on September 22, 2003, by the Los Angeles coroner's office, and on November 20, Spector was charged with her murder. Bail was posted at one million dollars until the trial four years later.

Many saw the whole affair as a "twisted tail of uncontrollable ego" ("Phil Spector," *True Crime*), and it seemed to be of little surprise that Spector had been accused of shooting someone as he had for a long time harbored an obsession with firearms. There were a lot of loaded guns found in Spector's house, and he was often seen screaming at people and waving guns. According to ex-Ronette Nedra Talley, Phil carried guns and surrounded himself with bodyguards, as a defense against regular attacks from random strangers ("Phil Spector," *True Crime*). John Lennon's ex-girlfriend May Pang, who had known Spector during her time with Lennon, was not too surprised at the whole affair, claiming that Spector's obsession with guns was "a ticking time bomb waiting to go off," while ex–Teddy Bears singer Annette Kleinbard (now Carol Connors) echoed Pang's remarks ("Phil Spector," *Dominick Dunne's*). Even though he always appeared to have an exaggerated sense of self, he seemed to use guns as a way to make him seem more important and powerful, possibly as a way of dealing with his insecurities over his physical weakness and stature.

Spector's defense pleaded suicide. Spector had claimed that "I don't even know her and she comes to my house to blow her brains out" ("Phil Spector," *True Crime*), but many women gave testimony at the trial that Spector had held them captive in his castle for as long as seven days, and he would be violent and controlling toward them, which made his testimony regarding Clarkson's suicide seem implausible. The fact that he had kept his ex-wife Ronnie Spector a prisoner in their home didn't really help Spector's case either, and the strange tales of him putting a gold coffin in his mansion, telling Ronnie it was for her, also didn't help ("Phil Spector," *Dominick Dunne's*).

TV presenter Dominick Dunne, in his TV special on Spector's murder trial, suggests Spector relished all the attention since his years in obscurity and seclusion; he presented himself to the media as a persecuted Jew, comparing the DA's team of lawyers to a group of Nazis, and ranted and raved about the injustices of the whole affair on his website.

Much of the evidence, however, seemed to pile up against Spector, particularly the quite damning testimony given by his limousine driver that night: Adriano de Souza, a former Brazilian military officer, claimed that Spector had come out of his house holding a gun, saying he thought he had shot somebody. Whether he had intentionally killed Clarkson or whether his obsessive and controlling behavior, along with his unhealthy obsession with guns and power that ended in this inevitable nightmare for him and Clarkson, Spector was clearly the architect of his own downfall. The *Word* magazine would suggest as much when it wrote, "Spector's personal disaster stems from the same source as his musical brilliance" (M. Brown, i). Spector was finally charged with murder in the second degree and sent to prison for nineteen years to life.

Spector's former executive assistant Michelle Blaine feels that Spector didn't like to be on his own; having people about gave him a "presence of importance." Blaine felt Spector was like a child. Blaine also felt Spector was insecure and that he was a person who had an awkward life and as a result wanted to control everything and everyone around him ("Phil Spector," *True Crime*). Psychologist Stephen A. Diamond, the author of *Anger, Madness, and the Daimonic: The Paradoxical Power of Rage in Violence, Evil, and Creativity*, sees genius, creativity, and evil as being closely connected and blames Spector's inability to control his inner demons of "inferiority feelings, narcissistic rage, traumatic loss, [and] fear of abandonment" to be the cause of his own destruction, echoing what the *Word* magazine had ultimately concluded (Diamond).

In Spector's defense there are a number of things that may have been brought into question, things that respected playwright and director David Mamet focused on in his film *Phil Spector: The Truth Is Somewhere in the Mix* (2013). Mamet's film takes the view that there was not enough evidence to convict Spector—no fingerprints found on the gun and the nature of the blood splatter (or the lack of it) on Spector's coat, and so forth. Spector's defense claimed that De Souza's English was not fluent and he could possibly have misunderstood Spector when he came out of his house that night. The defense also claimed that Clarkson was depressed and that Spector, as he would claim on his own website, had no motive. The fact that the first trial was declared a mistrial may give some weight to the feeling that there was not sufficient evidence to have convicted Spector. In his documentary *The Agony and the Ecstasy of Phil Spector* Vikram Jayanti also empathized with Spector:

Everyone asks me if I think he did it, and I always surprise them by saying, "I think there's a reasonable doubt." I have to look out for Stockholm Syndrome, because you're spending so much time with somebody and you fall in love with them. My primary concern was trying to do this act of empathic imagination, to feel his torment. I mean, there's stuff I could have put in there that made him look like the devil. (E. Douglas)

Although Jayanti was attempting to document the emotional state of a "great artist" in a major crisis whose world has been turned upside down and inside out, comparing him to both Oscar Wilde and Napoleon (E. Douglas), his empathy with Spector and his situation seems to obscure the fact that Spector is on trial for murder, not like Wilde who was persecuted for his lifestyle choices.

Throughout the two trials Spector became more of a curiosity to people, who were becoming to regard him as a freak, while the groundbreaking work he had done as a producer was slowly being forgotten. This unfortunately was the sad outcome for Spector, whose reputation has been indelibly tarnished, completely eclipsing his contribution to popular music and culture.

Spector has claimed the murder charges are nothing more than a vendetta against him, going back to the sixties, because he had upset the establishment. If you played rock 'n' roll and didn't support the war in Vietnam in the sixties, he claimed, then you were not liked and not wanted and the press would turn against you. "If the media doesn't like you they make it difficult for you," he told Jayanti, while the question of Spector's celebrity, and the tendency not to convict celebrities in Los Angeles, seemed to be a major motivating force behind deputy DA Alan Jackson to ensure Spector's prosecution ("Phil Spector," *True Crime*).

Spector feels he has not had the same acceptance that some of his contemporaries from the sixties have had. Dylan, for instance, Spector believes, has been seen as an artist who took a social position, while Spector was simply seen as an entertainer, nothing significantly important (Jayanti). Jayanti keenly points out that Spector had produced much of Lennon's more politically and socially oriented music, as well as George Harrison's great solo work, full of philosophical and spiritual ideology. As well, he says it is ignorance to overlook Spector's achievements in the recording studio, as many of his records are pieces of great sonic art, akin to Warhol's pop art in terms of a visual medium or that of

Dylan's in terms of lyrical poetry, and has contributed as much to American culture and art as have both of these individuals.

CONCLUSION

Spector: The Genius That the Geniuses Go To

SPECTOR KEPT ROCK 'N' ROLL ALIVE

After Elvis had been conscripted into the army, in March 1958, a major gap appeared within the arena of popular music. Not only had the King temporarily been absent from the rock 'n' roll scene, but also other notable contributors to rock 'n' roll's worthy cause had made a sudden exit. In October 1957 while on a tour of Australia, Little Richard suddenly decided to give up his hedonistic life in rock 'n' roll and turned to God; Buddy Holly came to a tragic end when his plane crashed, in February 1959; and ten months later on December 23, 1959, Chuck Berry was imprisoned for allegedly "immoral purposes." The time was ripe for someone, such as Phil Spector and his radio-friendly style of pop, to fill the gap. The time was ripe for a new pop sound, a sound that would focus primarily on the production values of the record itself.

It was essentially Spector who, for the first two years of the sixties, kept pop music interesting and relevant, while at the same time evolving the rock 'n' roll style, expanding it, making it more musical, and ultimately making the music of the British Invasion more palatable to American audiences, while also encouraging writers of pop music, such as Brian Wilson, to expand their songwriting and production skills. Fundamentally, to quote John Lennon, "Spector kept rock 'n' roll alive while Elvis was in the army" (Miles, *British Invasion*, 42).

THE GLITTERING CAREER OF AN OUTRAGEOUS FANTASIST

Though there are many such as Brian Wilson, Andrew "Loog" Oldham, John Lennon, George Harrison, Don Kirshner, Sonny Bono, and Jack Nitzsche, who all virtually idolized Spector, others felt differently toward him and dismissed his "greatness" as a producer as being more a result of the hype and publicity that the music industry thrives on. Some, such as Jerry Leiber and Mike Stoller, who had been Spector's mentors, were critical of Spector's production style, as well as his arrogance, though the objectivity of their criticism toward Spector may be seen more as jealousy, since Spector had more or less stolen their thunder and made their style of music redundant by 1961. Others, however, such as Johnny and Dee Dee Ramone, may have had more genuine reasons for dismissing Spector's talent after their disappointing collaboration with the "great" producer. In the Ramones' case, clashes of egos and personal ambitions certainly muddy the waters in regard to Spector's involvement, but at the same time it is unfair to expect an individual to continue to produce great work twenty-odd years after his heyday.

Producer Robert "Bumps" Blackwell, who had made Little Richard a big name in the fifties, never gave Spector the esteem that the music press had given him and thought he had stolen too much from black producers and artists (*Phil Spector: He's a Rebel*). Meanwhile, author and musicologist Albert Goldman also thinks little of Spector, saying that "Phil Spector is the voice of American popular music, the era that followed the beginning of rock 'n' roll, wiped out by a moral panic, symbolized by the payola scandal, which created a gap which Phil Spector filled." Goldman thinks Spector's records are "schlock," "vulgar," "gross," and "calculating and commercial" and that they "fascinate you through horror rather than delight"; he compares Spector's approach to a "mad Jewish Blitzkrieg." Goldman complains that Spector seems to suffer from "imaginative and emotional impotence, always adding more. Calling for more reinforcements. An element of more is less."

The result for Goldman was not the Wall of Sound so much as "the wall of schlock" (*Phil Spector: He's a Rebel*).

Despite all his success and his influence on the pop music industry, even if many such as Leiber and Stoller or Albert Goldman felt he was undeserving of all the acclaim, Spector, now in his seventies, will probably spend the remaining years of his life in prison, a sad end to what should have been a glittering career and life. It was not just these last few years of Spector's life that cast their shadow; throughout his life Spector seemed to have been subjected to torment and rejection, which he only momentarily escaped while creating his epic pop symphonies in the studio, but even that brought its pressure and its despair. The picture Richard Williams paints, in his article, of this lonely and insecure figure is worth quoting:

> But now it was five years since Spector's last big hit, five years since he retired in disgust after the American record industry took revenge on his refusal to play the payola game. He was 26 years old then, already a multimillionaire, and he walked away. . . . Weeks later, in London, there were glimpses of a different Spector. On a couple of long evenings in his hotel suite, as darkness fell over Park Lane, an outrageous fantasist emerged. This was the mask of a lonely and insecure man for whom no degree of acclaim and material success could quite override the tragedy of his father's suicide or the mental scars of humiliations at the hands of bigger and stronger boys during his school days. . . . For him they were art, no question. But also the best revenge. (R. Williams, "Other Side")

Without a doubt, pop music would have been the poorer without Spector, or possibly not even existed as it had done throughout the sixties. The major figures of pop music, from the Beach Boys and the Beatles to the Rolling Stones and the Who; the surf music, the girl group genre, and Motown; and the garage and underground music of the late sixties, all owe a huge debt to Spector. The late seventies pop sensibilities of the New Wave movement headed by groups such as Blondie, the Go-Go's, and others all borrowed from Spector's sound, and even in more recent times music producers and recording artists such as the Smiths; Mike Stock, Matt Aiken, and Pete Waterman; Amy Winehouse; the Spice Girls; Vivian Girls; the Pipettes; and many others have something of Spector's pop approach in them.

Spector was an individual who resonated very precisely and sensitively with his time. He created his art in accordance with the environment in which he lived, thought, and felt, and for this reason his music was a direct expression of teenage sensibility. It is most probably because he was so intrinsically in touch with the zeitgeist and the teenage sensibility of the time that other young musicians of the time, such as the Beatles and the Stones, and songwriters like Gerry Goffin and Carole King, related to him as a kind of pied piper.

THE LAST WORD

While "He's a Rebel" had grabbed the pop music industry by the scruff of the neck and made everyone stand up and take notice of the young "punk," Phil Spector, his next few Philles releases, two singles with the Crystals and his following one with the Ronettes, catapulted Spector into the realm of mega-stardom. What made it all the more impressive was that Spector was only twenty-two with just a small independent label behind him and was also not willing to bow down to the demands of the industry; instead, Spector chose to take the established industry on and play by his own rules. He controlled everything himself—finding the artists, cowriting the songs, production, publicity, and quality control—because he made the sound and the sound was what sold; he became unique for making the producer bigger than the artists.

Senior vice president and general manager of Legacy Recordings (Sony Music's catalog division) Adam Block, who reissued Spector's recordings in 2010, summed up Spector's legacy and his contribution to popular culture by saying, "There may be no pop music more iconic than 'Be My Baby' or 'Da Doo Ron Ron.' The Philles Wall of Sound is embedded in our musical DNA[;] the craft of these recordings, the quality of the songwriting and the power of the productions have established a standard that continues to inspire artists and musicians" (Kubernik). Others claim that Spector's sonic achievements, coupled with his music business acumen, have helped us all hear the world (Kubernik), while one newspaper, who paid tribute to Spector's talent and his impact on popular culture, stated that "what is beyond dispute is that the ambition of Spector's productions and their thematic consistency constitute a heartfelt love letter to teenage rebellion, infatuation and betrayal that remains unparalleled" (*Guardian*, "10 (Nuttiest) Produc-ers").

The last word on Spector, however, can be left to the son of Spector's onetime friend, collaborator, and admirer, John Lennon, who described Spector as "the genius that the geniuses come to" (Corliss, "Phil Spector and the New Film").

FURTHER READING

Abbott, Kingsley. *Little Symphonies: A Phil Spector Reader*. London: Helter Skelter, 2011.

Ames Carlin, Peter. *Catch a Wave: The Rise, Fall and Redemption of Beach Boy Brian Wilson*. London: Rodale, 2007.

Anderson, Paul. *Mods: The New Religion; The Style and Music of the 1960's Mods*. London: Omnibus, 2013.

Antonia, Nina. *The New York Dolls: Too Much Too Soon*. London: Omnibus, 2005.

Auslander, Philip. *Performing Glam Rock: Gender and Theatricality in Popular Music*. Ann Arbor: University of Michigan Press, 2006.

Barnard, Stephen. *Rock: An Illustrated History*. New York: Schirmer, 1986.

Barnes, Richard. *Mods!* London: Plexus, 1979.

Betrock, Alan. *Girl Groups: The Story of a Sound*. New York: Delilah Books, 1983.

Billig, Michael. *Rock 'n' Roll Jews*. Nottingham, UK: Five Leaves, 2000.

Blaney, John. *John Lennon: Listen to This Book*. N.p.: Paper Jukebox, 2005.

Block, Avital, and Lauri Umansky. *Impossible to Hold: Women and Culture in the 1960s*. New York: New York University Press, 2005.

Brown, Len. *Meetings with Morrissey*. London: Omnibus, 2009.

Brown, Mick. *Tearing Down the Wall of Sound: The Rise and Fall of Phil Spector*. New York: Bloomsbury, 2007.

Campbell, Michael. *Popular Music in America: The Beat Goes On*. Belmont, CA: Thomson Schirmer, 2005.

Che, Cathay. *Deborah Harry: The Biography*. London: Andre Deutsch, 2014.

Clayson, Alan. *Beat Merchants: The Origins, History, Impact and Rock Legacy of the 1960's British Pop Groups*. London: Blandford, 1995.

Clayton, Marie. *Madonna: An Illustrated Biography*. London: Transatlantic, 2010.

Clemente, John. *Girl Groups: Fabulous Females That Rocked the World*. Iola, WI: Krause, 2000.

Clerk, Carol. *Madonnastyle*. London: Omnibus, 2002.

Cross, Mary. *Madonna*. Westport, CT: Greenwood, 2007.

Davis, Stephen. *Old Gods Almost Dead: The 40-Year Odyssey of the Rolling Stones*. New York: Broadway, 2001.

DeBeauvoir, Simone. *The Second Sex*. Translated and edited by H. M. Parshley. London: Vintage, 1997.

de Forest, G. A. "Rock Music—Beach Boys vs Beatlemania." *Garbonza's Weblog*, February 20, 2008. http://garbonza.wordpress.com/.

Devereux, Eoin, Aileen Dillane, and Martin J. Power, eds. *Morrissey: Fandom, Representations and Identities*. Bristol, UK: Intellect, 2011.

Dillon, Mark. *Fifty Sides of the Beach Boys: The Songs That Tell Their Story*. Toronto: ECW Press, 2012.

Doggett, Peter. *The Man Who Sold the World: David Bowie in the 1970's*. London: Vintage, 2012.

———. *There's a Riot Going On: Revolutionaries, Rock Stars, and the Rise and Fall of the '60s*. New York: Canongate, 2007.

———. *You Never Give Me Your Money*. New York: Harper Paperbacks, 2011.

Douglas, Susan. *Listening In: Radio and the American Imagination*. Minneapolis: University of Minnesota Press, 2004.

———. *Where the Girls Are: Growing Up Female with the Mass Media*. New York: Times Books, 1994.

Downes, Julia, ed. *Women Make Noise: Girl Bands from Motown to the Modern*. Twickenham, UK: Supernova, 2012.

Du Noyer, Paul. *Conversations with McCartney*. London: Hodder & Stoughton, 2015.

———. *In the City: The Celebration of London Music*. London: Virgin, 2010.

———. *John Lennon: We All Shine On; The Stories behind Every John Lennon Song, 1970–1980*. London: Carlton, 2006.

Early, Gerald. *One Nation under a Groove: Motown and American Culture*. Hopewell, NJ: Ecco, 1995.

Egan, Sean. *The Mammoth Book of the Beatles*. Philadelphia: Running Press, 2009.

Elliott, Martin. *The Rolling Stones: Complete Recording Sessions, 1962–2002*. London: Cherry Red, 2003.

Emerson, Ken. *Always Magic in the Air: The Bomp and Brilliance of the Brill Building Era*. London: Forth Estate, 2006.

Everett, Walter. *The Beatles as Musicians: The Quarrymen through Rubber Soul*. London: Oxford University Press, 2001.

Examiner.com. "The Complicated History behind 'River Deep-Mountain High.'" Accessed March 27, 2016. http://www.examiner.com/.

Fletcher, Tony. *Dear Boy: The Life of Keith Moon*. London: Omnibus, 2010.

———. *A Light That Never Goes Out: The Enduring Saga of the Smiths*. London: Windmill, 2013.

Foster, Mo. *Play Like Elvis! How British Musicians Bought the American Dream*. Bodmin, UK: MPG Books, 2000.

Friedan, Betty. *The Feminine Mystique*. London: Penguin Modern Classics, 2010.

Friedman, Roger. "Spector Rips Tina at Ike Turner's Funeral." *Fox News*, December 22, 2007. http://www.foxnews.com/.

Gaar, Gillian. *She's a Rebel: The History of Women in Rock and Roll*. Exp. 2nd ed. New York: Seal, 2002.

Gluck, Sherna Berger. *Rosie the Riveter: Women, the War and Social Change*. New York: Meridian, 1988.

Goddard, Simon. *Mozipedia: The Encyclopedia of Morrissey and the Smiths*. London: Ebury, 2009.

———. *The Smiths: Songs that Saved Your Life*. London: Reynolds and Hearn, 2004.

Gordy, Berry. *To Be Loved: The Music, Magic, Memories of Motown*. Boston: Rosetta, 2013.

Grieg, Charlotte. *Will You Still Love Me Tomorrow? Girl Groups from the 50s On*. London: Virago, 1989.

Harrington, Richard. "Madonna: Siren of Success." *Washington Post*, June 3, 1985.

Harrison, George. *I, Me, Mine*. San Francisco: Chronicle, 2007.

Hartman, Ken. *The Wrecking Crew: The Inside Story of Rock and Roll's Best Kept Secret*. New York: Thomas Dunne, 2012.

Hewitt, Paolo. *The Sharper World: A Mod Anthology*. London: Helter Skelter, 2009.

Heylin, Clinton. *From the Velvets to the Voidoids*. London: Helter Skelter, 1993.

Jackson Joe. *A Cure for Gravity: A Musical Pilgrimage*. Cambridge, MA: Da Capo, 2000.

Jayanti, Vikram. *The Agony and the Ecstasy of Phil Spector*. DVD. London: Arena, BBC, 2009.

Johnstone, Nick. *The Amy Winehouse Story*. London: Omnibus, 2008.

Judt, Tony. *Postwar: A History of Europe since 1945*. London: Vintage, 2010.

Keenan, Elizabeth K. "Puppets on a String? Girl Groups of the 50s and 60s." In *Women Make Noise: Girl Bands from Motown to the Modern*, edited by Julia Downes. Twickenham, UK: Supernova, 2012.

King, Carole. *A Natural Woman*. London: Virago, 2013.

Kirby, Michael Jack. "The Paris Sisters: I Love How You Love Me." Way Back Attack. Accessed January 30, 2016. http://www.waybackattack.com/.

Kirkpatrick, Rob. *Magic in the Night: The Words and Music of Bruce Springsteen*. London: Souvenir Press, 2009.

Koojiman, Jaap. "From Elegance to Extravaganza: The Supremes on the Ed Sullivan Show as a Presentation of Beauty." *Velvet Light Trap* 49 (2002): 4–17.

Kureishi, Hanif, and Jon Savage, eds. *The Faber Book of Pop*. London: Faber and Faber, 1995.

Kurlansky, Mark. *Ready for a Brand New Beat: How "Dancing in the Street" Became the Anthem for a Changing America*. New York: Riverhead, 2014.

Levering, Stephen. *Time (and Newsweek) Is on My Side: Pop/Rock Coverage in Time and Newsweek during the 1960s*. Ann Arbor, MI: ProQuest, 2006.

Levine, Larry. "The Pet Sounds Sessions" (liner notes). *The Beach Boys*. CD. Los Angeles: Capitol, 1997.

MacDonald, Ian. *Revolution in the Head: The Beatles Records and the Sixties*. 3rd rev. ed. London: Vintage, 2008.

MacInnis, Colin. *Absolute Beginners*. London: Allison and Busby, 2011.

MacLeod, Sean. *Leaders of the Pack: Girl Groups of the 1960s and Their Influence on Popular Culture*. Lanham, MD: Rowman & Littlefield, 2015.

Madinger, Chip, and Mark Easter. *Eight Arms to Hold You*. Chesterfield, MO: 44.1 Productions, 2000.

Magee, Bryan. *Aspects of Wagner*. London: Panther, 1972.

Marable, Manning. *Malcolm X: A Life of Reinvention*. London: Penguin, 2011.

Marcus, Greil. *The History of Rock 'n' Roll in Ten Songs*. New Haven, CT: Yale University Press, 2014.

McRobbie, Angela, ed. *Zoot Suits and Second Hand Dresses: An Anthology of Fashion and Music*. London: Macmillan, 1982.

Melnick, Monte A., and Frank Meyer. *On the Road with the Ramones*. London: Bobcat, 2007.

Miles, Barry. *The Beatles: A Diary; An Intimate Day by Day History*. London: Omnibus, 2002.

———. *The British Invasion*. London: Sterling, 2009.

———. *Paul McCartney: Many Years from Now*. New York: Owl Books, 1998.

Moorefield, Virgil. *The Producer as Composer: Shaping the Sounds of Popular Music*. Cambridge, MA: MIT Press, 2010.

Morrissey, Stephen. *Morrissey: Autobiography*. London: Penguin, 2013.

Music Moguls: Masters of Pop–Money Makers (documentary). London: BBC, 2016.

Newkey-Burden, Chas. *Amy Winehouse: The Biography*. London: John Blake, 2008.

Norman, Philip. *John Lennon: The Life*. New York: HarperCollins, 2008.

———. *Mick Jagger*. New York: Harper, 2013.

———. *Shout! The Beatles in Their Generation*. New York: Simon and Schuster, 2011.

Oldham, Andrew Loog. *Stoned*. London: Vintage, 2000.

———. *Stone Free*. Vancouver, BC: Because Entertainment, 2012. Kindle ed.

Padel, Ruth. *I Am a Man: Sex, Gods, and Rock and Roll*. London: Faber and Faber, 2000.

Pegg, Nicholas. *The Complete David Bowie*. London: Reynolds and Hearn, 2009.

Philo, Simon. *The British Invasion: The Crosscurrents of Musical Influence*. Lanham, MD: Rowman & Littlefield, 2015.

Porter, Dick, and Kris Needs. *Blondie: Parallel Lives*. London: Omnibus, 2012.

Priore, Domenic. *Smile: The Story of Brian Wilson's Lost Masterpiece*. London: Sanctuary, 2005.

Quirk, Tom. *Endlessly Horny for Wonder and Magic: How Jim Steinman's "Bat out of Hell" Perfectly Captured the Pre-Pubescent American Id (and Nearly Ruined Me for Life)*. New York: Feedback Press, 2012.

Ramone, Johnny. *Commando: The Autobiography*. New York: Abrams, 2012.

Reed, John. *Paul Weller: My Ever Changing Moods*. London: Omnibus, 1996.

Reeves, Martha. *Dancing in the Street: Confessions of a Motown Diva*. New York: Hyperion, 1995.

Ribowsky, Mark. *He's a Rebel: Phil Spector, Rock and Roll's Legendary Producer*. Cambridge, MA: Da Capo, 2006.

Richards, Keith. *Life*. New York: Back Bay. 2011.

Riley, Tim. *Fever: How Rock 'n' Roll Transformed Gender in America*. New York: Picador, 2005.

Rinny. "Exclusive: Beyonce Guitarist Bibi McGill Talks Music, Hair and Healthy Living." Black Girl with Long Hair, January 12, 2012. http://blackgirllonghair.com/.

Robb, John. "Sex Pistols 'Never Mind the Bollocks': A Re-evaluation." Louder than War, November 15, 2011. Accessed November 15, 2016. http://louderthanwar.com/.

Rolling Stone. "100 Greatest Singers of All Time." December 2, 2010. http://www.rollingstone.com/.

Rosewarne, Lauren. *Part-Time Perverts: Sex, Pop Culture, and Kink Management*. Santa Barbara, CA: Praeger, 2011.

Rutherford, Paul. *The World Made Sexy: Freud to Madonna*. Toronto: University of Toronto Press, 2007.

Salewicz, Chris. *Mick and Keith*. London: Orion, 2002.

Sandford, Christopher. *Bowie: Loving the Alien*. New York: Little, Brown, 1996.

———. *McCartney*. London: Arrow, 2006.

Shaw, Arnold. *The Rockin' 50s: The Decade That Transformed the Pop Music Scene*. New York: Da Capo, 1987.

Shepherd, John, David Horn, and Paul Oliver, eds. *Continuum Encyclopedia of Popular Music of the World*. Part 1, vol. 1, *Media Industry and Society*. New York: Continuum, 2003.

Spector, Ronnie, with Vince Waldron. *Be My Baby*. London: MacMillan, 1991.

Spitz, Bob. *The Beatles: The Biography*. Boston: Little, Brown, 2005.

Stanley, Bob. *Yeah, Yeah, Yeah: The Story of Modern Pop*. London: Faber and Faber, 2013.

Stras, Laurie, ed. *She's So Fine: Reflections of Whiteness, Femininity, Adolescence and Class in 1960s Music*. Farnham, UK: Ashgate, 2011.

Taraborrelli, J. Randy. *Diana Ross*. London: Sidgwick and Jackson, 2007.

Taylor, Marc. *The Original Marvelettes: Motown's Mystery Girl Group*. New York: Aloiv, 2004.

Taylor, Steve. *The A to X of Alternative Music*. London: Bloomsbury, 2004.

Thesander, Marianne. *The Feminine Ideal*. London: Reaktion, 1997.

Thompson, David. *Phil Spector: Wall of Pain*. London: Sanctuary, 2004.

True, Everett. *Hey Ho Let's Go: The Story of the Ramones*. London: Omnibus, 2010.

Turner, Steve. *The Beatles: A Hard Day's Write; The Stories behind Every Song*. New York: MJF Books, 2009.

Warner, Jay. *American Singing Groups: A History from 1940s to Today*.

Warwick, Jacqueline C. *Girl Groups, Girl Culture: Popular Music and Identity in the 1960s*. London: Routledge, 2007.

Welch, Chris. *David Bowie: The Stories behind the Classic Songs, 1970–1980*. London: Carlton, 2010.

Whitely, Sheila. *Women and Popular Music: Sexuality, Identity and Subjectivity*. New York: Routledge, 2000.

Williams, Richard. "The Other Side of Phil Spector." *Guardian*, April 13, 2009. Accessed March 15, 2016. http://www.theguardian.com/.

———. *Phil Spector: Out of His Head*. London: Omnibus, 2003.

Wilson, Brian, with Todd Gold. *Wouldn't It Be Nice: My Own Story: Brian Wilson, the Creative Genius behind the Beach Boys*. London: Bloomsbury, 1996.

Wilson, Mary. *Dreamgirl: My Life as a Supreme*. New York: Cooper Square Press, 1999.
———. *Supreme Faith*. New York: Cooper Square Press, 1999.
Wilson, Terry. *Tamla Motown: The Stories behind the UK Singles*. London: Cherry Red, 2009.
Wolf, Naomi. *The Beauty Myth: How Images of Beauty Are Used against Women*. London: Vintage, 1991.
Wolfe, Tom. *The Kandy Kolored Tangerine Flake Streamline Baby*. New York: Bantam, 1989.
Womack, Kenneth. *Long and Winding Roads: The Evolving Artistry of the Beatles*. New York: Bloomsbury, 2007.

FURTHER LISTENING

Phil Spector had recorded and released more than a hundred singles, of which more than fifteen entered the top ten in the United States, while four of these went to number one, including George Harrison's "My Sweet Lord," the Teddy Bears' "To Know Him Is to Love Him," the Crystals' "He's a Rebel," and the Righteous Brothers' "You've Lost That Lovin' Feelin'." While Spector's medium was mainly the single, particularly during the late fifties and early sixties, Spector also produced and coproduced a significant number of very successful albums, including John Lennon's *Imagine*, George Harrison's *All Things Must Pass* and the Beatles' *Let It Be*. There are too many records (singles and albums) to mention them all here, but below is a list, for recommended listening, of some of Spector's best work.

PRE-WALL OF SOUND PERIOD

Albums

The Teddy Bears Sing. The Teddy Bears. Imperial Records, 1959. Spector's first album recorded with school friends when he was still only a teenager.

Twist Uptown. The Crystals. Philles Records, 1962. Spector's first since his *Teddy Bears Sing.* The album was simply only to cash in on the success of the Crystals' singles "There's No Other" and "Uptown." Albums were not the major works that they would come to be a few years later, particularly with the Beatles' *Revolver* and *Sgt. Pepper*.

Singles

"Don't Worry My Little Pet." The Teddy Bears. B-side to "To Know Him Is to Love Him."
Dore Records, December 1, 1958. The song is a curiosity piece as it was Spector's first
ever recording showing the many influences that would shape his future hit records.

"To Know Him Is to Love Him." The Teddy Bears. Dore Records, December 1, 1958, #1. A
song that revealed the deep effect the suicide of Spector's father had on him. It was
Spector's first number one, which has become a classic of the pop ballad tradition, recorded by numerous artists over the years, including most recently Amy Winehouse.

"Corrina, Corrina." Ray Peterson. Dunes Records, November 21, 1960, #9. Spector's first
major hit as a producer and ultimately the beginning of his career as such. The song had
been given to him by his mentors Jerry Leiber and Mike Stoller; little did they know that
this move was, unwittingly, the beginning of the end of their own career as they would be
unable to compete with Spector's productions over the next three years.

"Pretty Little Angel Eyes." Curtis Lee. Dunes Records, July 3, 1961, #7. Another hit for
Spector as a producer though he was still working toward creating his infamous Wall of
Sound.

"Every Breath I Take." Gene Pitney. Musicor Records, September 11, 1961, #42. Spector
would record many major artists outside his own stable of stars. Here is one of his first
collaborations with an iconic artist. Though not a huge hit for either Spector or Pitney,
both would go on to become major figures in their own right.

"Be My Boy." The Paris Sisters. Gregmark Records, April 24, 1961, #56. The first of Spector's wonderful productions with the Paris Sisters. Still searching for his hit sound, not
only is the work he did with the Paris Sisters tasteful and very effective but also its
minimalist nature was proof that Spector was not just a one-trick pony with his bombastic
Wagnerian Wall of Sound, which would become his trademark just a year later. The Paris
Sisters' records and sound was created entirely by Spector, who took them away from
their outdated Andrew Sisters style, and is a period in music that just simply should not be
ignored.

"I Love How You Love Me." The Paris Sisters. Gregmark Records, October 30, 1961, #5.
Probably the climax of the Spector/Paris Sisters collaboration "All through the Night," B-
side to "I Love How You Love Me." More upbeat than the other Spector/Paris Sisters
productions. The track is slightly throwaway but still perfectly captures the joyousness of
the girl group genre, which he would soon dominate with his many girl group acts.

"Under the Moon of Love." Curtis Lee. Dunes Records, November 27, 1961, #46. A minor
hit for Spector at the time, but the song would prove to have longevity as it became a
major hit for British rock 'n' roll revivalists Showaddywaddy a decade or so later.

"There's No Other (Like My Baby)." The Crystals. Philles Records, January 22, 1962, #20.
The first song that Spector recorded both with the Crystals and also for his own Philles
label. The song was the real turning point for Spector, finding the artists, producing the
artist, and promoting the song, and all on his own label.

"Uptown." The Crystals. Philles Records, March 3, 1962, #13. A major hit for Spector and
the beginning of his collaborations with Don Kirshner's Aldon group of songwriters, this
time with Barry Mann and Cynthia Weil. The song was a whole new direction for Spector
and for pop music in general displaying an element of social conscience that had not
existed in pop music before. Spector began to realize the sound he wanted to create with
this song as well as the black girl group the Crystals, realizing they were the perfect
vehicle for his songs. "Uptown" was the first time all the elements fell into place for
Spector, the right songwriters, the right song, and the right group to sing it, and best of all,
being on his own label, he had no one to tell him what he could or could not do.

"Second Hand Love." Connie Francis. MGM, June 9, 1962, #7. Another of Spector's collaborations with iconic artists, this time Connie Francis, which gained both Spector and
Francis a top ten hit, while keeping Spector relevant and also in demand by other big
artists keen for him to work his magic on them. Spector at this point, however, was
beginning to realize that he was the only star he wanted to work with. Spector began to

work with singers who were talented enough to carry his records but not big enough to overshadow his star role as producer.

THE WALL OF SOUND PERIOD

Albums

He's a Rebel. The Crystals. Philles Records, March 16, 1963, #131. Another token album to cash in on the success of the Crystals singles. Also the same year on the Philles label.

The Crystals Sing the Greatest Hits Vol. 1. The Crystals. Philles Records, 1963.

A Christmas Gift for You from Phil Spector. Various artists. Philles Records, 1963. The first and probably only major album produced solely by Spector. It was to be his magnum opus, presenting the world with a Christmas gift from the world's greatest pop producer, the only one, at least in his eyes, that could popularize classic Christmas songs by some of the greatest composers of popular song in the twentieth century. The album, though considered by many today as one of Spector's best achievements, was a flop, most probably because it was released just before the tragic killing of J. F. Kennedy, after which the whole nation went into mourning.

Presenting the Fabulous Ronettes Featuring Veronica. The Ronettes. Philles Records, December 26, 1964, #96. Apart from the Christmas album, Spector was not smitten by albums. It was with singles that stars were made, and Spector wanted his star to shine brighter and brighter. The unsuccessful Christmas album possibly reconfirmed his belief that singles were what people wanted and was where artistic and commercial success lay. However, with the number of great songs Spector had recorded with the Ronettes he could easily have produced one of the first classic albums of all time, before the album would gain prominence by the midsixties. With just a little more thought put into it, this album could have been a major work, but Spector just never bothered.

River Deep, Mountain High. Ike and Tina Turner. Philles Records, 1966 (in UK; only rereleased September 27, 1969, in United States), #102. Once again Spector threw away the opportunity to create a major album with one of soul music's greatest performers: Tina Turner. Spector put all his energy into just one song with her, the single of the same title. The song of course became a milestone in pop music, and many felt it was his greatest work, though some were less impressed, particularly in America. The single hit big in the UK, even if the United States ignored it. It was probably just as well that Spector hadn't put as much energy into recording the album.

Singles

"He's a Rebel." The Crystals. Philles Records, November 3, 1962, #1. Spector's first number one since the Teddy Bears and his first number one in his girl group era. The song was not a Wall of Sound, but it was the beginning of his conception of the idea, employing a large number of musicians to produce a big sound. The song made Spector the most important musician of the day, and this was just the beginning of his chart domination for the next two years.

"Christmas (Baby Please Come Home)." Darlene Love. Philles Records, 1963. One of the highlights from Spector's Christmas album *A Christmas Gift for You from Phil Spector.*

"Zip-a-Dee-Doo-Dah." Bob B. Soxx and the Blue Jeans. Philles Records, January 12, 1963, #8. Spector gives the Disney song his first real Wall of Sound treatment.

"He's Sure the Boy I Love." The Crystals. Philles Records, January 19, 1963, #11. Spector was beginning to shape the sound he was searching for, and with this track the Wall of

Sound can be heard as a definite concept, which he would employ for the rest of his sixties music, tweaking and perfecting it for every next single.

"(Today I Met) The Boy I'm Gonna Marry." Darlene Love. Philles Records, May 11, 1963, #39. Though Darlene Love would sing on most of the Crystals' songs, even though she was not a member of the band, this was the first track Spector recorded for her as a solo artist. The song shows the brilliance of her vocal and is the first time she is credited properly for her talents. The song, however, caused a major rift between her and Spector since he was supposed to sign her to a solo contract with this song. He never let her perform as a solo artist, possibly insecure that she would outshine him.

"Da Doo Ron Ron (When He Walked Me Home)." The Crystals. Philles Records, June 8, 1963, #3. One of Spector's most significant Wall of Sound productions and one of his most well-known singles.

"Then He Kissed Me." The Crystals. Philles Records, August 17, 1963, #6. Spector continues to have success with his Wall of Sound productions.

"Be My Baby." The Ronettes. Philles Records, October 12, 1963, #2. The song showcased the Ronettes, Spector's new discovery, the girl group from New York that would replace the Crystals as the vehicle for his pop masterpieces, and the unique voice of Ronnie Bennett. This was the first of the Spector/Bennett love songs that would chart their developing love affair, which they committed to record. Spector would marry Bennett some years later, but it was not a happy marriage. The song was also the first of his collaborations with his most successful writing partners Ellie Greenwich and Jeff Barry. The song would be a major influence on many recordings since, particularly the open drum part, and would be a major influence on the music of Brian Wilson.

"Baby, I Love You." The Ronettes. Philles Records, November 1963, #24. One of the best songs Spector ever recorded by Spector and the Ronettes. Another Greenwich and Barry composition. It should have done as well as the previous single "Be My Baby," but for some reason the public were just not interested.

"A Fine, Fine Boy." Darlene Love. Philles Records, November 23, 1963, #53. Darlene Love at her vocal best and one of Spector's best girl group productions. It should have done better in the charts, but Spector probably wasn't too keen on Love having any success and kept the song quiet.

"(The Best Part of) Breakin' Up." The Ronettes. Philles Records, May 16, 1964, #39. Another Spector/Ronettes classic, but still no one wanted to know; the Beatles had arrived.

"Walking in the Rain." The Ronettes. Philles Records, December 5, 1964, #23. Spector would record this track with the Ronettes at a last attempt to have another hit with them. The public appreciated the song but only enough to bring it to number twenty-three. The British Invasion had happened, and no one was interested in American producers or their female protégés.

"You've Lost That Lovin' Feelin'." The Righteous Brothers. Philles Records, February 6, 1965, #1. Spector would finally pose a challenge to the Beatles with his first major hit in three years. The song was a slow boil and required a good deal of promotion to get it going. The song however has since been confirmed as the most played song on American radio.

"River Deep, Mountain High." Ike and Tina Turner. Philles Records, June 18, 1966, #88; UK #3. This would be Spector's ambition to make the "greatest record" of all time. His ambitions may have been too big; it annoyed its composer Ellie Greenwich, who felt Spector's ego had gotten in the way. The song would become a hit in the UK, but in the United States nobody cared; it seemed Spector had lost patience with the American music industry and the public too. He went into semiretirement, which would last until the end of the decade. The sixties were over for Spector after this track flopped.

POST–WALL OF SOUND PERIOD

Albums

Let It Be. The Beatles. Apple Records, May 20, 1970, #1. Spector was called in to patch up the confused and clumsy recordings of the Beatles' unreleased album

All Things Must Pass. George Harrison (Spector, coproducer). Apple Records, December 19, 1970, #1. Harrison, always a big fan of Spector and his Wall of Sound, brought Spector in on his first solo album. Although things didn't go quite as planned and much tension developed between Spector and the "quiet" Beatle, the album became a major success both commercially and artistically, finally giving Harrison the recognition he deserved as a songwriter; it also put Spector back on top.

Plastic Ono Band. John Lennon and the Plastic Ono Band (Spector, coproducer). Apple Records December 26, 1970, #6. Spector was brought in by Lennon to produce his "warts and all" album after Spector had impressed him with his production on Lennon's "Instant Karma" single. Spector had kept his ego in control and aided Lennon in revealing the most delicate and personal music he had yet recorded.

The Concert for Bangladesh. George Harrison and Friends (Spector, coproducer). Apple Records, January 8, 1971, #2. Spector was to record Harrison's live concert in aid of refugees of the Bangladesh Liberation War genocide. It seems that Spector had been more of a hindrance then a help. The album would include some live recordings of Harrison as a solo artist, as well as capture Bob Dylan live for the first time in years.

Imagine. John Lennon and the Plastic Ono Band with the Flux Fiddlers (Spector, coproducer). Apple Records, September 18, 1971, #1. Spector again helped Lennon capture his innermost feelings, though sprinkled with chocolate "for commercial consumption." The album would not be quite as raw as *Plastic Ono Band*.

Born to Be with You. Dion. Polydor Records, 1975. UK only. The record may have been a commercial failure, but it went on to be a tremendously influential album remarked upon as such by individuals like the Who's Pete Townshend. The record was conceived by Spector and Dion as a return to their beloved doo-wop; Dion had been a successful doo-wop singer in the fifties, while Spector had grown up surrounded by the genre, much of which would influence many of his records recorded throughout his career.

Rock 'n' Roll. John Lennon (Spector, coproducer). Apple Records, 1975. An album conceived by Lennon, as a way to get him out of a depression, as well as a quick way to make some money for the broke ex-Beatle. Lennon, however, got more than he bargained for when Spector's ego went AWOL and Lennon had to abandon the project.

Death of a Ladies' Man. Leonard Cohen. Warner Bros. Records, 1977. While the great poet and producer collaboration was anticipated to be something special, Spector's Wall of Sound treatment didn't particularly marry well with Cohen's more intimate style. Perhaps, once again Spector's ego got in the way. It may have served the project better if Spector had approached Cohen's songs in the same manner as he had done with Lennon's *Plastic Ono* and *Imagine* albums.

End of the Century. The Ramones. Sire Records, February 23, 1980, #44. This was hoped to be the Ramones' breakthrough album. Their earlier recordings were pop/punk at its finest, but commercial success had eluded them. Bringing a big-name producer was to transform their fortunes, but Spector once again sabotaged the project by totally disregarding the dynamics of the band and producing their singer Joey Spector, as if it was one of his Philles acts.

Silence Is Easy. Starsailor. Capitol, 2003 (Spector, coproducer). Spector's last recording before facing accusations of murder, a murder trial, and a life sentence for which he is still imprisoned.

Singles

"Instant Karma (We All Shine On)." John Lennon. Apple Records, March 28, 1970, #3. The song was Spector's first occasion to produce the Beatles or at least one of them. The recording was considered a kind of audition for Spector prior to his work on the *Let It Be* album. Lennon was so impressed with Spector's production of the song that he recommended him for the *Let It Be* remixes. Harrison would also be impressed enough to invite Spector to produce his masterpiece *All Things Must Pass*.

"The Long and Winding Road." Apple Records, June 13, 1970, #1. Spector had taken the very poor and confused recordings of the Beatles' aborted *Let It Be* sessions and had brought them up to a standard that they could be released to the public. Though some had considered his efforts quite commendable, others felt Spector had interfered with the Beatles sound too much. This song became the most controversial of Spector's reworking of the Beatles material and particularly upset Paul McCartney, who felt Spector had destroyed the authenticity of what was to be a simple piano ballad. McCartney would release his initial vision of the song many years later with the *Let It Be, Naked* album. Spector's production, however, didn't stop McCartney from accepting a Grammy Award for the album the year it was released.

"My Sweet Lord." George Harrison. Apple Records, December 26, 1970, #1. This was Harrison's hit song from his *All Things Must Pass* album, a song that Spector had encouraged him to release, feeling it was the most commercial, and one didn't argue with Spector's gift for recognizing a hit single.

"What Is Life." George Harrison. Apple Records, March 27, 1971, #10. Another single offering from the Spector/Harrison–produced *All Things Must Pass* album. Not quite having the commercial potential of "My Sweet Lord," the song is still a good representation of what the rest of the album has to offer.

"Power to the People." John Lennon/Plastic Ono Band. Apple Records, May 15, 1971, #11. Spector had helped Lennon to express his innermost feelings on the Plastic Ono album, while this time he gave Lennon the fire he needed to produce one of his significant political anthems.

"Try Some, Buy Some." Ronnie Spector. Apple Records, May 22, 1971, #77. Though Spector and Ronnie had been estranged, Spector had offered to produce a number of songs for her, which had been written by George Harrison. Harrison had been a big fan of Ronnie's and generously offered to write her some songs in order to reignite her fading career. Spector, however, didn't give the project the attention it deserved, and Ronnie's career remained stagnant. This song, however, was of a particularly good standard, and Spector's production managed to create a certain ambience in which Harrison recorded his own vocal over Spector's production and included it on his *Living in the Material World* album. David Bowie was also so impressed with Ronnie's version of the song that he covered it on his 2003 *Reality* album.

"Imagine." John Lennon. Apple Records, November 13, 1971, #3. Spector produced Lennon's most successful ex-Beatle number. A song, which many have voted the greatest song of all time, was without doubt the most successful and probably the most powerful peace anthem of the twentieth century.

"Rock 'n' Roll High School." Ramones. Sire Records, August 4, 1979, UK #67. One of the first tracks Spector worked on with the Ramones, a kind of trial record to see if Spector was the right producer for the band's next album.

"Baby, I Love You." Ramones. Sire Records, February 4, 1980, UK #8. The Ramones' biggest hit. The song was a reworked cover of the Ronettes song. Unfortunately, it was more of a solo project for Joey Ramone playing the role of Ronnie Spector as Spector had ignored the band, undermining their abilities and concentrating all his attention on Joey, whom he saw as a male Ronnie Spector. The result was devastating to the band members, who never quite gelled together after this experience with Spector.

"Silence Is Easy." Starsailor. Capitol Records, January 9, 2003, UK #8. Spector's last single, which did well in the UK.

BIBLIOGRAPHY

Abbott, Kingsley. *Little Symphonies: A Phil Spector Reader*. London: Helter Skelter, 2011.

"The Action." *Twentieth Century Focus* (TV documentary series). London: BBC1, 1967.

Ames Carlin, Peter. *Catch a Wave: The Rise, Fall and Redemption of Beach Boy Brian Wilson*. London: Rodale, 2007.

Anderson, Paul. *Mods: The New Religion; The Style and Music of the 1960's Mods*. London: Omnibus, 2013.

Ankeny, Jason. "The Paris Sisters." AllMusic. Accessed May 7, 2017. http://www.allmusic.com/.

Antonia, Nina. *The New York Dolls: Too Much Too Soon*. London: Omnibus, 2005.

Auslander, Philip. *Performing Glam Rock: Gender and Theatricality in Popular Music*. Ann Arbor: University of Michigan Press, 2006.

Barnard, Stephen. *Rock: An Illustrated History*. New York: Schirmer, 1986.

Barnes, Richard. *Mods!* London: Plexus, 1979.

BBC. "Vietnam, 1954–1975: How the US Got Involved." GCSE Bitesize. Accessed January 16, 2016. http://www.bbc.co.uk/schools/gcsebitesize.

BBC Radio 2. "Sold on Song: 'River Deep Mountain High'; In-Depth." Accessed May 17, 2017. http://www.bbc.co.uk/.

The Beatles Anthology. Directed by Kevin Godley, Bob Smeaton, and Geoff Wonfor. Apple Corps, 1995.

Beatles Bible. "Rock 'n' Roll." Accessed July 17, 2015. http://www.beatlesbible.com/.

Bergstrom, John. "George Harrison: All Things Must Pass." PopMatters, January 13, 2011. Accessed March 11, 2016. http://www.popmatters.com/.

Betrock, Alan. *Girl Groups: The Story of a Sound*. New York: Delilah Books, 1983.

Billig, Michael. *Rock 'n' Roll Jews*. Nottingham, UK: Five Leaves, 2000.

Blaney, John. *John Lennon: Listen to This Book*. N.p.: Paper Jukebox, 2005.

Block, Avital, and Umansky, Lauri. *Impossible to Hold: Women and Culture in the 1960s*. New York: New York University Press, 2005.

Brown, George Martin Fell. "Walls of Sound." *GMF Brown* (blog), July 2, 2010. http://gmfbrown.blogspot.ie/.

Brown, Len. *Meetings with Morrissey*. London: Omnibus, 2009.

Brown, Mick. *Tearing Down the Wall of Sound: The Rise and Fall of Phil Spector*. New York: Bloomsbury, 2007.

Buskin, Richard. "David Bowie and Tony Visconti." *Recording Reality*, October 2003. Sound on Sound. Accessed October 9, 2014. http://www.soundonsound.com/.

The Byrds: Under Review. New Malden, UK: Sexy Intellectual, 2007.

Campbell, Michael. *Popular Music in America: The Beat Goes On*. Belmont, CA: Thomson Schirmer, 2005.

Charlie Is My Darling: Ireland 1965 (documentary). Directed by Peter Whitehead. New York: ABKCO Films, (1965) 2012.

Che, Cathay. *Deborah Harry: The Biography*. London: Andre Deutsch, 2014.

Classic Albums: Meatloaf; Bat out of Hell (documentary). Directed by Bob Smeaton. London: Eagle Rock Entertainment, 1999.

Clayson, Alan. *Beat Merchants: The Origins, History, Impact and Rock Legacy of the 1960's British Pop Groups*. London: Blandford, 1995.

Clayton, Marie. *Madonna: An Illustrated Biography*. London: Transatlantic, 2010.

Clemente, John. *Girl Groups: Fabulous Females That Rocked the World*. Iola, WI: Krause, 2000.

Clerk, Carol. *Madonnastyle*. London: Omnibus, 2002.

Corliss, Richard. "Phil Spector and the New Film About His Lovin' Feelin.'" *Time*, July 3, 2010.

———. "Phil Spector's Greatest Hit." *Time*, March 21, 2013.

Cross, Mary. *Madonna*. Westport, CT: Greenwood, 2007.

Curtis, Adam. *The Century of Self* (documentary). London: BBC, 2002.

Davis, Stephen. *Old Gods Almost Dead: The 40-Year Odyssey of the Rolling Stones*. New York: Broadway, 2001.

DeBeauvoir, Simone. *The Second Sex*. Translated and edited by H. M. Parshley. London: Vintage, 1997.

de Forest, G. A. "Rock Music—Beach Boys vs Beatlemania." *Garbonza's Weblog*, February 20, 2008. http://garbonza.wordpress.com/.

DeMartin, Michael. *Pet Sounds at 40: An Appreciation* (blog). http://pet-sounds40.blogspot.ie.

Deming, Mark. "The Paris Sisters: The Complete Phil Spector Sessions." AllMusic. Accessed April 24, 2017. http://www.allmusic.com/.

Devereux, Eoin, Aileen Dillane, and Martin J. Power, eds. *Morrissey: Fandom, Representations and Identities*. Bristol, UK: Intellect, 2011.

Diamond, Stephen A. "Dangerous Genius: The Rise and Fall of Phil Spector." *Psychology Today*, March 24, 2013. https://www.psychologytoday.com/.

Dillon, Mark. *Fifty Sides of the Beach Boys: The Songs That Tell Their Story*. Toronto: ECW Press, 2012.

Doggett, Peter. *The Man Who Sold the World: David Bowie in the 1970's*. London: Vintage, 2012.

———. *There's a Riot Going On: Revolutionaries, Rock Stars, and the Rise and Fall of the '60s*. New York: Canongate, 2007.

———. *You Never Give Me Your Money*. New York: Harper Paperbacks, 2011.

Douglas, Edward. "Exclusive: The Agony and the Ecstasy of Phil Spector." ComingSoon.net, July 2, 2010. http://www.comingsoon.net/.

Douglas, Susan. *Listening In: Radio and the American Imagination*. Minneapolis: University of Minnesota Press, 2004.

———. *Where the Girls Are: Growing Up Female with the Mass Media*. New York: Times Books, 1994.

Downes, Julia, ed. *Women Make Noise: Girl Bands from Motown to the Modern*. Twickenham, UK: Supernova, 2012.

Du Noyer, Paul. *Conversations with McCartney*. London: Hodder & Stoughton, 2015.

———. *In the City: The Celebration of London Music*. London: Virgin, 2010.

———. *John Lennon: We All Shine On; The Stories behind Every John Lennon Song, 1970–1980*. London: Carlton, 2006.

Early, Gerald. *One Nation under a Groove: Motown and American Culture*. Hopewell, NJ: Ecco, 1995.

Egan, Sean. *The Mammoth Book of the Beatles*. Philadelphia: Running Press, 2009.

Ellen, Barbara. "Was 1966 Pop Music's Greatest Year? The Beach Boys—Pet Sounds." *Guardian*, January 31, 2016.

Elliott, Martin. *The Rolling Stones: Complete Recording Sessions, 1962–2002.* London: Cherry Red, 2003.

Emerson, Ken. *Always Magic in the Air: The Bomp and Brilliance of the Brill Building Era.* London: Forth Estate, 2006.

End of the Century: The Story of the Ramones (documentary). Directed by Jim Fields and Michael Gramaglia. Dallas: Magnolia Pictures, 2003.

Everett, Walter. *The Beatles as Musicians: The Quarrymen through Rubber Soul.* London: Oxford University Press, 2001.

Examiner.com. "The Complicated History behind 'River Deep-Mountain High.'" Accessed March 27, 2016. http://www.examiner.com/.

Fletcher, Tony. *Dear Boy: The Life of Keith Moon.* London: Omnibus, 2010.

———. *A Light That Never Goes Out: The Enduring Saga of the Smiths.* London: Windmill, 2013.

Foster, Mo. *Play Like Elvis! How British Musicians Bought the American Dream.* Bodmin, UK: MPG Books, 2000.

Friedan, Betty. *The Feminine Mystique.* London: Penguin Modern Classics, 2010.

Friedman, Roger. "Spector Rips Tina at Ike Turner's Funeral." *Fox News,* December 22, 2007. http://www.foxnews.com/.

Gaar, Gillian. *She's a Rebel: The History of Women in Rock and Roll.* Exp. 2nd ed. New York: Seal, 2002.

Gallagher, Paul. "Roy Wood: The Talent behind the Move, Elo, and Wizzard." Dangerous Minds, August 11, 2011. http://dangerousminds.net/.

George Harrison: Living in the Material World (documentary). Directed by Martin Scorsese. N.p.: Grove Street Pictures, 2011.

Gerson, Ben. "George Harrison: All Things Must Pass." *Rolling Stone,* January 21, 1971, http://www.rollingstone.com/.

Girl Groups: The Story of a Sound (documentary). Based on the book by Alan Betrock. Directed by Steve Alpert. Beverly Hills, CA: Delilah Films, 1983.

Gluck, Sherna Berger. *Rosie the Riveter: Women, the War and Social Change.* New York: Meridian, 1988.

Goddard, Simon. *Mozipedia: The Encyclopedia of Morrissey and the Smiths.* London: Ebury, 2009.

———. *The Smiths: Songs That Saved Your Life.* London: Reynolds and Hearn, 2004.

Gordy, Berry. *To Be Loved: The Music, Magic, Memories of Motown.* Boston: Rosetta, 2013.

Grieg, Charlotte. *Will You Still Love Me Tomorrow? Girl Groups from the 50s On.* London: Virago, 1989.

Guardian. "The 10 (Nuttiest) Producers." November 20, 2005. https://www.theguardian.com/.

Harrington, Richard. "Madonna: Siren of Success." *Washington Post,* June 3, 1985.

Harrison, George. *I, Me, Mine.* San Francisco: Chronicle, 2007.

Hartman, Ken. *The Wrecking Crew: The Inside Story of Rock and Roll's Best Kept Secret.* New York: Thomas Dunne, 2012.

Hewitt, Paolo. *The Sharper World: A Mod Anthology.* London: Helter Skelter, 2009.

Heylin, Clinton. *From the Velvets to the Voidoids.* London: Helter Skelter, 1993.

Hochman, Steve. "Wall of Sound Lost and Found." *Los Angeles Times,* Special to the Times, February 6, 2005.

Howe, Sean. "How Madonna Became Madonna: An Oral History." *Rolling Stone Magazine,* July 29, 2013. http://www.rollingstone.com/.

Inside Pop: The Rock Revolution (documentary). New York: CBS News Special, 1967.

Jackson, Joe. *A Cure for Gravity: A Musical Pilgrimage.* Cambridge, MA: Da Capo, 2000.

Jayanti, Vikram. *The Agony and the Ecstasy of Phil Spector.* DVD. London: Arena, BBC, 2009.

Johnstone, Nick. *The Amy Winehouse Story.* London: Omnibus, 2008.

Judt, Tony. *Postwar: A History of Europe since 1945.* London: Vintage, 2010.

Keenan, Elizabeth K. "Puppets on a String? Girl Groups of the 50s and 60s." In *Women Make Noise: Girl Bands from Motown to the Modern*, edited by Julia Downes. Twickenham, UK: Supernova, 2012.

King, Carole. *A Natural Woman*. London: Virago, 2013.

Kirby, Michael Jack. "The Paris Sisters: I Love How You Love Me." Way Back Attack. Accessed January 30, 2016. http://www.waybackattack.com/.

Kirkpatrick, Rob. *Magic in the Night: The Words and Music of Bruce Springsteen*. London: Souvenir Press, 2009.

Koojiman, Jaap. "From Elegance to Extravaganza: The Supremes on the Ed Sullivan Show as a Presentation of Beauty." *Velvet Light Trap* 49 (2002): 4–17.

KSHE 95. "Flashback: George Harrison's 'My Sweet Lord' Hits Number One." December 24, 2014. http://www.kshe95.com/.

Kubernik, Harvey. "Phil Spector: The Musical Legacy." *Goldmine: The Music Collector's Magazine*, March 10, 2011. http://www.goldminemag.com/.

Kureishi, Hanif, and Jon Savage, eds. *The Faber Book of Pop*. London: Faber and Faber, 1995.

Kurlansky, Mark. *Ready for a Brand New Beat: How "Dancing in the Street" Became the Anthem for a Changing America*. New York: Riverhead, 2014.

Lambert, Molly. "In Which We Go beyond the Valley of Gwangi with Phil Spector." This Recording, November 23, 2008. http://thisrecording.com/.

Levering, Stephen. *Time (and Newsweek) Is on My Side: Pop/Rock Coverage in Time and Newsweek during the 1960s*. Ann Arbor, MI: ProQuest, 2006.

Levine, Larry. "The Pet Sounds Sessions" (liner notes). *The Beach Boys*. CD. Los Angeles: Capitol, 1997.

Life Could Be a Dream: The Doo-Wop Sound (documentary). West Long Branch, NJ: White Star, 2002.

Little, Michael H. "Graded on a Curve: Dion, *Born to Be with You*." Vinyl District, June 30, 2014. http://www.thevinyldistrict.com/.

Love, Darlene. *My Name Is Love: The Darlene Love Story*. New York: William Morrow, 2013.

MacDonald, Ian. *Revolution in the Head: The Beatles Records and the Sixties*. 3rd rev. ed. London: Vintage, 2008.

MacInnis, Colin. *Absolute Beginners*. London: Allison and Busby, 2011.

MacLeod, Sean. *Leaders of the Pack: Girl Groups of the 1960s and Their Influence on Popular Culture*. Lanham, MD: Rowman & Littlefield, 2015.

Madinger, Chip, and Mark Easter. *Eight Arms to Hold You*. Chesterfield, MO: 44.1 Productions, 2000.

Magee, Bryan. *Aspects of Wagner*. London: Panther, 1972.

Marable, Manning. *Malcolm X: A Life of Reinvention*. London: Penguin, 2011.

Marcus, Greil. *The History of Rock 'n' Roll in Ten Songs*. New Haven, CT: Yale University Press, 2014.

McGee, Alan. "ELO: The Band the Beatles Could Have Been." *Guardian*, October 16, 2008.

McRobbie, Angela, ed. *Zoot Suits and Second Hand Dresses: An Anthology of Fashion and Music*. London: Macmillan, 1982.

Melnick, Monte A., and Frank Meyer. *On the Road with the Ramones*. London: Bobcat, 2007.

Miles, Barry. *The Beatles: A Diary; An Intimate Day by Day History*. London: Omnibus, 2002.

———. *The British Invasion*. London: Sterling, 2009.

———. *Paul McCartney: Many Years from Now*. New York: Owl Books, 1998.

Moorefield, Virgil. *The Producer as Composer: Shaping the Sounds of Popular Music*. Cambridge, MA: MIT Press, 2010.

Morrissey, Stephen. *Morrissey: Autobiography*. London: Penguin, 2013.

Music Moguls: Masters of Pop-Money Makers (documentary). London: BBC, 2016.

Musicneverdies. "The Wagner in Spector's Pop." *Music Never Dies's Blog*, March 11, 2009. https://musicneverdies.wordpress.com/.

Myers, Marc. "Bill Medley on Phil Spector." *JazzWax*, July 2012.
The Nation's Favourite Beatles Number One. Directed by Stephen McGinn and John Piper. London: ITV, 2015.
Newkey-Burden, Chas. *Amy Winehouse: The Biography*. London: John Blake, 2008.
Norman, Philip. *John Lennon: The Life*. New York: HarperCollins, 2008.
———. *Mick Jagger*. New York: Harper, 2013.
———. *Shout! The Beatles in Their Generation*. New York: Simon and Schuster, 2011.
O'Hagan, Sean. "Was 1966 Pop Music's Greatest Year? The Beatles—Revolver." *Guardian*, January 31, 2016.
Oldham, Andrew Loog. *Stoned*. London: Vintage, 2000.
———. *Stone Free*. Vancouver, BC: Because Entertainment, 2012. Kindle ed.
Padel, Ruth. *I Am a Man: Sex, Gods, and Rock and Roll*. London: Faber and Faber, 2000.
Pegg, Nicholas. *The Complete David Bowie*. London: Reynolds and Hearn, 2009.
The People's History of Pop (documentary series). London: BBC4, 2016.
Philo, Simon. *The British Invasion: The Crosscurrents of Musical Influence*. Lanham, MD: Rowman & Littlefield, 2015.
"Phil Spector." *Dominick Dunne's Power, Privilege and Justice* (TV series). Directed by Patrick Taulère. Atlanta: truTV, 2009.
"Phil Spector." *True Crime with Aphrodite Jones* (TV series). Directed by Tom Jennings. New York: Peacock Productions, 2010.
Phil Spector: He's a Rebel (documentary). Directed by Binia Tymieniecka. London: BBC, 1983.
"Phil Spector: The Gift, the Demons, the Mystery." Biography Channel, A&E Television Networks, UK, 2006.
Pinnock, Tom. "The Making of . . . : The Beach Boys' 'Good Vibrations.'" Uncut, June 8, 2012. http://www.uncut.co.uk/.
Porter, Dick, and Kris Needs. *Blondie: Parallel Lives*. London: Omnibus, 2012.
Priore, Domenic. *Smile: The Story of Brian Wilson's Lost Masterpiece*. London: Sanctuary, 2005.
Quirk, Tom. *Endlessly Horny for Wonder and Magic: How Jim Steinman's "Bat out of Hell" Perfectly Captured the Pre-Pubescent American Id (and Nearly Ruined Me for Life)*. New York: Feedback Press, 2012.
Ramone, Johnny. *Commando: The Autobiography*. New York: Abrams, 2012.
Reed, John. *Paul Weller: My Ever Changing Moods*. London: Omnibus, 1996.
Reeves, Martha. *Dancing in the Street: Confessions of a Motown Diva*. New York: Hyperion, 1995.
Ribowsky, Mark. *He's a Rebel: Phil Spector, Rock and Roll's Legendary Producer*. Cambridge, MA: Da Capo, 2006.
Richards, Keith. *Life*. New York: Back Bay. 2011.
Riley, Tim. *Fever: How Rock 'n' Roll Transformed Gender in America*. New York: Picador, 2005.
Rinny. "Exclusive: Beyonce Guitarist Bibi McGill Talks Music, Hair and Healthy Living." Black Girl with Long Hair, January 12, 2012. http://blackgirllonghair.com/.
Robb, John. "Sex Pistols 'Never Mind the Bollocks': A Re-evaluation." Louder than War, November 15, 2011. Accessed November 15, 2016. http://louderthanwar.com/.
Rock and Roll: In the Groove (documentary). South Burlington, VT: WGBH; London: BBC, 1995.
Rolling Stone. "100 Greatest Singers of All Time." December 2, 2010. http://www.rollingstone.com/.
Rosewarne, Lauren. *Part-Time Perverts: Sex, Pop Culture, and Kink Management*. Santa Barbara, CA: Praeger, 2011.
Rutherford, Paul. *The World Made Sexy: Freud to Madonna*. Toronto: University of Toronto Press, 2007.
Salewicz, Chris. *Mick and Keith*. London: Orion, 2002.
Sandford, Christopher. *Bowie: Loving the Alien*. New York: Little, Brown, 1996.
———. *McCartney*. London: Arrow, 2006.

Savage, Jon. *1966: The Year the Decade Exploded*. London: Faber & Faber, 2016.

The Secret History of Rock 'n' Roll (documentary). N.p.: Frozen Television, 2001.

Shapiro, Marc. *Behind Sad Eyes: The Life of George Harrison*. New York: St. Martin's, 2002.

Shaw, Arnold. *The Rockin' 50s: The Decade That Transformed the Pop Music Scene*. New York: Da Capo, 1987.

Shepherd, John, David Horn, and Paul Oliver, eds. *Continuum Encyclopedia of Popular Music of the World*. Part 1, vol. 1, *Media Industry and Society*. New York: Continuum, 2003.

The Sixties: The Years That Shaped a Generation (documentary). Directed by David Davis and Stephen Talbot. Alexandria, VA: PBS, 2005.

Spector, Ronnie, with Vince Waldron. *Be My Baby*. London: MacMillan, 1991.

Spitz, Bob. *The Beatles: The Biography*. Boston: Little, Brown, 2005.

Stanley, Bob. *Yeah, Yeah, Yeah: The Story of Modern Pop*. London: Faber and Faber, 2013.

Staunton, Terry. "Roy Wood: Santa Claus of Pop Music." *Sunday Express*, December 11, 2011.

Steinman, Jim. "Filled with Speculation." Dream Pollution. Accessed May 8, 2017. http://www.jimsteinman.com/spector.htm.

Stras, Laurie, ed. *She's So Fine: Reflections of Whiteness, Femininity, Adolescence and Class in 1960s Music*. Farnham, UK: Ashgate, 2011.

Taraborrelli, J. Randy. *Diana Ross*. London: Sidgwick and Jackson, 2007.

Taylor, Marc. *The Original Marvelettes: Motown's Mystery Girl Group*. New York: Aloiv, 2004.

Taylor, Steve. *The A to X of Alternative Music*. London: Bloomsbury, 2004.

Thesander, Marianne. *The Feminine Ideal*. London: Reaktion, 1997.

Thompson, David. *Phil Spector: Wall of Pain*. London: Sanctuary, 2004.

True, Everett. *Hey Ho Let's Go: The Story of the Ramones*. London: Omnibus, 2010.

Turner, Steve. *The Beatles: A Hard Day's Write; The Stories behind Every Song*. New York: MJF Books, 2009.

Twenty Feet from Stardom (documentary). Directed by Morgan Neville. N.p.: Gil Friesen Productions, 2013.

UltimateGuitar.com. "New York Dolls: 'We Re-hatched Iggy Pop's Career.'" February 28, 2001. https://www.ultimate-guitar.com/.

U.S. Diplomatic Mission to Germany. "An Outline of American History," chap. 11, "Postwar America." About the USA. Accessed April 20, 2017. https://usa.usembassy.de/etexts/history/ch11.htm.

Wald, Gayle. "'Deliver de Letter': 'Please Mr. Postman,' the Marvelettes, and the Afro-Caribbean Imaginary." *Journal of Popular Music Studies* 24, no. 3 (September 2012): 325–32.

Walk on By: The Story of Popular Song (documentary). London: BBC, 2001.

Warner, Jay. *American Singing Groups: A History from 1940s to Today*.

Warwick, Jacqueline C. "'And the Colored Girls Sing': Backup Singers and the Case of the Blossoms." In *Musicological Identities: Essays in Honor of Susan McClary*, edited by Susan McClary, Raymond Knapp, Steven Baur, and Jacqueline C. Warwick. Aldershot, UK: Ashgate, 2008.

———. *Girl Groups, Girl Culture: Popular Music and Identity in the 1960s*. London: Routledge, 2007.

Welch, Chris. *David Bowie: The Stories behind the Classic Songs, 1970–1980*. London: Carlton, 2010.

White, Charles. *The Life and Times of Little Richard*. London: Omnibus, 2003.

Whiteley, Sheila. *Women and Popular Music: Sexuality, Identity and Subjectivity*. New York: Routledge, 2000.

A Whole Scene Going (TV series). London: BBC, 1966.

Williams, Richard. "The Other Side of Phil Spector." *Guardian*, April 13, 2009. Accessed March 15, 2016. http://www.theguardian.com/.

———. *Phil Spector: Out of His Head*. London: Omnibus, 2003.

Williams, Zoe. "Lady Gaga, Miley Cyrus and the Rape Generation." *Guardian*, June 24, 2014.

Wilson, Brian, with Todd Gold. *Wouldn't It Be Nice: My Own Story: Brian Wilson, the Creative Genius behind the Beach Boys*. London: Bloomsbury, 1996.

Wilson, Mary. *Dreamgirl: My Life as a Supreme*. New York: Cooper Square Press, 1999.

———. *Supreme Faith*. New York: Cooper Square Press, 1999.

Wilson, Terry. *Tamla Motown: The Stories behind the UK Singles*. London: Cherry Red, 2009.

Wolf, Naomi. *The Beauty Myth: How Images of Beauty Are Used against Women*. London: Vintage, 1991.

Wolfe, Tom. *The Kandy Kolored Tangerine Flake Streamline Baby*. New York: Bantam, 1989.

Womack, Kenneth. *Long and Winding Roads: The Evolving Artistry of the Beatles*. New York: Bloomsbury, 2007.

INDEX

ABOUT THE AUTHOR

Sean MacLeod is a songwriter, music producer, and lecturer from Dublin, Ireland, and has been writing and producing music for over twenty-five years. Since he was a child, Sean has had a keen interest in the pop music and culture of the 1960s. This period has been a major influence on his own work and still continues to fascinate and inspire him today. Sean is the author of *Leaders of the Pack: Girl Groups of the 1960s and Their Influence on Popular Culture in Britain and America* and currently lives in Limerick where he teaches courses in music technology and media at the Limerick College of Further Education.

CPSIA information can be obtained
at www.ICGtesting.com
Printed in the USA
BVOW08*0444091117
499615BV00003B/3/P